JESUS SAID IT ...

*Dedicated
to my brother Ted,
and Peg his wife and best friend,
both deceased.
They knew the Promises,
accepted them without question,
and now enjoy the fullness of all they contain*

Jack McArdle SS CC

# Jesus said it ...
# and I believe it

PROMISES IN THE GOSPELS

the columba press

First published in 2004 by
the columba press
55A Spruce Avenue, Stillorgan Industrial Park,
Blackrock, Co Dublin


Cover by Bill Bolger
Origination by The Columba Press
Printed in Ireland by ColourBooks Ltd, Dublin

ISBN 1 85607 442 0

# Table of Contents

# Introduction

My generation grew up on promises! I was making promises to God day and night, New Year's Day, Ash Wednesday, Annual Retreats, thunder storms, and every time an aeroplane went 'iffy' in the sky! I have now reached my 'free pass' stage and, in the hope that it may be 'wisdom, age, and grace', I'm beginning to review all those promises, and to learn something from them. I wouldn't have to be a rocket scientist to know that I have never scored too highly in the promises stakes! Some time ago the Lord suggested another (better!) way of doing things. 'Jack, I know you meant well, and I don't "knock" you, because you had the goodwill, even when you were off target. For whatever time you have left in life, I suggest a very different approach. The only promise I ask from you now is that you make no more promises! I am the one making the promises, and I am the only one who can keep promises.' 'Heaven and earth will pass away before my promises pass away' (Mt 24:35).'

I searched through the gospels, and came up with 157 promises. Not one 'might', 'maybe' or 'perhaps' in the whole lot! I took some liberty with those that are not direct promises, but actually contain a promise. I grouped them, and came up with 22 different headings, which I chose to deal with as chapters. This presented a problem, which was easily overcome. For example, the first chapter has 19 promises, while the last one has three. To give some balance I reflect on 11 promises in Chapter One, and add the other 8, without comment, so the readers have the freedom to do their own reflecting. While all reflections are basically the same length, the chapters taper off, and the final chapter has but three promises. I have added an index, while should greatly help in locating a particular promise, and the page on which the reflection is to be found.

Elizabeth said to Mary, 'All these things happened to you because you believed that the promises of the Lord would be fulfilled' (Lk 1:45). Jesus said 'The sin of this world is unbelief in me' (Jn 16:9). I found that reflecting on these promises has been a source of wonderful blessings for me. That is what encourages me as I put this book into the hands of my readers. The promises can be used in any way the reader chooses. I can read the reflection on a particular promise each morning, and that could give me food for thought for the day. I could select a particular chapter, e.g., eucharist, and concentrate on those promises over a week or two. Prayer Groups, Bible Study Groups, and homilists may also find thoughts, insights, and inspirations from reading these reflections in any way they choose. With these people in mind, I deliberately went to the trouble of giving chapter and verse for every reference to scripture, so that the quote can be read in context by those who wish to do so. Because these words are taken directly from the words of Jesus in the gospels, they already have a value and a power that does not require my augmentation in any way. The word of God is shot-through with the Spirit of God. While I had the wonderful privilege of writing these reflections, it is only the Spirit of God who can convey these words to the heart of the reader. Might I suggest that, before reading any reflection, the reader should whisper a little prayer to the Holy Spirit. This will greatly bridge the gap between writer and reader, because I myself whispered such a prayer before writing any of these reflections. My wish for you, gentle reader, is that you experience some of the joys and inspirations that I experienced as I put these reflections on paper.

# Belief in Jesus

*Heaven and earth will pass away,*
*but my word will never pass away. (Mt 24:35)*

I chose this to begin with, because it underpins all the promises of Jesus. He is giving us his word, and he wants us to take him at his word. Staking heaven and earth against his word is a very strong endorsement of that word. There is no way that he could be more emphatic about how sure and certain his promises are. He lays it on the line for us. He cannot do any more to convince us of his sincerity, and his reliability. Jesus is caught in a bind, in that he makes a promise, he emphasises how serious that promise is, but then he leaves the rest to us. We may choose not to believe him, or to ignore his promise, which is just another way of expressing our unbelief. No wonder Jesus said that the sin of this world is unbelief in him. (Jn 16:9) Without a response from us, his promises hang in the air. Jesus doesn't *give* us anything; he *offers* us everything. Nothing happens until we accept his offer.

It was the absence of a response that caused him to weep, as he overlooked Jerusalem. (Lk 19:41) Our indifference, of course, is a response, because 'no' is also an answer. The opposite to love is not hatred, but indifference. Love or hatred is to feel strongly, one way or another. Indifference is just not to care at all. In the Book of Revelations – the last book in the Bible – God says: 'I wish you were either hot or cold, but, because you are lukewarm, I will begin to vomit you out of my mouth.' (Rev 3:15-16) In simple English, 'you make me sick'. Strong words from God! Imagine the following scenario: Jesus arrives back in heaven on the Ascension Day. 'Welcome home, son … and I'm sorry' was the Father's greeting. Jesus replied, 'It wasn't the nails that hurt as much as the kiss.'

Refusal to accept or believe this word is a very serious thing. The gospels contain many solemn promises, and we are rejecting the core of the message if we refuse to believe those promises. Elizabeth said to Mary 'All these things happened to you, be-

cause you believed that the promises of the Lord would be fulfilled.'(Lk 1:45) Faith is a response to love. I will only trust those
people whom I believe are interested in my welfare. Not to believe Jesus is to throw the whole offer of incarnation, and all that
stems from that, back in his face. The whole purpose of his mission, and everything he achieved for us, is rejected. What is left
for us? Nothing; nothing at all. We are lost sheep who choose to
remain lost, and exposed to the ravages of the world. Jesus
would certainly weep once again, if this was our response.

It is absolutely impossible to grasp the enormity of the rewards and blessings that are ours when we accept the truth of
his promises. We are safe and happy for life, and for eternity.
His promises protect us, like some superb insurance policy. We
are insulated against evil, against sin, against death. When we
walk in the certainty of those promises, we enjoy the happiness
of heaven now. It is uniquely the work of the Holy Spirit to lead
us into such belief. 'I believe, Lord, help my unbelief.'(Jn 9:38);
'Lord, increase my faith.'(Mk 9:24) Belief in his promises is not
some magic formula, nor is it a question of gritted teeth, clenched
fist, or flexed muscles. It is a simple response to a sincere and
genuine offer of love. This offer has no small print, or no hidden
agenda. It is an offer that is made for my sake only, and accepting the offer brings nothing but untold blessings. It is important
to be a person of my word, to be as good as my word, to be true
to my word. Jesus is all of that, and all he asks is that we believe
him. He pledges that word against heaven and earth. Heaven
can cease to be, and the earth can no longer exist, but his word
still stands. Right now I can stake my whole happiness for life,
and for eternity, on that word.

I have to seriously search my heart, to ensure that I actually
do accept his word. This is not something that I presume, without any serious reflection. Acceptance and belief is more than
the absence of doubt. It is the presence of something strong,
powerful, and tangible; something around which I live my life.
It effects everything I do, and everything I hope to do. My hope
and purpose for now, and for eternity, rests on believing the
promises of Jesus. Yes, Lord, I believe that your word will never
pass away, and that I can safely stake my life and happiness, for
now and for eternity, on you being faithful to your word.

*Everyone who believes in me will have eternal life.*
*(Jn 3:15)*

I entitled this book *Jesus said it ... and I believe him*. When I read this promise, I repeated those words of the title to myself. It is a simple, direct, and uncomplicated promise. The result of believing it, however, reaches as far as eternity. In chapter three of his letter to the Romans, St Paul makes a very clear statement about how we can attain to salvation. 'We are made right with God when we believe that Jesus shed his blood, sacrificing his life for us.' (Rom 3:25) Notice the balance between the two elements. Jesus died for us, and we believe that. In another translation it is 'his blood and our faith that secures our salvation.' It is what Jesus has done, and whether we believe and accept that. There is a serious onus on us regarding our salvation. Once again, we need to remember that God *offers* us salvation; he doesn't *give* it to us. I could hold out a book until I get a pain in my arm, and have to lower my arm, and it doesn't become yours, until you step forward and accept it.

There is no might or maybe in any of Jesus' promises. If I believe in him, I will have eternal life. In practice, what does believing in him mean? It means listening to his word, accepting that he is speaking the truth, and acting on what he says. There is a difference between faith and belief. You decide you want to have your car serviced. You are a visitor to these parts, so you ask me where you should go. I recommend a particular garage. You go there, because I said so, and you are acting on belief. You get your car serviced; you are satisfied with the job, and the price is reasonable. The next time you are here, you decide to get your car serviced again, and you go back to the same garage. This time, you are acting on faith, because now you yourself know that they will do a good job, and the price will be reasonable. I learn to believe in Jesus by acting on his word and, when I discover that his word is trustworthy and reliable, I grow in faith.

My particular reason for wanting to reflect on these promises is to answer this question for myself: What difference does it make for me to accept this promise as truth, and to entrust my whole future to the certainty of that promise being fulfilled for me? It should make a profound difference. It should make all the difference in the world. I am alive now, but I will die some day. This promise tells me that I possess a life that will never end. Physical death is of no importance, if I believe that I, the real me, and not the body, will continue to live for all eternity. Not only will I live for all eternity, but this eternity will be spent sharing the fullness of life with the Trinity, the angels, saints, and those people belonging to me who believed these promises of Jesus. I sometimes say that I would not like to live to be a hundred, because, no matter how alert I might be, I would surely depend on others for most things. The promise we are now considering tells me that I will live forever, and that, in that next stage my life will be completely free to enjoy it to the full, in a way that would be completely impossible now, in this mortal body. Lord Jesus, I believe in you, and I know that my belief opens the door for me to enter a life, right now, that is eternal. Today is the beginning of that life, as I walk the way of faith with you. I depend totally on your Spirit to increase and strengthen my faith.

The *Imitation of Christ* tells of a monk before the Blessed Sacrament, who kept repeating, 'If I only knew I would persevere. If I only knew I would persevere.' After a while a voice from the tabernacle spoke, 'And if you knew you would persevere, what would you do? Do now what you would do then, and you will persevere.' What a profound difference it should make to my life when I believe this promise of Jesus. Living my life, while keeping this promise in mind, and knowing how my life will end, that is faith, that is belief. Speaking to the crowds on the morning of Pentecost, Peter said, 'He is the one all the prophets testified about, saying that everyone who believes in him will have their sins forgiven through his name.' (Acts 3:17-18) Belief in Jesus is at the core of the gospel. This must surely be the work of the Spirit because, being human, my belief seems to always be accompanied by doubts. I cannot hope to be any other way, unless the Spirit comes to my rescue. I believe that an honest heartfelt cry to the Spirit to implant a conviction about this promise in my heart, is a prayer that will surely be answered. Even to make the cry is a very clear declaration: I believe, Lord, help my unbelief.

*Those who believe in me will never thirst.*
*(Jn 6:35)*

There is a thirst, as much as a hunger, within the human heart, and it can never be satisfied apart from God. 'You have made us for yourself, O Lord, and our hearts will never be at rest until they rest in you', was the prayer of St Augustine. Mother (now Blessed) Teresa used speak of a yearning to be loved as being a greater hunger than that for food. Jesus offers himself as a gift that will satisfy the longings of every human heart. We are familiar with compulsions, addictions, and drives to meet human appetites. We are also familiar with the scrap-heap of humanity that results from such self-will run riot. Many people die long before their time, because of the abuse of food, alcohol, or other kinds of drugs. These compulsions send people to self-destruction and death, because the drug, or the high life, cannot deliver what we believe it promises. Jesus made the promise we are now considering, to a Samaritan woman who was with her seventh partner. She obviously was not happy, because she listened to him and, being deeply impressed by him, she brought out her friends to meet him.

Alcoholics, in a Twelve Step programme of recovery, are introduced to a spiritual programme, and they learn to turn their will and their lives over to God, as they understand God. They are told that, by themselves, they will never stay sober. If they try to do this on their own, then, they can be sure, they will thirst again! The compulsion for satisfaction makes us restless and, unless it is satisfied, we can never be at peace. If I accept what Jesus says in this promise, I will look towards him to satisfy my human longings. There is no one way to do this. I just tell him that I want him to satisfy all the inner longings of my heart. I invite him to make his home there, and to fill my heart with his Spirit. When I have Jesus in my heart, there is no room for anything else. Many of us do experience a drive for pleasure, for creature comforts, for personal aggrandisement. We try to satisfy that thirst by going on a shopping spree, or having a make-over from head to toe, with beauty treatments, clothes, etc. After a while we discover that this satisfaction is short-lived and, despite all the beauty treatments, and the health programmes, the years keep rolling by, and the signs of aging are unstoppable. Our thirst is an inner one and, when that is quenched, we feel good about everything else in our lives. I can waste so much time and money and, when I discover the futility of that waste, I may then turn to Jesus, and begin to listen to his promises. I would save myself so much heartache by going to Jesus right at the beginning. This promise was made many years ago. I may only now be adverting to it for the first time.

Once again, I ask the question: What difference does it make when I believe this promise, and apply it to my life? It must surely bring a great peace, and a sense of inner satisfaction. It is as if the great search is over. I have found the pearl of great price. This is something that will never be taken from me. I ask the Holy Spirit to confirm in my heart that no earthy satisfaction compares with having Jesus, and with believing that his promises are for me. 'Having given us Christ Jesus', says Paul, 'will he not surely give us everything else?'(Rom 8:17) 'Keep your eyes fixed on Jesus, the author and finisher of our faith' is a word in the letter to the Hebrews (12:2) that we should keep in mind. I ask the Holy Sprit to help me focus my attention on Jesus, to enlighten my mind to the security that this brings, and to treat all other distractions as lies, as offers that do not, and cannot deliver. The Spirit leads us into truth, and the truth is that only Jesus can satisfy our thirst. He has made the offer, and I accept it, and this should make all the difference. What is left now is that I continue to remind myself of this, and not let the lures of false satisfaction draw me away from the true, and only source of my happiness.

*I have given you authority over all the power of the evil one; nothing will harm you. (Lk 10:19)*

This is an extraordinary promise, and, believing it and acting on it would completely transform the life of a Christian. When we think of how easy it was for Satan to deceive our first parents with his lies, and deceit, and now we know that Jesus is giving us full authority over Satan, this must surely be a complete reversal of the evils of Original Sin. Notice that Jesus is saying, 'I have given you ...' In other words, this is not some promise to be fulfilled in the future. This authority has already been given to us. If Jesus gives us this authority, it is so that it be used. If we want nothing to harm us, then we have to exercise that authority. It is important that we use this authority wisely and correctly. It is not something that can be flaunted, and exercised as a magical power. Satan would be very pleased if we did this, because we would be acting as if the power was our own. Of ourselves we have absolutely no power over Satan and, while we might forget that, Satan certainly doesn't. This power is pure gift, and it can only be used with humility and gratitude. I can use it firmly, of course, as long as I remember that I am using the power of Jesus, with his specific permission. Any confidence I have in using this power stems directly from the fact that I take this promise of Jesus seriously. It is extraordinary that Jesus should choose to let us share his power, but that's what he has chosen to do.

A very important part of the ministry of Jesus was driving out demons who had taken over within someone. Jesus was very definite in letting Satan know that he had come to put him in his place. Satan tested Jesus right from the start (Lk 4:1-13) because, like any bully, he was terrified of being challenged. Satan spoke through people, including Peter (Mk 8:33), and he did everything in his power to thwart the plans of Jesus. From the time I was a child, I always got a great kick out of seeing a bully getting his comeuppance. Satan had it his own way for too long. Indeed, in today's world, he seems to be having a field day. The human heart is made in such a way that it yearns for the spiritual. When the Spirit of God is absent, the evil one takes over. There is always some spirit speaking to me at any one time. It is either the Holy Spirit, the human spirit, or the evil spirit. Discernment is a gift of the Holy Spirit that enables me discern the spirits. Jesus told us to 'watch and pray'. (Mk 14:34) It is not enough to pray. Satan is also listening when I pray, and he is always ready to thwart my every effort at doing the good. It is vital that I accept the authority that Jesus offers me in this promise, and to use this authority wisely, firmly, and constantly.

This is a prayer that should constantly be on my lips:

*I use the power, authority, and precious Blood of Jesus, and I bind in his name every presence and influence of Satan within me. In the name of Jesus, and through the authority he has entrusted to me, I command you, Satan, to depart from me, to go to Jesus, and let him dispose of you in whatever way he chooses.*

When I speak of exercising this authority, I am not speaking of exorcism. It is nothing that dramatic. When I find myself drawn towards some situation, action, or train of thought that that does not lead to my good, I can exercise the authority, and discover that I become free from the bind. Using this authority means freedom from bondage. I know of recovering alcoholics who use this authority over the demon drink. When I constantly exercise this power that is entrusted to me, I become more and more aware of exactly what it means. It is only through exercising this authority that I come to fully appreciate just how important and powerful it is. For those who do not understand, no words are possible, and for those who understand, no words are necessary.

St Peter tells us to stand up to Satan and, because he is a bully, he will run from us, if we are strong in our faith. (1 Pet 5:9) Without claiming any special knowledge, it is my experience that this authority is not exercised to any great extent. That is a great pity, and Satan is the only one who benefits from this. I can sprinkle myself with holy water, wear a religious object, or have religious artifacts in my home, but if I do not do this with authority, with boldness and with expectation, then I am not exercising my authority. Jesus is the model for all our actions. He asks us to follow him, to imitate him, to do as he did. It makes an enormous difference in the life of a Christian when this promise is fully accepted, and firmly acted on. If I don't accept this power, I do not have it. If I accept it, I must use it, and only then will I appreciate the strength that is mine because of the promises and the power of Jesus.

*If you trust me, you are really trusting God who sent me.*
*(Jn 12:44)*

Although we joke about God being a hoary old man in the sky, complete with white flowing beard, there are people who still retain this image. Jesus came to reveal the Father to us. He was very definite in portraying a Father of great love, and of constant loving care; a Father who ran to meet and hug the Prodigal Son, or who provides food for the birds of the air, and for the lilies of the field. Jesus spoke a language of love, forgiveness, and of family, and he told us that he never said anything unless the

Father told him. (Jn 8:28) 'They who hear me hear the Father', Jesus said. (Jn 14:24) Some people listen to what Jesus has to say, and they find his words very reassuring; but they still cling to the idea of there being some other kind of God, who will be there waiting for them when they die. There seems to be a real problem in accepting this package deal, if I may call it that, where there is only one voice speaking for all three Persons in the Trinity. Jesus said what the Father told him, and the Spirit would remind us of what Jesus had said. They would speak with one voice, because they are united in love, and there could never be conflict or double-speak between them.

Jesus came to us with a mission from the Father. The terms of reference of that mission were clearly defined, just as it would be when passed on to his followers to complete, at a later date. The gospels can be summarised in one sentence: God loves me, and in one word: Father. The Father was speaking to us through his Son Jesus. If we accept Jesus, we accept the Father, and if we reject Jesus, we reject the one who sent him. 'They who hear me, hear the Father', Jesus tells us. (Jn 14:24) 'Anyone who has seen me, has seen the Father … Don't you believe that I am in the Father and the Father is in me? … Anyone who hates me hates my Father also …'(Jn 14:9) In other words, Jesus and the Father are inseparable. That is why it is important that, when we think of Jesus, we do so in the context of the Trinity. Jesus is making this promise on behalf of the Trinity. This means that if I trust Jesus, I am also trusting the Spirit. Notice that this translation reads, 'If you trust me, you are really trusting God who sent me.' My trust is in God in totality, Father, Son, and Spirit. This trust draws me into the life of the Trinity and, as Jesus said, he, the Father, and the Spirit will come and make their home in such a heart. This is a wonderful promise because it makes it possible for me to share in the life of the divinity. What a privilege for us mere humans!

*Spirit and breath of God, you are the loving whisper of the Trinity, who has come to complete the work of Jesus, now that he has returned to the Father. I ask you, please, to sharpen the scope of my spiritual vision, so that I can embrace the Trinity in all my dealings with God. I want to avail of all that Jesus made possible, and I depend on you to bring that to completion within me.*

It is absolutely OK to approach the Trinity in the way that is most meaningful for me. There are times when I feel that I am more open to Jesus; at other times, I find that I can turn with great ease to the Spirit; and yet again, there are occasions when I find it easier to speak to God as my Father. It makes no difference whatever, because no matter which way I pray, I am coming face to face with the Trinity. It may help to develop my trust in Jesus, and then to develop that trust to include the Father and the Spirit. If I accept and act on this promise, my spiritual life will be greatly enriched. Like any other promise, this bears fruit only when I accept it, believe it, and act on it.

### *Those who believe in me, even though they die, will live again.* *(Jn 11:25)*

This is a promise that is certainly well worth taking to heart. A promise that transcends death, and that gives certain assurances for beyond the grave, is surely something very special. It is a simple promise, very clearly spoken, with no ambiguity whatsoever. If I believe in Jesus, I will continue to live, even if the body dies. Belief in Jesus, and in his promises, provides a bridge over which we can safely cross into eternal life. We say, 'Dying, you destroyed our death; rising, you restored our life ...' Jesus overcame death, and we all are invited to share in that victory. This is the extraordinary story of redemption, where Jesus did all that was necessary, where he paid the price, and where we can come along and reap all the benefits of something we did nothing to earn. It is very important that we repeat this truth like a mantra: Our salvation is based on his Blood, and on our faith. (Rom 3:25) We are saved through what Jesus has done, and because of our faith in what he offers.

There is no magic formula for impressing this truth on our minds. This happens through the inner enlightenment of the Holy Spirit. I could write, 'Jesus is Lord' on a page and, to someone in China, with absolutely no knowledge of English, or of our alphabet, it would look like what Chinese writing looks to me. There is a truth behind that phrase, however, and by simply looking at it, it is impossible to have any idea of what that truth is. It is at this stage that revelation enters in, and the lights come on, the coin drops, and suddenly, I grasp the truth and it makes a profound impression on me. This is uniquely the work of the Holy Spirit. Jesus said that the Spirit would teach us all about him. Certainly, it is the work of the Spirit to reveal the truth of Jesus' promises to us. I cannot hope that any words I write during this brief reflection will go any length towards convincing you of the wonder of this promise. I am asking the Holy Spirit, however, to be in the words I write, so that you read an inspired word, a word that enters your heart as you read it, a word that becomes flesh within you.

Jesus is our Moses, who divides the Red Sea, so that we can pass over, dry-shod, into the Promised Land. He asks us to follow him and, if we do so, we will not walk in darkness, but will have the light of life. (Jn 8:12) We follow him to Calvary, when we join our struggles to his, and this brings us, with him, right through to Easter and to ascension. This promise of Jesus holds up through life, and through death. It is an eternal promise and, as Jesus says, heaven and earth will pass away before his word passes away. If we believe in him, then, even if we die, we will live again. There is no time limit on this promise. It is difficult to define the exact meaning of 'believe'. It has nothing to do with clenched fists, gritted teeth, or flexed muscles. It is simply a quiet conviction that grows in our heart, because the seed of that belief is sown there by the Spirit. Faith is a gift of the Spirit. Not only is eternal life a gift, but even the ability to accept it and believe in it is also a gift. Earlier in this chapter, we reflected on another promise, where Jesus promised eternal life to those who believe in him. In this promise, he goes one step further, when he states that death does not deprive us of that eternal life. Our human life will end anyhow, because our days in the body are limited. The body is not me. I am living in the body for just a relatively short time. When the body breaks down, and is no longer habitable, I will have to change residence, and go to live elsewhere. It is then that my mortal, earthly life, will be replaced by eternal, unending life. Praise God, for the wonders of his promises!

*I am going away, but I will come back to you.*
*(Jn 14:28)*

When it came time for Jesus to return to the Father, the apostles were sad to see him go. He explained to them that it was necessary for them that he left them because, if he did not leave, the Spirit would not come. He told them that when he returned to the Father, he would send the Spirit to complete his work. A spirit on its own cannot do anything. An evil spirit needs somebody's hand to plant the bomb, or somebody's tongue to tell the lie. When the Holy Spirit came, the apostles, and ourselves, would provide the body so that the Spirit could carry on the work of Jesus through us. I provide the voice to speak God's word, or the hands to provide his healing touch. I just have to provide the body, and the Spirit provides the power. I am a channel of his power, his peace, his love. I never become a generator or a transformer!

Jesus promises his apostles that he will return. This is very important for them. He came in humanity, and suffered all the slings and arrows of being human, even to death. When he returns, he will come in glory. The kingdom of this world will end, and the kingdom of Satan will be confined to hell for all eternity. No longer will Satan be able to tempt, or bully any of God's children. No longer will the false values of this world persist. There will only be one kingdom, and Jesus will be Lord in that kingdom. The kingdom, the power, and the glory will be his.

Belief in this promise must have been at an all-time low on Calvary. How could he come back from this? When he came to them on Easter Sunday, their belief in this promise was resurrected. Anything was possible now. They had witnessed the many ways in which his plans were thwarted, his teachings rejected, and his promises derided. They had seen the success of deceit and lies in bringing him to an ignominious end. The thought that he would return in glory, and would put all his enemies under his feet, was something wonderful. They had felt so helpless to defend him, and they were afraid of what would happen to them if they went public in his defence. Now they believed that he was quite capable of defending himself, and he would prove to all the world that he had the final victory.

After Pentecost, we have several long sermons from Peter. These sermons usually are based on five points of good news: The Messiah who was promised has come; his name was Jesus of Nazareth; you put him to death, but he rose again from the dead; he returned to the Father in triumph where he can no longer be subjected to human degradation; he will return in triumph to reap the harvest into his kingdom and to proclaim his eternal victory over all the powers of the evil one. Notice that his return is also proclaimed as good news. The Jesus they knew would be welcome to return anytime. As a matter of fact, many of them expected him to return during their lifetime. St Paul refers to this in his letters, and the very last words of the Bible are *Maranatha! Come, Lord Jesus!* (Rev 22:20) Having watched him exercising his power over the forces of evil, they longed for him to return to put an end to the wiles and attacks of the enemies, both human and demonic.

Finally, please note the positive nature of the promise: 'I am going away, and I *will come back* to you.' There is no room left for doubt here. This is a sure and certain promise. It is something I can build on. I can stake my whole future, for time and eternity, on the truth of this promise. This is something that I need to pray through. In other words, I need to pray about it, chat to the Lord about it, and constantly ask the Spirit to impress this promise indelibly on my mind and heart. I depend on the Spirit to remind me, as Jesus said he would. (Jn 16:12) When I have a deep conviction about the reality of this promise, I can open my fists, ungrit my teeth, and relax my muscles. I get on with life, giving it all I have, in the sure and certain hope that my eternal destiny is in safe hands. Jesus holds my future, so I need not worry what my future holds.

> *Anyone who believes in me, will do the same works I do,*
> *and even greater works, because I am going to my Father.*
> *(Jn 14:12)*

This promise must have made a profound impression on the apostles. They had seen Jesus calm the storm, heal the blind, cleanse the leper, and even raise the dead. Now he tells them that they will be able to do the very things he did, if they believe in him. He passes his power on to those who hear his word, and accept that word. 'Blessed are they who hear the word of God, and keep it.'(Lk 11:28) This surely is an extraordinary promise. I just wonder, if a spot check was taken in a church any Sunday morning, how many people would admit that they actually believe this, and how many of them actually avail of it. The average person would be amazed to witness a miracle, because it would come as a completely unexpected surprise. The scandal is that there are so few miracles. 'These are the signs that shall accompany those who believe in me ... They will cast out devils in my name ... They will place their hands on the sick, and heal them.'(Mk 16:17-18)

I think it important that we give serious consideration to what exactly this promise means for us. Firstly, the promise is very specific, very definite, and very clear. It is obvious what is meant by the words Jesus uses. I can understand the promise, and I can easily have a good idea of what it would entail if this promise held up. The question I have to ask, of course is: Do I believe it? Can I believe it? It is absolutely essential that I keep out of my head when I reflect on this. I can understand what the words mean, and yet not understand the message they convey. I can reflect on it, of course, and, like Mary, I can ponder it in my heart. (Lk 2:19) In the final analysis, however, getting to the level of believing, in that I accept it and am ready to act on it, is entirely the work of the Holy Spirit. The promise comes from God, and the grace to respond to it also comes from God. I can read this promise very slowly, many many times. I can read it for my head, to understand what the words say. I can read it for my heart, to be open to the message those words contain. I can pray the words, meditate on them, and talk to God about them. I can listen to Jesus as he actually speaks those words to me, or I can ask the Spirit to please reveal the truth of the promise to me. Elizabeth told Mary that all these things had happened to her, because she believed that the promises of the Lord would be fulfilled. (Lk 1:45) Someone in the crowd said to Jesus, 'Happy is the womb that bore you, and the breasts that gave you suck', to which Jesus replied, 'Happy are those who hear the word of God and keep it.' (Lk 11:27-28) It would be good, then, to include Mary in my prayers for the grace to accept and believe this promise, and, indeed, any other promises in the gospels.

What would it mean if I really accepted and acted on this promise? Before attempting to answer that question, may I draw your attention to another very important question? Jesus speaks about believing in him, not believing the promise. It would be a total contradiction to try to believe in a promise, if I didn't trust the person who made the promise. Once again, we are faced with the question: What exactly does it mean to believe in Jesus? Believing in Jesus involves accepting the whole package of redemption. Jesus was sent by the Father. He never said anything unless the Father told him to say it. (Jn 8:28) If we hear him, we hear the Father; if we believe him, we believe the one who sent him. (Jn 14:24) Jesus overcame all the damage done to our humanity by Original Sin. He overcame sin, sickness, and death. He is totally victorious over all the power of the evil one. If I accept him, believe what he tells me, and am prepared to walk with him, then I too can share in the spoils of his victory. The answer to my first question, then, is that I have full access to all the power of Jesus, and that I too am now beyond the power of the evil one. I can live with a Higher Power, who brings me to a life beyond my wildest dreams. Coming into an experience of this promise is like setting out on a journey. The journey begins with the first step. Bit by bit, step by step, I come to discover that this promise holds up. My faith grows when I exercise it. I learn to pray by praying, not by reading a book about it!

*All who trust me will no longer be in the darkness.*
*(Jn 12:46)*

St John's gospel has wonderful contrasts between light and darkness, life and death, good and evil. Jesus is seen as a light that came into the darkness of this world. John the Baptist announced that he was not the light. (Jn 1:20) Jesus claimed that he was the Way, the Truth, and the Life. (Jn 14:6) At the end of the gospel, he tells his disciples that they are now to become the light of the world(Mt. 5:14). They were to let their light shine before people, so that their good works might be seen as evidence of the goodness of their Father in heaven. They were not to hide their light under a bushel, but let it shine for all to see. (Mt 5:16)

Trusting in Jesus brings us closer to him. The closer we come to him, the brighter the light. We are no longer children of darkness, because the angel of darkness no longer has any control or power over us. Living in darkness implies several limitations. We cannot see, we cannot read, we cannot know what surrounds us. When we trust Jesus, we are brought into the light of revelation. We come to know his mind, we come to learn his will. If we are to follow him, we need to know what way he wishes us to travel. To remain in darkness is to remain in ignorance. Jesus calls us his friends. He said that we are no longer slaves, because a slave does not know what his master is doing. (Jn 15:15) We, however, know because Jesus has told us everything. He came to lead us out of the darkness of ignorance. He told us that, if we followed him, we would not be walking in darkness, but would have the light of life. (Jn 8:12)

The gifts of the Spirit include wisdom, discernment, knowledge. When we exercise these gifts, we are not walking in darkness. If someone comes to me, and is extremely disturbed and confused, I can expect to have wisdom, discernment, and knowledge in dealing with that person. If I am walking in the power of the Spirit, I expect the gifts to be available when needed. Only God can do a God-thing. If the Spirit is not working through me, I cannot be involved in God's work. It can happen that, when the person leaves me, he may well express wonder at how insightful and intuitive I had been. I may have given the impression that I could almost read the other person's mind. As soon as that person has left my office, I may not know what day it is! The gift was present when needed, and it is no longer present, because it is not needed. The gift is not mine, but I can draw on a gift of the Spirit if that is needed to do God's work. There is no excuse for a Christian stumbling around in the dark. Jesus is like the bright sun that came into a dark cave; there can never be darkness there again.

Again and again, in these reflections, we have to look at that word 'trust', and see what it really means. Trust could be defined as having a firm belief in the honesty, veracity, or justice of a person. It implies reliance on the truth of a statement, even without testing it. This trust comes from us, but it has its roots in the goodness of the other. Faith is a response to love. When I reflect on why Jesus came, what he did and said when he did

come, and what Christians have discovered since about his message and mission, it is hardly asking too much that I should trust
him. Someone who has died because of love for me, is not very
likely to deceive me. In other words, if I don't trust Jesus, who
can I trust?

We are all familiar with people who are confused, uncertain,
lacking confidence, not sure where to turn, or where to go. There
are varying amounts of darkness in their lives. This promise is
especially addressed to them. It is a wonderful gift to be able to
walk in the light, not to be stumbling, and to be deeply aware.
Awareness is a gift of the Spirit. It is an inner vision that can see
over, through, and beyond all obstacles. It contributes greatly to
inner peace, and to a feeling of accompaniment. I feel that I'm
not alone, but am being led. Jesus has entrusted the continuance
of this promise to the Holy Spirit, who continues his work
among us.

*Here on earth you will have many trials and sorrows.*
*But take heart, because I have overcome the world. (Jn 16:33)*

This is a very consoling promise. Jesus warned us that we would
be tested because we belong to him. The world has little time or
concern for someone who is trying to follow Jesus. For those
who judge work and endeavour by the monitory results accru-
ing from it, then Christian love would rate very low on the scale
of things. The Christian is an exile in this world. He does not belong here, but is just passing through. We are a pilgrim people,
on our way to the Promised Land. Like the Israelites in the
desert, there are many trials and tribulations along the way.
Moses was prevented from entering the Promised Land, but
Jesus has already entered there. That is why he can assure us
that our destiny is sure and certain. He has the victory, and he
assures us that nothing along the way of life can prevent us
moving towards our eternal destiny. St John says, 'Little children, there is a spirit within you that is more powerful than any
evil spirit you will meet on the road of life.'(1 Jn 3:9)

When a person is being wheeled into an operation theatre,
the main concern is that the operation be a success. I would be
more at ease, in such a situation, if I could be given definite

guarantees that all would go well. As I encounter the trials and sorrows of life, it is much easier to deal with them when I am assured that everything will be alright in the end. Not only will I survive them, but my survival will be eternal. In an earlier reflection, we considered the outcome of a promise where Jesus gave us full authority over all the power of the evil one. He told us that nothing would harm us. In that promise, he told us that we were protected from the attacks of Satan. In the promise on which we now reflect, he assures us that we are also protected against the attacks of the world. Jesus offers to share his power and strength with us. We should claim that strength. We can claim all the strength we need for any situation. Jesus has given us a right to claim it, and we should exercise our right. A beggar supplicates, a child appropriates. We are children of the Father, who sent Jesus to reveal the Father's love to us. If he cares so much for the birds of the air, and the lilies of the field, how much more can we be assured that he will care for us? (Mt 6:26)

There are two certainties in this promise. The first is that, on earth, we will have many trials and sorrows. The second is that Jesus has overcome the world, and we can share in his victory over everything that burdens us. We all probably have ample proof about that first part of the promise. We may not, however, have discovered the reality of the promise itself, at the end. That would be a great pity. The Christian is an eternal optimist, someone who lives with the victory of Jesus, who walks in his strength, and who relies totally on his promises. There are many solutions on offer for the trials and tribulations of life. These range from medicine, to psychiatry, to drugs, to one of the many self-help programmes available. Some people even look to suicide as a solution. Unfortunately, this is a permanent solution for a temporary problem. While medicine, psychiatry, and other treatments all have a valid and real part to play in our struggles with the pains and aches of life, it would be a tragedy if the Christian saw this as a first option, and turned to God, when all of this has failed. God's phone number should never be listed under 'Emergencies Only'!

'Somebody else had a heavier cross than the one I bear today, and the cross were far too much for me, had not Somebody led the way.' What a freedom it is for us to accept the promises of

Jesus, without question or equivocation; to simply believe it, because Jesus said it. The only way I can ever discover whether the promises hold good is when I accept them, act on them, move on, and expect everything to turn out as Jesus promised. Jesus will never disappoint you. If you expect him to answer your prayers, he will. Can we expect him to answer, when we refuse to believe that he will? I cannot give a definite answer to this question, because I refuse to believe that Jesus is spiteful and he will get his own back on us for not believing him. I can accept that his answer may well be 'no', if that's what it takes to get us to take him seriously. 'When a man finds himself lying on the ground, face downwards, with his nose buried in the rubble of his achievements, he is ready to be wafted by the breath of God across the chasm of infested waters, into a land of hope, of new birth, and of new beginnings.' What Patrick Kavanagh is telling us here is that, when we've been broken enough, we may be ready to submit, let God take over, and bring us to where we never could go of ourselves.

### *Those who believe in me will place their hands on the sick, and heal them. (Mk.16:18)*

This promise is listed below in its entirety. The full promise speaks of casting out devils, speaking new languages, handling snakes, drinking poison, and healing the sick. I believe that healing the sick is the one most applicable to us in our Christian ministry and, so, I have chosen this part separately. When Jesus ascended into heaven, he brought the body he had with him. He sent down his Spirit, and he asked us to supply the body, through which the Spirit could do his work. If I supply the voice, the Spirit will speak God's word. 'When you stand up to speak on my behalf, don't worry what you shall say, because the Spirit will give you words that no one will be able to oppose.'(Mt 10:20) If I supply the hands, and lay them on the sick, the Spirit will effect healing through them. I couldn't heal anyone, nor am I expected to heal anyone. Only God can do a God-thing. 'The kingdom, the power, and the glory are his.' If I supply any of the power, I will be tempted to steal some of the glory. I am not a generator or a transformer for God's power. I am simply a channel of that power, when I allow the power and life of God flow through me to others.

There is a difference between sickness and suffering. Suffering is a special vocation, and it is from God. I have met people in hospital and they were profoundly edifying, through their patience, compassion for others, and gratitude for everything that is done for them. They are a great source of affirmation to the staff who care for them. On the other hand, there are patients who are forever complaining about the tea being too cold, the porridge being too hot, or the way in which they are not getting the attention from the staff that they expect. 'By their fruits you'll know them.'(Mt 12:33) This latter group are sick, and I mean sick! Sickness is not from God. Enough cigarettes, alcohol, or food, and we shouldn't blame God for what happens to us. What I am saying is that suffering is from God, and sickness is not. Before praying with someone who is ill, it is important to discern whether that person is suffering, or is sick. For the one who is suffering, I pray for continued strength to carry the cross, and, if it is God's will, that the suffering might be shortened. St James writes: 'Are any among you suffering? They should keep on praying about it, and those who have reason to be thankful should continually sing praises to the Lord. Are any among you sick? They should call for the elders of the church, and have them pray over them, anointing them with oil, in the name of the Lord. And their prayer, if offered in faith, will heal the sick, and the Lord will make them well. And anyone who has committed sins will be forgiven.'(Jas 5:13-15)) James is saying that anyone who is suffering has reason to be praising God. Those who are sick, however, are in trouble, and there is a hint that the sickness may have been caused by some sin. There are a lot of sicknesses today that are self-inflicted. Such people should ask for help, and they should be given help. It is here that the laying on of hands comes in. Once again, this is an exercising of the authority that Jesus has entrusted to us.

The distinction I have made between sickness and suffering is not always so evident, and it doesn't always hold up. When I think of a baby who is sick, I cannot define this as either sickness or suffering. I know, however, that this is a very definite opportunity for parents to carry out the Lord's injunction. Nobody loves this baby as much as the parents, and it is reasonable to assume that no one is better suited to be an instrument of healing for that baby than those same parents. Parents should always be encouraged to place their hands on a sick child, and to ask the Lord to anoint their touch with the gift of healing. Once again, as in coming to claim and exercise the promises, this is done only by practice. When I exercise this mandate given to me by Jesus, it becomes almost second nature to me. I find myself automatically stepping out to claim the strength that is offered, and that is available.

### *Other promises under the heading: Belief in Jesus.*

The sin of this world is unbelief in me. (Jn 16:9)

I have come to give sight to the blind. And to show those who think they can see, that they are blind. (Jn 9:39)

They are given eternal life for believing in me, and will never perish. (Jn 11:26)

Don't be afraid. Just trust me, and she'll be alright. (Lk 8:50)

Just believe that I am in the Father, and the Father is in me. (Jn 14:11)

I have told you these things before they happen, so that you will believe when they do happen. (Jn 14:29)

All who reject my message will be judged on the day of judgement by the truth I have spoken. (Jn 12:48)

These are the signs that will accompany those who believe in me:
> They will cast out devils in my name.
> They will speak new languages.
> They will handle snakes with safety.
> If they drink anything poisonous, it won't hurt them.
> They will place their hands on the sick, and heal them.
> (Mk 16:17-18)

*(This last line is treated separately above.)*

# Holy Spirit

*If I go away, the Comforter will come, because I will send him.*
*(Jn 16:7)*

Without wishing to be too simplistic, I might suggest that there are three parts to the story of salvation. Firstly, the Father's love was so great that he just had to come up with a rescue plan for us, so that we would not be separated from him for all eternity. The second part of the story is Jesus coming to carry out the will of the Father in putting that rescue plan into operation. The third part is when the Holy Spirit took over, after Jesus ascended into heaven, to complete his work, and to bring us to the fullness of redemption. It was necessary, therefore, that Jesus should leave, because it was only when he had left that the Spirit would come to take over. The words of Jesus are very definite, and leave no room for doubt. 'The Comforter *will* come, because *I will send* him.' There is no maybe, might, or perhaps in this.

I often imagine Mary in the Upper Room with the apostles, preparing for Pentecost. If I had the talent, I consider that there is material for a drama there. There were no recriminations coming from Mary for all these macho fishermen, who ran away and deserted her and Jesus on Good Friday. They had ridden the crest of the wave for several years. Being with Jesus gave them a special status, and they were often quite impatient and intolerant with the crowds, and with the mothers and their babies. (Lk 16:18) In that Upper Room, they were totally deflated. Mary consoled and supported them. Their personalities would not have changed, however, and one can well imagine the problem Mary had to keep some of them in a room for nine days, while there was nothing happening. After a few days, Peter would have been restless, and would have demanded some action. Thomas wanted proof that something was going to happen, or he was going home. All the while, Mary reassured them that the Spirit would come, because Jesus had said that he would send the Spirit. In other words, the Spirit came, because the Spirit was expected to come. Mary believed the promise of Jesus, and she had no doubt that it would be fulfilled.

Notice that Jesus calls the Holy Spirit 'the Comforter'. Both the apostles and ourselves are in need of a comforter. The normal use of the word 'comforter' is to describe something we put in a baby's mouth to keep it from crying. It is the nearest thing to actual food we can give. We also speak of a 'security blanket' as being some sort of comforter. The comforter calms, reassures, and accompanies. 'You're not alone, my friend, any more.' In another promise, Jesus tells us that the Spirit will never leave us. (Jn 14:16) In God's eyes we are children. Even if we live to be a hundred, that is just a moment of time compared to the eternity of God. We are children who are afraid, worried, anxious, and often discouraged. We need a presence to be with us on our journey.

Jesus shows extreme sensitivity to his apostles in this promise. The thought of him leaving them was frightening. They found it difficult to believe in anything they couldn't see. They could see, hear, and touch Jesus. Jesus knows their fears, and he gently reassures them that he himself will continue to care for them through the Comforter he would send. The Spirit had been present at all great moments of the world. The Spirit was present at creation, and was breathed into the clay. The Spirit hovered over the waters, bringing order out of chaos. The Spirit came upon Mary, so that incarnation would be possible. Now Jesus was promising that the same Spirit would come upon them for the next part of their journey. Their very lives were part of an ongoing plan of salvation; they were part of the Father's plan.

When I consider that the gospel is now, and I am every person in the gospel, then I must accept this promise as being made to me. Jesus promises me that he will send the Holy Spirit. The highlight of my own church year is the novena for Pentecost. It is then that we all have an opportunity to go into the Upper Room and open our hearts to the Spirit. The heart can become a prayer room, a Pentecost place, an Upper Room, a place of the Spirit. Pentecost is on-going. I can open my heart to this promise every single day. It is a source of wonderful blessings to accept this promise as being made to me, and to act on it, and allow it be fulfilled.

*Stay in the city until the Spirit comes*
*and fills you with power from heaven. (Lk 24:49)*

I cannot resist a smile when I read this promise. Jesus is asking his apostles to do nothing till the Spirit comes. He knows them only too well. With all the best intentions in the world, they are liable to rush in where angels fear to tread. There is a vital lesson to be learned, and they must be slowed down until that lesson has been fully assimilated. They are to go nowhere until the Spirit comes to lead them. The Spirit will lead them into truth, and will guide their feet into the way of peace. They were never too strong in the humility stakes, and may not have been fully convinced just how weak they were. Only God can do a God-thing. The Spirit is coming to complete the work of Jesus. It is God all the way, from the initiative of the Father, through the life and death of Jesus, into the work of the Spirit, and on through until Jesus comes in glory.

There are times in the gospels when the apostles seem to be full of themselves. They resented babies and children wasting Jesus' time. (Lk18:16) They argued about which of them was the greatest. (Mk 9:34) The mother of two of them came to Jesus, to put in a good word for her sons, to ensure that they got posts of responsibility when he set up his kingdom. (Mt 20:20) In this promise, Jesus speaks of the Spirit filling them with power from heaven. To make room for that power, there was some emptying that needed to be done. Perhaps their failure to be with him on Calvary went a long way towards deflating their egos. One of the conditions for being open to the Spirit is to have a deep conviction of my own weakness, and my need for a power greater than myself.

There is a kind of a matter-of-factness about these words of Jesus. There is no doubt that the Spirit will come, and there is no doubt what the Spirit will do when he does come. This is a profound happening, and yet it is spoken in such simple, straightforward language. We need to pause to reflect on the ramifications of these words. We need to do so, because these words are also spoken to us. Not only are we promised power from on high, but we will be filled with that power. There is no way we could get our heads around the concept of being filled with

God's power, but it certainly is very profound, and truly extraordinary. Of ourselves, we never would dare presume that we
could be filled with God's power. To even think of such a thing
would appear to be very presumptuous. Once again we have to
remind ourselves that we are speaking of pure free gift here.
With our own experiences of rewards, merits, bonuses, and benefits, it is not easy to grasp the concept of gifts that are totally
free, with absolutely no strings attached. The gifts do have a
come-back on them, of course, in that they are given to us for a
purpose. The gifts are free, but they are given so that I can live a
Christian life, and live with the power of God within.

It really should make all the difference in the world to know
that I have access to the fullness of God's power. What a tragedy
it would be not to avail of that. Jesus said that the Spirit would
remind us of everything he told us. Our problem can be that we
forget. We can find ourselves calling out to God when everything else has failed. It would be wonderful if we began with
God, and it certainly would save us a lot of heartache. I suggest
that we should whisper a prayer to the Spirit from time to time,
asking him to remind us, and not let us forget the power that is
at our disposal. When I do this on a regular basis, it becomes impressed on my mind, and I have a better chance of working and
living out of that power. I then act out of that power, and I discover that it is there for me. Availing of the power, and using
that power is the only way to make it part of my life. The gift is
given to be used, and the greatest thanks I can give God for his
gift is to make full use of it.

*I will ask the Father, and he will give you another Comforter,*
*who will never leave you. (Jn 14:16)*

Once again, we have a simple, plain statement that is easily understood. I read it once for my head, to learn what it says. I read
it again for my heart, to get a feeling about what it is saying. As
in so many of his promises, Jesus speaks of what he *will* do, and
what *will* happen. He doesn't speak of what he *might* do, or of
what *may* happen. His promises are firm, uncomplicated, and
unambiguous. Because his promises are definite, and uncomplicated, I believe that they call for a similar kind of response. I

should have no maybe or might in my response. 'Let your "yes" be yes, and your "no" be no.' (Mt 5:37) Jesus made this promise to his apostles and, in turn, he is making it to us, and to me as an individual. I will not be able to come to grips with this promise if I think of it as something that was said to some people one time, and was intended only for those people. The gospel is now, and I am every person in it.

Jesus told us to ask the Father for anything in his name. In this promise, it is Jesus himself who is asking the Father. It is reasonable to presume, then, that his prayer will be answered. He is going to ask the Father to send us the Holy Spirit. In another place he says, 'Will the Father not surely give the Spirit to those who ask?'(Lk 11:13) Are we ready for the Spirit, then? Do we really want the Spirit in our lives? If we do, then, we can just open our hearts and expect to be filled with that Spirit. This is a very definite promise. Giving us the Spirit is an essential part of the plan of salvation. When Jesus has completed his work, he will return to the Father. He will then send the Spirit to complete his work on earth. The coming of the Spirit is just as central as was the coming of Jesus. The coming of the Spirit, as mentioned in this promise, however, is that the Spirit will come to each of us. Not only will he come to us, but he will never leave us. This is wonderful good news. Any of us can feel good for a few hours, but we probably don't expect this to last. We are always waiting for the other shoe to drop. This is not true when it comes to the Holy Spirit. Jesus tells us that the Spirit will never leave us. This is a very important part of the promise, and something that should be a great consolation to all of us. I don't want the Spirit to leave, but I sometimes think that the presence of the Spirit is determined by the fact of whether I am good enough or not. I feel that, because of my own fault, I will do something that will drive a wedge between the Spirit and me. If I understand the heart of Jesus, I must realise that the more broken I am, the more the Spirit sticks with me. The Spirit is but another expression of the unconditional love of the Trinity. God loves me because he's good, and not because I am good.

'I hope in your word. My eyes watch through the night, to ponder your promise.' (Ps118) The promise on which we now reflect merits our serious consideration. We are told that Jesus is going to ask the Father, and, because of that, the Father will send us the Holy Spirit, and that Holy Spirit will never leave us. I say 'Yes' to that with all my heart. I ask the Spirit to impress this truth deep in my heart. I want to hold and cherish it deeply within my being, so that I am always conscious of it. I can even take it that all of this has already happened. Jesus has already asked the Father, the Father has sent the Spirit, the Spirit is with us, and will never leave us. When I begin to act out of this conviction, when I begin to enter into situations and circumstances where I am deeply conscious of the truth of what has happened, things become totally different. Life is never the same again. I am not on my own.

The promises of Jesus call us to action. It is only when we act on them that they become operative. To act on them is to act with the conviction that they are true. When we do this, we discover that they hold up, and this, in turn, deepens our conviction of their truth. I have the Spirit, because Jesus asked the Father, and the Father has given me the Spirit. That Spirit will never leave me. I will have that Spirit within me until the day I die, in each and every circumstance of life, and of death.

### *He will come to you from the Father, and will tell you all about me. (Jn 15:26)*

St John concludes his gospel with the following words: 'This is that disciple who saw these events, and recorded them here. And we all know that his account of these things is accurate. And I suppose that if all the other things that Jesus did were written down, the whole world could not contain the books.' (Jn 21:24-25) Jesus lived on this earth for thirty-three years. Three of those years were spent in the public forum. He was open and forthright in everything he did and said. When the High Priest questioned Jesus after his arrest he replied, 'What I teach is widely known, because I have preached regularly in the synagogues and the Temple. I have been heard by people everywhere, and I teach nothing in private that I have not said in public … Ask those who heard me. They know what I said.'(Jn 18:19-21).

Since that time to this many thousands and thousands of

books have been written about Jesus. I myself wrote a book called *Jesus, the Man and the Message*, and, while I had nothing new to say, I think I may have had a different way of saying it. The personality, the life, and the message of Jesus seems to be inexhaustible. When the apostles first met Jesus they asked him, 'Where do you live?' He said, 'Come and see.' (Jn 1:38-39) They went with him, and spent the whole day with him. They got to know something about him on that first occasion. They spent the next three years travelling with him, night and day. At the end of that time, it is extraordinary just how little they knew him, and how little they knew about him. Even when he ascended into heaven, we are told that some of his disciples 'still doubted him'. (Mt 28:17) In view of this, it is interesting to read the writings of Peter, James, John, and Jude, after Pentecost, when the Spirit came. For the first time in their lives they seem to have a real conviction as to who Jesus was, and why he came. This was the work of the Spirit, as foretold in the promise we are now considering. It is the role of the Spirit to reveal Jesus to us. When Jesus asked the question, 'Who do you say that I am?', Peter replied, 'You are the Christ, the Son of the living God.' (Mt 16:15) To which Jesus replied, 'You are blessed, Simon Barjona, for it is not flesh and blood that revealed this to you, but my Father in heaven.' At another time Jesus said, 'No one knows the Father except the Son, and those to whom the Son chooses to reveal him.' (Lk 10:22) It is the role of Jesus to reveal the mind of the Father to us, just as it has become the role of the Spirit to reveal Jesus to us.

How does the Spirit tell us about Jesus? I can call them whisperings, or I can call them inspirations. I can call them insights, or I can label them discoveries. Whatever I choose to call them, they come from the Spirit within. I can learn a lot about Jesus from books, from attending theology classes, or from listening to talks. However, I can only get to know Jesus personally through the revelation of the Spirit within. The ears and eyes of the heart don't need glasses or hearing aids. They need a complete realignment, a complete new focusing, which is the work of the Spirit.

Christianity is not about producing nicer people with better morals. I could be a pagan, and be a good person. Neither is it about prayer and fasting. I could be a Muslim and do all of that in a much more consistent way than most Christians ever do. Christianity is about a person, Jesus Christ. It is about knowing him, and his message; about following him, and living his message. It is the Spirit who introduces me to this way of living. As Jesus says in this promise under review, the Spirit tells us all about Jesus. The Spirit has already come. It is up to us to ask the Spirit to tell us all about Jesus. It is about opening our hearts to the Spirit, and continually stating our willingness to listen, and to follow the promptings. I will be very aware of the journey, as I discover that Jesus is becoming more and more real with each passing day.

### When the Spirit comes, he will guide you into all truth.
### (Jn 16:13)

Original sin was a lie, brought about by Satan, whom Jesus called 'the father of lies'. The Holy Spirit is the perfect antidote for the poison of that lie. The Holy Spirit is the antibiotic for the infection of the evil one. It is a wonderful thought to be guided into truth. There is great freedom in truth. 'The truth will set you free.' (Jn 8:32) The liar has to have a good memory, because the lie has to be backed up by several other lies. To leave the lies, the deceit, the deviousness, the cunning, and the denial behind, is like coming out of prison. It is just wonderful to live in the truth. It is not always easy to know the truth, however. The human mind can be very stubborn, and the human heart can be very blind. Some of the most prejudiced and bigoted people in the world could be completely convinced that they are right in what they believe. The work of God's Spirit is to refocus the vision, so that we can see what is true, and see what is false. This saves us from some of the many pitfalls awaiting those who stumble along blindly. In this promise, we are told that the Spirit will guide us. Zechariah, the father of John the Baptist, spoke of the coming Messiah in these words: 'the light from heaven is about to break upon us, to give light to those who sit in darkness, and in the shadow of death, and to guide our feet into the way of peace.' (Lk 1:78-79)

Once again, I must draw our attention to the matter-of-factness of this promise. It is said without the slightest hint that it might not happen. It is spoken of as something definite, dependable, and entirely reliable. The Spirit is certainly coming, and when he does come, he will lead us into all truth. No doubt about what's being said here. Leading us into all truth is to complete the work of redemption and salvation. We were in bondage because of original sin. We were outside of the garden. The Spirit will now lead us back to the garden, and we will be back where we were before the fall. What an extraordinary grace from God! God never wastes a thing. He continues to write straight on crooked lines; he continues to bring good out of evil. St Augustine says: 'O happy fall, that merited so great a redeemer!' In some ways we are better off now than we were before original sin. It is impossible, of course, for us to know what life might have been like had we not left the garden. However, it is an extraordinary blessing to have all of that restored, and to have Jesus' revelations of the Father, and the Spirit's on-going revelations about Jesus to accompany us on our journey of life.

Last weekend, I was looking across towards the Gap of Dungloe in Killarney, and it was completely shrouded in mist. I couldn't see a thing. Within an hour the mist had lifted, and the Gap was clearly visible. It is that way with truth. The truth is always there, but it is not always possible for us to see it. The Spirit dispels the mists and the fog and, in the words of the song, 'I can see clearly now.' In order for the Spirit to effect his work in me, it is necessary that I have a deep longing for the truth. In my heart, I really do want to know the truth, and I really do want the grace to live that truth, and to be led into it. Like Mary, I say 'yes' to the Spirit, again and again. Jesus says that the Spirit will guide us into all truth. Nothing left to chance here. Of myself, I could easily become very selective of the truth, so I need the assurance that the Spirit will present me with truth all the way. When the Spirit came upon Mary, it is easy to imagine that she was totally open to that event. She also helped the apostles, so when the Spirit came at Pentecost, they were ready and willing to welcome him. I open my heart, with a sigh of longing, with a sincere desire to be free, with a deep longing to live the truth. The Holy Spirit will do the rest. 'You will know the truth, and the truth will set you free.' (Jn 8:32)

*When he comes, he will convince the world of its sin,*
*of God's righteousness, and of the coming judgement. (Jn 16:8)*

While I understand what Jesus is saying here, I am faced with a question. I do believe that the Spirit can reveal the presence of sin, and the facts of God's righteousness, and of the coming judgement. What puzzles me, however, is how he can convince the world, when the world is not interested, and doesn't want to know? The only way I can deal with this is to speak of you and me as representing the world. As citizens of the world, the Spirit can fulfill this promise for us. In the last promise we considered, we were told that the Spirit would guide us into all truth. One of those truths is our own sinfulness. Sin, by its very nature, denies its own existence. Without the presence of the Spirit, I would be totally blind to sin in my life, because my head could justify and excuse anything. Another of the truths revealed by the Spirit is the goodness and holiness of God. It is difficult for our human minds to grasp the concept of someone who is totally honest, open, and fair in every possible situation, and who never deviates from love and from justice in all things. Yet another of the truths revealed by the Spirit is the fact that we must all face God's judgement on how we have done, and what we have done with the gift of life entrusted to us by God. We can easily get so involved in the worries, cares, and concerns of life, that we forget we are a pilgrim people, that we are just passing through, and that our lives must be held up to scrutiny at the end. God is generous with his gifts, but we are held responsible for what we do with those gifts.

Jesus promises us that, when the Spirit comes, he will let us know those things that we should know, in order to lead meaningful lives. We are not going to be left in the dark about anything. We will be deeply aware of our sinfulness, of the goodness and holiness of God, and of the fact that we will be held responsible for what we do with the gift of life. It is very important that we keep those things in perspective. Whether the world wants to or not, it is going to have to face up to reality, sooner or later. Those of us within the Christian fold have the wonderful advantage of being familiar with the words and promises of Jesus. We are, of course, part of this world, but we can be *in* the world, but not *of* it. We can remind ourselves that 'we have not here a lasting city, but we look for one that is to come.' (Heb 13:14) There are people with a worldly mind-set who seem to live as if there's no tomorrow. If they have enough money, they can delay the onslaught of age, and live in total denial of their mortality. Money, power, and pleasure is their god, and they are accountable to nobody. It is tragic that such people would never listen to this promise, because they would never consider that it has anything to do with them. I'm sure that God, in his infinite mercy, will ensure that they are given equal opportunity. In the meantime, however, those of us who claim Jesus as our Saviour must pay heed to this promise. It is not a warning, of course; rather is it wonderful good news. For our own freedom, we badly need to be convinced and convicted when it comes to sin. Denial means bondage, and the Spirit frees us from the darkness of ignorance. The more convinced we are of our sinfulness, the more open we become to the offer of a Saviour. We also need to be very certain about the goodness of God. All good comes from God. If we want what is good for us, we go to God. God is infinitely just, and he calls on us to align our lives with what is just and fair. It is only right that he should hold us accountable for the gift of life he has given us. God gives us nothing for ourselves. Our life is given that it may be spent in the service of others. Only those who live this way are ever truly happy. We should also hold ourselves accountable for how we live our lives. We are entrusted with a great responsibility, and we should ensure that we act responsibly.

The result of all this is peace and happiness, in this life, and for eternity. God wants what is best for us. The Spirit is called the Comforter, someone who is there to accompany us through the struggles of life. When I learn to live and to walk in the Spirit, I experience a whole new freedom, and I begin to get a foretaste of what awaits me in heaven.

### *He will tell you about the future.*
### *(Jn 16:13)*

Jesus is Saviour of the room of my past, he is Lord of the room of my future, and he is God in the space that is today. Some people get trapped in the room of the past, with its guilt, regrets, and hindsights. Others are trying to live in the room of the future, with its worries, anxieties, and fears. In this promise, Jesus puts our minds at ease about the future, if we choose to listen to what he says. The Holy Spirit grounds us, enables us to live in the now, and to walk with quiet confidence. We lose all fear of what the future holds, when we become convinced that God holds the future. Once again, we are reminded that the Spirit will remind us of everything that Jesus told us. Jesus spoke about the future, about heaven, about eternal life. It is so easy for us to get bogged down under the cares of life, to become discouraged, to lose hope. We need to be constantly reminded of the good news about what the future holds. St Paul tells us 'we have not here a lasting city, but we look for one that is to come.' (Heb 13:14)

We are a pilgrim people. For forty years the Israelites wandered through the desert, and there must have been many occasions when they wondered just where they were going, and when they might arrive there. I'm sure it must have been part of Moses' remit to keep up their hope, to encourage them, to remind them of what lay ahead. He had to do this, even when he himself was unsure. They complained a lot and, at one time, some of them wanted to return to Egypt. Moses had to continually point to the Promised Land, and to keep this held out before them.

We are told that the Spirit will tell us about the future. How exactly does he tell us, and what exactly does he tell us? My deeper beliefs are things that I discover to be part of my thinking, and I seem to have a conviction about them that has come from nowhere. It is as if a seed had been growing all the time, and then, one day, a new flower opened out. The Spirit works quietly, but constantly. Jesus said 'Just as you can hear the wind, but don't know where it comes from, or where it is going, so it is with the Spirit.' (Jn 3:8) It is constant revelation, constant whisperings. The Spirit gives us hope, he awakens in us a deep sense of something greater than ourselves being in charge of things. We just sense it, we know it, even if we cannot understand or explain it. The Spirit enables us cling to the sure and certain hope that 'all is well, all will be well, and all manner of thing will be well.' As each new day comes along, and each day includes the daily bread for that day, we grow in quiet confidence, as we move into the future. We learn to relax, to slow down, to live life one day at a time. The wonderful thing about all of this is that, while we don't need to have exact knowledge about the future, relative to day and date, we have some very definite information. Firstly, we know we shall die one day. That is a certainty. We don't need any great revelation of the Spirit to convince us about that; although, of course, we do need to be reminded from time to time. Secondly, we come before God, without any hope of excusing, denying, or hiding. The canvas of our lives will be opened out fully, right to the edges. Thirdly, because we have trusted Jesus to pay our debts, to take away our sins, to reclaim us from the bondage of the evil one, we will stand before God, totally redeemed, with a valid passport and visa for heaven. That is our hope, and it is the Spirit that strengthens that hope in us. Once again, I say that we need not fear what the future holds, because God holds the future.

> *When the Father sends the Comforter, as my representative,*
> *he will teach you everything, and will remind you*
> *of everything I myself have told you. (Jn 14:26)*

This is a beautiful and a wonderful promise. Jesus is going away and, through the working of the Spirit, he will always be among us. The Spirit will be his spokesperson, who will continue Jesus' work. He will continue the teaching of Jesus, and he will also remind us of everything that Jesus taught us. We need the consolation and the assurance of this promise. We need constant teaching on the truths of the gospel. We need on-going revelation, something that prevents us staggering forward in the dark. Notice the word 'everything' repeated in this promise. That is surely good news. We can ask for nothing more than that.

The Spirit will teach us everything. What I understand by 'everything' is all that I need to know. I have many questions for which I do not have an answer. I believe that if the Spirit thought that I should know something, he would tell me. If he doesn't tell me, I am happy not to know. I am certain, however, that the Spirit is more than willing to teach me everything that I need to know, on my journey towards the eternal kingdom of heaven. Teaching is not a one-way dynamic. While one is teaching, it is presumed that someone is learning. In order to be able to learn, it is necessary to listen. If I cannot hear, or I do not listen to what the teacher is saying, there is no way that I can learn anything. This listening to the Spirit is at the heart of prayer. Prayer is not so much me talking to God, who doesn't hear, but God talking to me, who won't listen. This listening to God is called reflection, meditation, contemplation. It comes from a hunger to know, a deep desire to learn, a thirst for God's word. There is no way that I could ever know all that is to be known about God, but I can experience the on-going revelation that comes from the whisperings of the Spirit. In order to hear those whisperings, it is important to have moments of quiet reflection, moments of silent contemplation. I live in a world that is getting louder and louder. It is becoming increasingly more difficult to get a moment that is not invaded with noise of one kind or another. There is a radio playing in most kitchens, or offices, even if there's no one listening. There is often a television set switched on in a living room, even if no one is watching it. A lot of people we meet on the street have earphones on their ears, as their hands or their feet attempt to keep time to the music blaring in their ears. It is only when we are faithful to the hunger and the thirst to which I referred earlier, that I can have any hope of being disciplined enough to take time out to listen, and to learn. There used be a radio programme some years ago on the Irish language called *Listen and Learn*. It was a good title and, in order of priorities, it got the order right. I have to learn to listen, and then I listen to learn.

We are told in this promise that the Spirit will remind us of everything Jesus has told us. We need that reminding. It is so easy for us to forget. When we worry, become anxious, feel guilty, or lose hope, we have forgotten the promises of Jesus. Sometimes God's phone number is among our Emergency listings. We call on him when everything else has failed, and the boat is about to sink. It would save us so much heartache if we listened to the Spirit, who reminds us of everything Jesus said to us. Part of the work of the Spirit is to sharpen our awareness, to raise our alertness, and to waken up our sensitivities. Being alive to the Spirit is like wearing antennae on our heads, so that we are very aware of all that is happening within us, and around us.

There is wonderful consolation in this promise. It is something that must be deeply imprinted on our minds, hearts, and souls. To live our lives with openness to this on-going work of the Spirit is to lead fulfilled, fruitful, and meaningful lives. Not to avert to the message in this promise makes us run the risk of leading aimless, purposeless, and undirected lives. We find ourselves on the sea with no rudder, or no oars. This promise is a wonderful safeguard against disaster and heartache. It is that only to the extent that we heed it, accept it, and live it. Jesus makes the promise in good faith. He hopes that we have the good faith to accept it.

### *Other promises under the heading: Holy Spirit*

I will send the Comforter, the Spirit of truth. (Jn 15:26)

How much more will your heavenly Father give the Holy Spirit to those who ask. (Jn 11:13)

I will send the Holy Spirit, just as the Father promised. (Lk 24:49)

You will receive power when the Spirit comes on you, and you will be my witnesses ... to the ends of the earth. (Acts 1:8)

# Eternal Life

*This is the will of God, that I should not lose*
*one of those he has entrusted to me, but that I should raise them*
*to eternal life on the last day. (Jn 6:39)*

Jesus told us that he never said anything unless the Father told him to say it. His mission was to do the Father's will in everything. Original sin was one of disobedience, and it would be set right by a life of total obedience. For whatever reason I don't know, we have been entrusted to Jesus by the Father. That is why we have had the wonderful blessing of meeting Jesus, even if it was in our brokenness. Jesus came looking for sinners, and we can be grateful that he has found us, no matter how that meeting came about. While I don't know why we should have met him, all I can think is that he chose to meet us. It is certainly no unique merit on our part. Because we are entrusted to him, he tells us that, if any of us went astray, he would leave the ninety-nine, and go after the one that is lost, and he would not give up until that person is found, and returned to the flock. (Mt 18:12) He calls himself the Good Shepherd. In his day, a shepherd was someone whose whole purpose in life was to care for the sheep entrusted to him. It was always expected that a shepherd would die in defence of his sheep. Jesus died for us, so determined was he that not one of us would be lost. Taking care of us was yet another way of fulfilling the Father's will. The whole purpose of Jesus' life was to obey the Father in everything.

When Jesus was dying on the cross, he cried out to the Father 'It is consummated'(Jn 19:30), it is finished, I have finished the work which you gave me to do. While it is a fact that Jesus has completed his work, we continue to enter into the fullness of the results of that work. In other words, we are already saved, but we have to continue to travel the road of salvation, until we enter the fullness of salvation. When we speak of Jesus in the Mass, for example, we use the past tense. 'Dying, you destroyed our death, rising you restored our life, … By your cross and resurrection, you have set us free.' Whereas Jesus has already paid in full the price of our salvation, the full results of that will not be achieved until all of us have entered into eternal life. That is the promise of Jesus. He was entrusted with the mission of caring for us, not losing any of us, and bringing us all the way into eternal life. At the Last Supper, Jesus prayed to his Father, 'And all of them, since they are mine, belong to you; and you have given them back to me, so they are my glory.'(Jn 17:24) It is as if Jesus wishes to parade us into heaven, as free people, whom he has redeemed from slavery. We are the spoils of war, we are the rescued ones, 'saved from the hands of our foes, so that we might serve him in holiness and justice all the days of our lives in his presence.'(Lk 1:74-75)

If it is the will of God that none of us should be lost, it is important that we join our will to his. We do have free will, and the possibilities of what we can do with that privilege are frightening. God will not drag us anywhere. Jesus didn't want Judas to go out and hang himself, but he wouldn't stop him. He offers us peace, but we're free to live in misery and die of ulcers if we choose to. Sheep tend to follow along behind the shepherd, but I remember a shepherd describing how a sheep can be so sick and disorientated that it is liable to wander off in any direction. We can develop a spiritual sickness of soul through undernourishment, with the absence of prayer, reflection, or social conscience. The love of God calls for a response. Love always calls for a response. There is nothing so hurtful as unrequited love. If I read this promise once again, very slowly, what do I feel should be my response? What does this promise call for from me? It is a promise with wonderful hope. We have a Saviour who is genuinely interested, and caring for us in every way. He is watching over us on our journey, and he will be there to ensure that the journey ends up in glory. We are truly blessed ...

*Spend your energy seeking eternal life,*
*which I, the Son of man, can give. (Jn 6:27)*

Another translation says 'Work then, not for perishable food, but for the lasting food that gives eternal life.' He tells us that his flesh is food indeed, and his blood is drink indeed (Jn 6:55). Not on bread alone do we live, but on every word that comes from his mouth. (Lk 4:4) In another place, we are told 'Seek ye first the kingdom of God … and everything else will be added onto you.' (Mt 6:33) It is a question of priorities. I could become so busy worrying about the 'everything else', that I have no time to be bothered with the kingdom of God. I can become so busy with the urgent that I can overlook the important. An interesting experiment: Sit down, and check out how you spent your time and your money over the previous twenty-four hours. It often gives a fair indication of priorities. I usually find time and money for the things that really interest me.

Let us look at the words of this promise in a different order. 'I can give you eternal life, so you must show that you really want it.' God fills the hungry with good things. 'Blessed are they who hunger and thirst after justice, for they shall have their fill.'(Mt 5:16) When God puts a desire or a hunger in my heart, he provides the means to satisfy that hunger. Eternal life is his to give, and he is more than anxious and willing to give it to anyone who seeks it. 'Seek, and you shall find.' (Mt 7:7) He asked the man at the pool, 'Do you want to be healed?' (Mt 5:6) He asks us what we want, and he hopes that our answer will be 'eternal life'. 'Lord, to whom else can we go? You, and you alone, have the words of eternal life.' (Jn 6:68) Jesus has what we want and need; he knows that, and he hopes that we know that also.

We are all familiar with investing, hoping for a return. This investing could be money, it could be energy, it could be time. We invest in the expectation that it will bring a dividend, and that we will be better off than before. In this promise, Jesus invites us to invest our energies in seeking eternal life. The returns here are sure, certain, and never-ending. This is the greatest investment possible for any of us. It is not a gamble, or a lottery. If I found the possibility of investing money in something (legal!), and was absolutely certain that it would give an enormous return, I would be most foolish to ignore it. This investment is offered in my best interests. There is no snag, no catch, no small print. Once again, as in all the promises, all Jesus asks is that we believe him. The more I reflect on these promises, the more I realise just how offensive it must be to Jesus that we should continue to doubt him, to question, or to ignore. In these promises, he is pouring out blessings in abundance for us. He is extremely careful not to compel or manipulate us in any way. He makes the offer, stands back, and awaits our response.

I don't understand the word 'energy', as used in this promise, as being physical energy, as in some sort of muscular endeavour. There can be no muscular Christianity, and we should never become card-carrying members of the 'white-knuckle club'. I think of 'energy' as being interest, priority, and taking it seriously. It calls for more than just some form of mental assent. The promise must be met with a genuine acceptance, and a willingness to avail of it, and to live with that promise in mind. Jesus can give me eternal life, and I declare my sincere desire to receive that, I ask him for it, and I live in the expectation that I will receive it. Eternal life is not simply something I'll receive when I die. 'They who eat my Body, and drink my Blood have everlasting life ...'(Jn 6:54) This is something that we already have. As Jesus says in another promise 'Even if they die, they shall live ...' (Jn 11:25) In other words, our human death is but a second's flight into the fullness of life. 'Life is changed, not ended', as the Preface for a funeral Mass puts it. When I accept this promise, I begin a journey that will never end. I will actually look forward to that instant switch from mortal life to eternal life. I can live what's left of this life with peace, patience, and a quiet confidence. Yes, indeed, eternal life begins right now ...

> *Everyone who has left everything to follow me, will have a*
> *hundred times as much in return, and will have eternal life.*
> *(Mt 19:29)*

For most of my life, I had a very limited understanding of this promise. I had what was passed on to me at the time. It was seen as having to do with people who had a vocation to priesthood or Religious Life, and especially to those who left home and country, and travelled on the missions. I no longer confine this promise to such limits. I think of it as a promise made to anyone who is prepared to leave aside anything in their lives that gets in the way of following Jesus, and living the Christian life. We all have our defects and short-comings. We all have our pet addictions and compulsions. Some of these are harmless (being a football fanatic!), but some are also very major barriers to the work of the Spirit in our lives. A pattern of sin, of self-will run riot, and of selfishness, all of this just has to go if we are to follow Jesus. That is what I believe Jesus is referring to, when he speaks of leaving everything. When we find the pearl of great price, we must be prepared to sell everything else to purchase it. (Mt 13:46) Nothing must get in the way of following Jesus.

Lest this be seen as very demanding, and even a little harsh, it is important for us to remember that, with the call to follow Jesus, comes the grace to answer that call. I do not have what it takes to make any great or generous offer. It goes against my nature to have to surrender those things I tend to cling to. It is only by the grace of God that I can have the courage and the generosity to follow Jesus on his terms. Jesus tells us that we cannot serve God and mammon. (Mt 6:24) We are either for him, or against him. Following Jesus involves a very deliberate decision. It involves an act of faith that the grace will be given to do that to which I feel called.

The promise made to those who leave all things to follow Jesus is prodigally generous. They are promised 100% in this life, and eternal life when they die. Surely, nobody could expect any more than that. When we look at this promise, we realise just how little Jesus is asking of us. It is a very small price to pay. Jesus paid an enormous price for us, and he asks for very little in return. If I were an alcoholic, I am asked to give up alcohol, and the drip-drip suicide of such insanity, for a life beyond my wildest dreams. I am offered a second chance at life, and I am offered a life full of happiness, peace, and fulfillment. Not a bad exchange on my little investment! If I am in a relationship that is harmful to others, and devoid of moral responsibility, I am offered freedom from the bondage of selfishness, dishonesty, and moral cowardice. I am offered the freedom of truth, and the peace of knowing reconciliation with myself, and with others. Peace is what I experience when my relationships are the way they ought to be. If I am involved in deceit or fraud, and stealing from others, whether that means the company for which I work, or from an individual, I am offered freedom from furtiveness, lies, cover-up, manipulation, and deception. I can breathe deeply once again, and no longer need to be looking over my shoulder all the time. I said earlier that the demands in this promise may seem to be harsh but, when we really look at what is involved, we are asked to do something which showers us with enormous blessings, not just for this life, but for all eternity.

There are many reasons why I should want to leave everything, by way of major adjustment of lifestyle, and they may not necessarily be spiritual ones. It could be for health reasons, out of fear of the law, or to preserve a marriage, and keep a home together. Once again, the result is a good, and will bring many blessings. If, however, my decision is because I want to be single-minded and sincere in following Jesus, and living as he wants me to, then the fullness of this promise holds good. It is important to remember that with the call comes the grace to follow the call. If I am depending on my own power, I will never be able to act with any kind of courage or generosity. The promise from Jesus to supply the power is in many of the promises reflected on throughout this book. The Holy Spirit is like Popeye's spinach and, with the Spirit, I have all that is needed to respond to every call. St Paul tells to 'learn to live and to walk in the Spirit.' (Rom 8:4) Opening out, and entering in to the full implications of this promise, is one sure way to live and walk in the Spirit. When I am ready, the Spirit is ready to supply what is needed.

*This is the way to have eternal life, to know you,*
*the one true God, and Jesus Christ, whom you have sent.*
*(Jn 17:3)*

These words are taken from the prayer of Jesus at the Last Supper. He spoke these words to the Father. One of the ways to really get to know someone is to listen to that person praying, especially if the prayers are spontaneous, rather than memorised prayers, or prayers from a book. Listening to the prayer, when the other is not aware of this, gives a very good glimpse of what's going on in that person's soul. I just don't know how the gospel writer captured so much of what Jesus said in this prayer to the Father, but I am deeply grateful that he did. It is a beautiful prayer, and it gives some wonderful insights into the mind of Jesus. In this promise he speaks about knowing him, and knowing the Father. Notice he does not speak of knowing about himself or the Father. Knowing him implies a whole lot of things.

A theologian is someone who makes a study of God, who

seeks to gather knowledge about God. 'Theos' is the Greek for God, and 'logos' is the Greek for knowledge. It is impossible, of course, to know God through knowledge. We can come to know something about him in that way, by studying his works, in the light of reason and of nature. To actually know God, however, is something that flesh and blood cannot reveal, as Jesus told Peter. (Mt 16:17) When it comes to knowing Jesus or the Father, we depend totally on revelation. Jesus said, 'No one knows the Son except the Father, and no one knows the Father except the Son, and those to whom the Son chooses to reveal him.' (Lk 10:22) He also said that, when the Spirit came, he would tells us all about him. (Jn 16:26) No matter how we approach it, we can only come to know a Person of the Trinity through the revelation of another Person. Thomas Aquinas says that, when we speak of God, there is only one thing we are sure of, and that is that we're wrong! God is so much more than anything we could possibly say about him.

Anyone who prays is a theologian; someone who is coming to know God. It is a question of crossing the bridge from academic knowledge to experiential knowledge. The apostles spent three years in the company of Jesus. They were familiar with his appearance, his accent, his habits, his sayings, and his works. Yet it must be said that they still did not know him. It was only at Pentecost, when the Spirit came, that the scales fell from their eyes, and they actually came to know him. It was only then that they could embark on the way to eternal life.

Jesus speaks of us having eternal life. It is not something away off in the future, but something we can have right now. I can ask Jesus to reveal the Father to me. I can ask the Spirit to reveal Jesus to me. It all comes down to prayer. To know the Father, or to know Jesus, is to get into the mind of both, to listen to what they say, to act on that, and to develop a sense of travelling with them in life. It is much less complicated to have an openness to the Trinity. The very first prayer I was taught was to bless myself, when I said 'In the name of the Father, and of the Son, and of the Holy Ghost ...' (as he was then!). I can do a lot of my praying in this way. Because of what Jesus has done, I can enter into the life of the Trinity, I can share the divine life, I can draw life from them.

This promise, like all the other promises, is very specific. It is a simple statement of fact. Jesus was speaking to the Father, and he had no reason to waffle, or to be obscure. It is a simple fact that if we come to know Jesus, and to know the Father, we have eternal life. Once again, we are issued an invitation. If we want to have eternal life, we know what to do. There is no particular formula of prayer, beyond asking Jesus and the Spirit to reveal this great mystery to us. Surely, it can be expected that Jesus is more than willing to answer such a prayer. He came to reveal the Father to us, and the Spirit came to reveal Jesus to us. It is over to us, then, to declare our desire to know Jesus and the Father. This is a prayer that we can repeat again and again, while being absolutely certain that it will be answered. What a privilege for us that we should have eternal life. Surely this should completely transform our day-to-day living ...

**The water I shall give shall become a perpetual spring within them, giving them eternal life. (Jn.4:14)**

Jesus spoke these words to the Samaritan woman he met at the well. She spoke of the water in the well, and he spoke of something entirely different. That particular well was where Jacob, his family, and his cattle drank. It was considered very special and, if I may be facetious, if we had a similar well today, the water would probably be bottled and sold! Jesus accepted the sacred history of the well, and he may even have made a detour to reach it. He used the theme of the water and the well to teach a simple lesson about what he had come to offer. Jacob, his family and his cattle drank from this well, but they are all truly dead and gone by now. The water Jesus offered, however, was from an eternal spring, and the life it gave was eternal.

Because of our baptism, deep within our beings is a deep deep well, with a gurgling spring of water at its base. Unfortunately, however, the well can get cluttered up with the wreckage of life, and the water cannot rise to the surface. The Greek word for conversion is *kinosis*, which literally means to empty out. Conversion is a process of dumping overboard the flotsam and jetsam of life, so that the water can rise to the surface, and overflow into the lives of those around us. Beneath the driest desert there is plenty of water, but there are very few places where the water can reach the top. Each oasis is a source of life to plant, beast, and human. There are people who are like that. This is what Jesus is speaking about. This is what he is offering.

Jesus speaks of this spring being a perpetual one, one that will continue, and never dry up. We all have a deep thirst for the divine. The apostles told Jesus 'Everybody is looking for you.' (Mk 1:37) Unfortunately, many people search for what Jesus has to offer in places and in ways where it never can be found. Alcohol can never satisfy this thirst; nor can money, sex, or all the excitement the human heart can muster. Jesus tells us: 'If anyone is thirsty, let him come to me; and let him who believes in me drink, for the scripture says "Out of him shall flow rivers of living water".' (Jn 7:37) What Jesus offers us is something permanent, something that will transform our lives, and give us the kind of life that will continue for eternity. It is interesting to note that the woman at the well must have got some idea of what he was talking about, because she ran off to bring all her friends to meet Jesus.

As I said earlier, we all have this thirst. If we can identify it, we can then turn to Jesus and ask him to satisfy it. With the woman, we can ask: 'Give me this water, that I may never be thirsty again.' (Jn 4:15) This is an offer made to all of us, and it is up to each one of us to decide whether to accept that or not. We are all familiar with those times when our spirit feels like a desert. We feel completely dried up. It is as if someone pulled the plug on the oasis, and all the water has gone down the drain. The sparkle is gone, the spring in the step, the smile on the face are no more. It is at such a point that we are invited to come to Jesus. We ask the Spirit to release that inner spring, to water the garden of our souls. We accept the promise included in these words, and we act on that acceptance. No more dryness for us; no more death; no more stagnation. Jesus came that we should have life, and have it to the full. (Jn 10:10) We open our hearts, we open every corner of our inner beings, and we express a bold and definite desire for the eternal water which Jesus is offering. We want to be an oasis for others; we want to be life-giving people; we want to be fully alive ourselves. In the course of writing this reflection, I can see one of my confrères watering the front garden. It was raining earlier in the day, but he knows rightly that a shower of rain only wets the surface, and does nothing for the roots of the flowers and plants. It takes so much more than just a sprinkle to make a difference. Jesus is speaking of water that is flowing, a perpetual spring, water that is gushing. Nothing less will do for our parched souls. If we do not do this, we will look for satisfaction elsewhere, and will destroy ourselves in a fruitless search for something that only Jesus can give. Yes, Lord, give us this water, please. Let it rise up within us, and overflow into the lives of those around us ...

*Those who have done good will rise to eternal life.*
*(Jn 5:29)*

As I approach this promise, there are many thoughts and questions coming to me. What is the 'good' of which Jesus speaks? What of those unfortunates who are so mentally disabled as to be incapable of doing good? The idea of 'doing good' implies that eternal life is earned, rather than being a totally free gift. Surely salvation is a totally pure gift, earned for us by Jesus, through his death on the cross? How much good should one do to merit this reward? What about those who, through no fault of their own, have never learned anything but violence and destruction? The questions go on and on. I understand, of course, that my undertaking is to reflect on the promise, and not write a thesis on reward and punishment. It is not my present remit to deal with all the questions that come to mind. Jesus is speaking about what happens at the end of time. We will have what is called the Day of Judgement. On that day, each of our lives will be measured on the scales of justice. That justice will certainly allow for those who were unaware of reality, as well as those who knew no other way but the way they travelled. Most of us will have no excuse. Conscience is part of the human psyche. A parent can look at a young child, and know that he has been up to something! When I was a child, I had a dog that looked very guilty once he did something wrong. He lay on his back, as I approached him, expecting a slap. When he got patted, he jumped up, all excited, and jumped all over me, because he knew he was forgiven.

One simple way to get some kind of handle on this is to reflect on the following: God doesn't send me anywhere when I die. Rather will he eternalise the direction in which I choose to travel now. I think it reasonable to spread this concept to embrace all peoples, because there must be some form of accountability for our use of the gift of life. Rather than get into endless debate about what God may, or ought to do, I prefer to consider what we should do to merit this promise. The fact that I am writing this, and you, dear reader, are reading this, is some indication that we are open to the good. Jesus promises that every good we do will not be forgotten. Even if it's only a cup of cold water, given in his name, it will be remembered for all eternity. (Mt 10:42) There are those who could be called Anonymous Christians. These are people whose conduct is very much in keeping with Christian teaching, even if they do not subscribe to Christianity. I could be a pagan, and be a very good person. I could be a Muslim, with a life of prayer and fasting. Christians certainly don't have a monopoly on goodness. In my own life, I have never come across anybody that I would describe as being intrinsically evil. Of course, there are such people, but the average person is good at heart.

If we take the promise just as given, we are told that those who try to do good, and make some use of their lives, will surely rise to eternal life. Alongside the words quoted is the statement that those who do evil will rise to be condemned. This latter part is more of a threat than a promise. It does not form part of our reflection, however, so I will leave it without comment. It is true that salvation cannot be earned, but the necessary conditions for salvation can be nurtured. St Paul tells us that our salvation comes from 'his blood and our faith.' (Rom 3:25) It comes from what Jesus has done, and how we respond to that. There is nothing automatic about God. God will never over-ride or by-pass my free will. Nothing happens if my 'yes' is missing. 'The way that you show you are my disciples is that you love one another.' (Jn 15:14) We give witness to our faith through our actions. 'Faith, without good works, is dead.' (Jas 1:17) That is why Jesus speaks of those who have done good; not those who had nice ideas, or good intentions, that never came to anything. There is nothing more powerful that an idea whose time has come. 'I shall pass this way but once. Any good deed that I can do, any good word that I can say, let me do it now, let me say it now, because I shall never pass this way again.' 'Now is the acceptable time; today is the day of salvation.' To summarise what Jesus is saying: He will certainly bring us to heaven when we die, if we spend our lives bringing heaven down here, while we are alive. It is much more difficult to get heaven into people than to get people into heaven!

> *(Those who love their life in this world will lose it.)*
> *Those who despise their life in this world*
> *will keep it for eternal life. (Jn 12:25)*

Once again, we are faced with a promise that requires some reflection and comment, to clarify what exactly it says. It is important for us to remember the mindset of those to whom this statement was made. Then we must try to interpret the same concept in language of today. To revamp this statement in today's language, I would suggest something like this: If you put your own life over and above everything else, and are totally preoccupied with your own interests, you are most to be pitied, because life is passing you by, and you're not living at all. On the other hand, if you don't take yourself too seriously, get outside of yourself, not make yourself your first and only love, you will become involved in the lives of others; you will have a life that is filled with people and purpose; a life that will never end. The word 'despise' can be misleading, just as we are given a translation where Jesus commends us for hating our father and mother. It is most unfortunate that such translations are still presented to us.

Once again, we are reminded of works of charity, which is the hallmark of the Christian. In a way, the life of a Christian involves a form of dying. 'Greater love than this no one has, that a person should lay down a life for a friend.' (Jn 15:13) Dying to myself, for the sake of others, is to be a life-giving person. Death, in the human sense, is like a pile of sand at the end of my life, that I can take, and sprinkle it, fist by fist, everyday of my life. If I do this, I will have done my dying during my life, and the end will be the ascension. If, on the other hand, I wait till the end of

my life to die, it may well be too late. In the course of loving others, I may have to die to my possessions, my pride, my opinions,
or my prejudices. This is not despising love, but it is putting
others ahead of myself, where Christian service requires this.
Everything I invest in the service of others gives an eternal return. On the other hand, all those things that I keep for myself in
life, will die when I die. Life is a gift, given to us to be spent in
the service of others. Those people who are people of service are
the happiest people on earth. For them heaven has begun, because the way to heaven is heaven.

'Seek first the kingdom of God, and its justice, and everything else will be added onto you.' (Mt 6:33) The three rules of
the kingdom of God are: Jesus is Lord; everybody is of equal importance; and the power to live there is provided by the Holy
Spirit. Because Jesus is Lord, I cannot claim anything above my
standard of being a servant of this Lord. If everybody is of equal
importance, I will strive for justice, equality, and fair play for
those around me. If I can live in this kingdom only by the power
of the Spirit, I can accept the privilege, and also the responsibilities that go with that. In other words, if I am to live in the kingdom, I must be a person of service, who willingly accepts that
the most disabled person on this earth is here with as much right
as the greatest genius that ever lived. The kingdom of God now
is heaven later on.

Jesus tells a story about a sower that went out to sow seed on
his farm. He threw the seed in all directions, with prodigal generosity. All he could do was sow; it was up to the ground to do
the rest. I can be like the rocky ground, or the thorns, where the
seed came to nothing. On the other hand, I can be the good
ground that produces a crop. Notice that Jesus applies the word
'good' to ground that produced anything, even if it were only 30
or 60%. He does not demand 100% from all of us; and, indeed,
very few people would be capable of giving such a return. This
promise speaks of those who invest the gift of life in the service
of others, something that gives a return of eternal life.

Selfishness is a form of idolatry. It is putting self before God,
and before others. Total selfishness is the equivalent of living in
solitary confinement, where there is no one in my life but myself. Scrooge was miserable, because he was a miser; a word that

is closely related to 'miserable'. It was only when he began to give away his goods to others that he experienced happiness. That's what this promise is about. God will never be outdone in generosity. 'The measure with which you give, is the measure which you will receive.' (Lk 6:38)

### *The very words I have spoken to you are spirit and life.*
### *(Jn 6:63)*

Words, in themselves, say very little. It's the spirit in the words that makes all the difference. I could call you an idiot, and you might fall around the place laughing. The next day, if I called you an idiot, you could be deeply hurt. There is a completely different spirit in my words that second day. I meet people who ask me how I am, and I don't really tell them, because I can sense they don't really want to know! I could meet someone else who asks me how I am, and I sit down and tell them ... to such an extent that they may regret having asked me in the first place! It is never the words, but the spirit in the words, that matters. That's what Jesus is speaking about in this promise.

The words in the Bible are totally different from any words I may read in a newspaper. The words of the Bible are the words of God. They are inspired, which is to say, they come shot through and through with a power that makes it possible for me to respond to the word I hear. With the call, comes the grace to follow the call. Jesus tells us that his words are spirit and life. They are living words, words that inspire, that give life, that become flesh in our lives, as we put them into action. 'They that have ears to hear, let them hear.' 'You have ears, but you hear not.' (Mt 13:13) 'Happy are they who hear the word of God, and keep it.' (Lk 11:28) 'They that come from God listen to God's word.' (Jn 8:47) A very good motto is: Learn to listen, and listen to learn. Listening is a refined art, and it is a real way of loving someone else. Creative listening generates creative sharing. Some people are good listeners by nature. Others have to work hard at it, because they are usually more preoccupied with themselves than the person speaking. If I really believed what Jesus is saying in this promise, I certainly would give my full attention to every word that comes from his mouth. In this is the secret of real prayer. Prayer is not so much me speaking to God, who doesn't hear, as God speaking to me who won't listen. There is a great difference between saying 'Speak, Lord, your servant is listening', and 'Listen, Lord, your servant is speaking.'

All of us would like to be filled with spirit and life. We recognise those times when this happens, and it's just wonderful while it lasts. To approach the words of Jesus with expectation that this will be the result, is something that we should always keep in mind. 'Not on bread alone do people live, but on every word that comes from the mouth of God.' (Lk 4:4) There is a hunger within our hearts for the word of God and, without that word, we are badly malnourished indeed. The word of God is food for the soul, it is nourishment for the spirit. Spirit and Life are interchangeable words. God breathed his Spirit into the clay, and human life began. Without that spirit and life, we are dead, even if we're still walking around. Jesus said that he came that we should have life, and have it to the full. One of the ways he has of giving us life is through his word. Notice he doesn't say that his words will give us spirit and life. His very words are spirit and life. I find myself getting enormous life from this writing, because it involves reflecting on the words of Jesus all the time. It is a wonderful privilege, something for which I am deeply grateful.

There are many graces awaiting those who take Jesus at his word, in what he is saying in this promise. It opens us up to more willingness to listen to him, to hear his word, and to respond to that word. We soon become aware of the results of this promise in our lives. We become aware of a fresh inner liveliness, a greater awareness of being grounded, and a quiet desire to hear more and more of the word of God. It generates a hunger in us, and we soon decide not to settle for living on bread alone.

### Other promises under the heading: Eternal Life

Those who listen to my message, and believe in God who sent me, have eternal life. (Jn 5:24)

There will be special favour for those who are ready, and waiting for his return. (Lk 12:37)

If you want to be perfect, go sell all you have, and give the money to the poor, and you will have treasure in heaven. (Mt 19:21)

# Joined to Jesus

*Those who remain in me, and I in them, will produce much fruit.*
*(Jn 15:5)*

Remaining, in this context, means to be attached to, or to belong. In this same passage of John's gospel, Jesus speaks of us being the branches, and of he being the vine. The branches won't last long if they become separated from the vine. To be joined to Jesus is to have a sense that he is always within reach. He said that he would never abandon us, that he would be with us always. To live with that awareness is to be joined, or united with him. St Paul says of himself, 'It is not I who live, but Christ lives in me.' (Gal 2:20) After his resurrection, Jesus often appeared to his disciples, as if he actually came through the wall. He can enter right through the crust of our nature, if we invite him to. This promise implies a bond, where I am joined to Jesus, and he is joined to me. The vine and its branches is a very good image to help us understand what Jesus means here. The branch is an entity in itself, but it depends totally on the vine for life and sustenance. 'Apart from me you can do nothing', Jesus tells us. (Jn 15:4)

To remain in Jesus, and to be conscious of him remaining in me, is to live with a constant awareness of the source of my life, my strength, and of anything good within me. Some plants grow particularly well in certain gardens. The shelter, the soil, and all the other conditions are ideal. In another garden, the plant would die. In writing these reflections, it is my hope that the reader will be prompted to respond to each promise as an invitation. In this particular promise, my response is to evoke a sincere desire to be attached to Jesus, and never to be separated from him. This desire is placed in my heart by the Spirit, and it is the Spirit who makes it possible for this desire to be fulfilled. 'Peace on earth to those of goodwill.' (Lk 2:14) Again and again, I must declare my willingness to be open to everything Jesus is offering. If I have the goodwill, and am prepared to act on it, Jesus will certainly do the rest. There is not much point in an alcoholic asking Jesus to help him stop drinking, as he walks into an off-licence to buy a bottle. If the prayer is sincerely offered, asking for help not to go into an off-licence, there is some hope of it being answered.

'Those who remain in me' implies an on-going situation. It is not just a once-off occurrence. It is a day-in day-out fact of life. I want to remain in Jesus, and I want him to remain in me throughout every moment of my life, and for all eternity. Jesus came that we should have abundant life. It is only by being attached to him that I can have any life at all. The more I am united to him, the more alive I am. When I am united with him for all eternity in heaven, I will be more alive than I ever could be during this stage of my existence. It's ironical that people will speak of me then as being dead! The secret of maintaining this union with Jesus is a daily expressed prayer that this should be so. I cannot live today on yesterday's resolutions. Each new day requires its own new 'yes'. Any one of these promises gives us central material for prayer. I can pray my way through any one of them, and thus I can imbed that promise, as it were, in my mind and heart. The secret is to assume and consume the promises, so that they become integrated within my being. As I live them, I discover that I am growing in my awareness of them, and in my dependence on them.

What is the fruit of which Jesus speaks? Obviously, it is the fruit of good works. The gifts of the Spirit are given so that we can produce the fruits of the Spirit. The fruits are as a return for what God has invested in us. We are like the soil, in which the sower has sowed the seed. We are good soil if the seed can grow, and produce a crop. We cannot accept the privilege without accepting the responsibility that goes with it. It must be quite obvious that, if we are united to Jesus, we will produce much goodness in our lives. 'By their fruits you will know them.' (Mt 12:33) 'By this will all people know that you are my disciples, if you have love for one another.' (Jn 13:35) It is by the fruits our lives will be judged. Jesus told a story about servants who were given certain gifts or talents, and each was called to account for what they did with what was given to them. (Mt 25:15) It must be a wonderful consolation, at the hour of death, to be conscious of God's goodness, and of having lived a life that was rich in abundance. The quality of that life before death, is a foreshadowing of what is to follow.

*I will reveal myself to each of them.*
*(Jn 14:21)*

The context of this promise is where Jesus is saying that those who love him are those who obey him. He says that the Father will love them, he will love them, and he will reveal himself to them. Knowing *about* Jesus, and knowing Jesus are two entirely different things. There is a vast difference between academic knowledge and experiential knowledge. Jesus is speaking about experiential knowledge here. He will reveal his innermost thoughts, and I can come to know the mind of Christ. Scripture asks, 'Who knows the mind of the Lord?' (Rom 11:34) And Paul says, 'We, however, have the mind of Christ.' (1 Cor 2:16) During his public life, it is possible that the apostles never really knew Jesus. They knew what he looked like, what his voice sounded like, and what his everyday habits were. It is very possible, however, that they didn't know his mind, and could not follow the logic of his thinking. It is funny, but it's only after he left them and the Spirit came that they really came to know him.

I think that what happened the two disciples on the road to Emmaus is a very good example of how we can come to know Jesus. We come to know him only when he reveals himself, or when the Spirit reveals him to us. The disciples were deeply troubled. All their dreams had been shattered. They were on their way home, dejected and disappointed. They thought they were on to a good thing, but it had just blown up in their face. They were joined by what they thought was a tourist. They saw what he looked like, and they heard his voice. As they went along, they came to know something about what he thought. When he broke bread with them, we are told that their eyes were opened. 'Their eyes were opened, and they recognised him.' (Lk 24:31) It is not suggested that their eyes had been shut, that they had walked from Jerusalem with their eyes closed! They were given a new vision, an ability to really see him for who he was. St Paul never actually met Jesus in person, but when Ananias placed his hands on his eyes, the scales fell from them, and Jesus was revealed to him in a way that he never was to the other apostles during his earthly life. (Acts 9:18) It is as if the eyes of our souls are opened, and we receive a whole new vision.

I can ask Jesus for this beautiful favour. He offers this to us in the promise we are now considering. He is always willing and ready to reveal himself to us. All he can do is make the offer, and wait for us to respond. The only handle on the door of our hearts is on the inside. He cannot enter unless we open that door. Bartimaeus, the blind man, was sitting by the roadside, when he was told that Jesus of Nazareth was passing by. (Mk 10:46) He had a choice. He could cry out for help, or remain silent and die a blind man. He called out to Jesus, and his sight was restored. It is the same for any one of us. Jesus offers to reveal himself to each of us; not just to certain people, to a select few, to some chosen souls. This offer is for anyone who wants it.

In John's gospel, chapter ten, Jesus gives us the wonderful image of he being a shepherd, and we being the sheep of his flock. It is highly significant that he says, 'I know mine, and mine know me.' It is not knowing *about* him, having heard of him, or read the book. The disciples on the road to Emmaus said they had heard a rumour that he was alive. At that same time, a group of women met him, saw him, listened to him. As they continued on the road to Jerusalem, they had more than a rumour. They had proof, and definite evidence. He had revealed himself to them. They were privileged, and they knew it. It must be wonderful to receive such a revelation. It is something to pray for, to long for, to wait for. Again and again I must ask him to reveal himself to me. This is a prayer that I can expect him to answer. As I said at the beginning of this reflection, these words are spoken within the context of Jesus speaking about those who show their love for him by obeying him. Obeying him is about living as he asks us to. It would be a contradiction to ask Jesus to reveal himself to me, if I refuse to do what he tells me. Once again, I cannot accept the privilege without also accepting the responsibility. This is the wonderful thing about all of these promises. While the promises are total gift, there is always the understanding that we must seek to conform to his wishes for us. His only wish is for what is best for us, so we cannot claim that he is laying any burden on us. His yoke is easy, and his burden is light. (Mt 11:30) When we take a promise in its entirety, we open ourselves to much greater gifts and blessings than are inherent in the promise itself. Revealing himself to us is but the beginning of many other wonderful blessings.

*If I don't wash you, you won't belong to me.*
*(Jn 13:8)*

I have chosen to see this as a promise, even though it could be construed as a veiled threat. I can easily restate it to say: If you let me wash you, you will belong to me. These words were spoken at the Last Supper, when Jesus was washing the apostles' feet. When he came to Peter, who expressed shock that Jesus should wash his feet, he was told that if he didn't allow Jesus wash his feet, he would not belong in his kingdom. With typical Peter spontaneity, came the reply, 'Lord, wash not just my feet, but my head and hands as well.' Washing the feet was both a service and a highly significant act. It was washing off the dust of all their yesterdays, and it was offering a ministry of loving and caring. It was presented as a real-life practical example of how Jesus wanted them to treat each other. 'Jesus came to do and to teach.' (Acts 1:1) He did the act himself, and then he told his disciples to do the same. He healed others, and then he sent them out to heal. He fed the hungry, he taught those who yearned for spiritual nourishment, and he commissioned his disciples to spread the good news all over the world.

The great symbol of this washing is a sign of forgiveness, of being cleansed of our sins. He is washing the dust of the past from our feet; he is freeing us from that past. To allow him do this is to accept him as Saviour. If I do not accept him as Saviour, he cannot become Lord in my life. In the gospel story, Jesus was Saviour. He was not Lord yet, because he was not yet glorified; he had not yet returned to the Father; he could not yet give the Holy Spirit. In our lives, Jesus has to be Saviour, before he can become Lord. That is why it is vital that I accept his ministrations as Saviour, when he wants to wash away my sins. 'Wash me yet more from my iniquities, and cleanse me from my sins.'(Ps 50) Jesus loves forgiving sins, and he was always ready and willing to say, 'You sins are forgiven.' He came to take away the sins of the world, and it gladdens his heart when a sinner de-clares a willingness to 'give up his auld sins'.

The first step of walking with Jesus is to invite him, and to allow him, to wash my feet. I do want to belong to him, so I have got to open my heart to his forgiveness, and to have my sins washed away. In the Divine Mercy image, Jesus is shown with two rays streaming from his heart. The red rays represents his blood, and the white ones the water, both of which flowed from his heart when his side was lanced on the cross. To stand be-neath the cross, so that I can be washed in that blood and water, that is salvation. Appealing to his compassion and mercy is a di-rect request to be washed clean. It is possible that my religious training prepared me for all I was going to do for Jesus. It would be a great pity if this meant shifting the focus away from what I am willing to allow him do for me. It is sad that Jesus, after giv-ing everything he had for us, should then have to turn to us and beg us to accept what he earned for us through his passion and death. One should expect that we would have a burning desire to open our hearts to every grace he offers, and to be filled with gratitude for that privilege. What a wonderful God we have! Jesus said that he did not come to be served, but to serve. (Mt 20:28) When he comes again in glory, he tells us that he will gird himself, and minister to those who are ready, awaiting his com-ing. This is not the general impression of God that most people have. Jesus told his disciples that the greatest among them are those who serve. (Mt 18:4) Our hearts should be filled with grat-itude that Jesus wishes to make such direct and effective contact with us. He is a very personal God, and he sees each of us as an individual. He asks personal questions. 'Who do you say that I am?' (Mt 16:15) 'Will you also go away?' (Jn 6:67) 'Do you love me?' (Jn 21:15) As I reflect on the promise under review, I tell him of my willingness and desire that he should wash me of my sins, and cleanse me of my selfishness. I can tell him this with confidence, because the idea came from him, in the first place. As with Peter, he insists that, unless we allow him wash away our sins, and all the wreckage of the past, we cannot belong to him. It is difficult to imagine anyone refusing such an offer, even though everything is possible.

*Be sure of this: I am with you always, even to the end of time.*
*(Mt 28:18)*

One can't help noticing that this promise begins with the words
'Be sure of this ...' Jesus is always concerned that we should believe him, and take him seriously. This is a very clear and definite promise. He assures us, beyond all doubt, that he is with us
always, and will continue to be with us until the end. It is a very
special grace to obtain the gift of faith to believe and accept this
promise exactly as given. Faith is a gift. It is not something I can
generate by myself. 'I believe, Lord, help my unbelief; ... Lord,
increase my faith.' (Jn 9:38; Mk 9:24) In my own experience, I
find that I turn to the Spirit to help me in this area. Faith is one of
the gifts of the Spirit. There is a virtue of faith, which is practised
and developed through use. This has to do with certain truths in
which I believe, and certain practices in which I engage. This
grows with practice, and becomes stronger with time. There is
also a gift of faith, which is something planted in my soul by the
Spirit. It is a pure free gift that is given without reference to my
worthiness or virtue. This gift enables me have a deep awareness and conviction about certain truths, and a confidence to act
on them, in the sure and certain knowledge that they will hold
up for me.

    With that gift of faith, this promise becomes a very powerful
force in my life. I just know that I am never alone. Jesus walks
with me into each and every situation. When I lie awake at
night, he is there with me. When I wander through the park he is
walking with me. Being aware of the reality of this is a source of
great comfort and reassurance. As a very limited human being, I
can feel totally alone in the midst of a crowd. The people are 'out
there', and I am not involved. With Jesus, it is entirely different.
Jesus is within me, and I carry him with me wherever I go. As a
Christian, I can be like Mary when she visited Elizabeth. She
brought Jesus into that situation. A very popular spirituality
some years ago was called 'practising the presence of God'. It involved developing an on-going sense of God's presence at all
times. For whatever reason, it is seldom spoken of now. This
promise brings us back to it. If Jesus is with me at all times, then
surely I need to develop a constant sense of that truth.

I have come across a few people who live with this belief. One elderly lady, living alone, is never conscious of being alone. 'I talk to him all day long', she told me. It was just wonderful to hear the conviction in her voice, as she described how she spends her day, and her waking night hours, very conscious of his presence. Another person I know is nervous of driving in the city. As she opens the door of the car to get in, she invites Jesus to enter first, and she clears away any items on the front passenger seat to make room for him! This is very real to her and, so far, it seems to work, so I wouldn't knock it. By the nature of my work, I spend long hours alone here in my office at the computer. I have succeeded in growing ever more conscious of his presence, and the most important part of the promise, for me, is that he will be with me till the end. It is so easy to fret and worry about the future. It helps a great deal when I am conscious that Jesus who is with me today, will be with me every other day as well.

Once again, I draw attention to the opening words of this promise 'Be sure of this …' This helps re-enforce the message. I can be absolutely sure of it. I can walk each day, with a sense that he is both with me, and one step ahead of me. 'They who follow me shall not walk in darkness, but will have the light of life.' (Jn 8:12) I don't want to walk in the dark. It is so easy for any of us to stumble, and to end up going down a different road. He is with me, and I must determine that I will stay with him. I can develop a sense of his presence, as I live out each day. I can use some short prayers to emphasise this. In the words of the song I can say, 'Jesus, I know you are near; standing always at my side. You guard me from the foe, and you lead me in ways everlasting.' In the words of the Psalmist, if I climb the mountain he is there; if I enter into the deep, he is also there. (Ps 139) It is said that it's better to be alone than to be in bad company! What better company could I have than Jesus and, because of him, I am never alone.

*Where two or three are gathered together in my name,*
*there I am in the midst of them. (Mt 18:20)*

I remember when Charismatic Renewal first came on the horizon, this was a phrase that was often used by those who felt uncomfortable with silence! Someone was always sure to drag it in, and I often wondered just how deep was the reflection which it evoked. This is a beautiful promise, and it is a wonderful assurance to any of us gathered together as a group of Christians. When Jesus ascended into heaven, he brought the body he had with him. He said he would send the Spirit, and he depended on us to provide the body. A spirit cannot do anything by itself. An evil spirit needs someone's hand to plant the bomb, or someone's tongue to tell the lie. Likewise, the Holy Spirit needs our hands, feet, and voice so he can minister to others through us. I place my hands on the sick, and the Spirit does the rest. I open my heart and my mouth to pray, and I can expect the Spirit to take it from there. 'When you are arrested, do not worry what you are to say; when the hour comes, you will be given what you are to say. For it will not be you who will speak, but it will be the Spirit of your Father in you.' (Mt 10:19-20)

What this promise is saying is that when a few of us gather together as Christians, that we form the Body of Christ. 'Christ has no body now but yours; no hands, no feet, no voice on earth but yours.' This certainly is a most extraordinary way of making us one with him. While waiting for Pentecost, we are told that Mary and the apostles 'prayed with one mind and one heart.' (Acts 1:14) This is the ideal for any gathering of Christians. When I pray, I am praying as an individual. When I unite with others, the Father looks down and sees the face of Christ. Praying with one mind and one heart results in powerful prayer. Jesus is certainly there in the midst of them. In fact, they represent him, and it is Jesus who is actually praying. 'If you ask the Father for anything in my name ...' (Jn 16:24) It is by being subsumed into Jesus, and becoming one with him, that I can come to the Father. The story of salvation can be summarised as follows: Imagine that my car was stolen. After some time, the car is recovered, and the person who stole it is brought into my presence. What would I do or say? I won't answer that question! If I were God, however, this is what I would do: I would forgive him, hand him the keys of the car, and provide him with a free petrol voucher for the rest of his life! Sounds crazy? It is crazy, and it is only God who could think of doing such a thing. Original sin was people trying to become as good as God. What did God do? He forgave them; he devised a plan of salvation that enabled them share in his divinity, and he sent the Spirit as the petrol to enable them live this way for the rest of their lives.

It is only when we take time out, like we're doing now, to really reflect on the full implications of what Jesus told us, that we get any idea of just how magnanimous and prodigally generous his promises are. What a tragedy it would be not to give serious thought to such wonderful offers. Every promise should serve to open my heart ever wider to receive his many graces. I say 'yes' again and again to each and every promise. The name I chose for this book is *Jesus said it … and I believe it.* Both parts of that title are equally important. If Jesus said it, and I didn't believe it, nothing happens. The key that opens the door of my heart is willingness. I offer him my goodwill, and I declare again and again that I am open to everything he is offering, and to everything he asks. Jesus is a personal God. If he is present in the gathering, I should be aware of that presence. It would be a mistake to imagine that he is somewhere among the crowd, if I don't experience him there. Mary and Joseph made that mistake one time. They presumed that Jesus was somewhere in the crowd and, when they got home, they discovered he wasn't there at all. By constantly reminding myself, and involving the help of the Spirit, I can develop a deep awareness of his presence, when I come together as part of a Christian community. It certainly will mean that my presence there will be much more meaningful.

*I am the light of the world. If you follow me,*
*you won't be stumbling through the darkness,*
*because you will have the light that leads to life. (Jn 8:12)*

Once again, we see this promise as an invitation. When Jesus speaks about his part of the promise, he is very definite. 'I *am* …; you *will* …' When he refers to us, he says, 'If you …' There is al-

ways that X-factor that no one else, not even God, can supply
without my consent. Many of us may be familiar with the Divine
Mercy picture where, written at the top of the picture are the
words 'Will you help me?' I must confess that, at first, I was puz-
zled by that. After some thought I came to accept it as meaning,
among other things, 'Will you help me to help you?' Without my
co-operation, he can do nothing for me. Jesus invites us to follow
him, and he makes a serious commitment to those who choose
to do so. They will walk in the light, on a road that leads to life.
They will not stumble, as people can do who walk in the dark.
Life can present us with many obstacles, and it is very easy to
get tripped up. I can easily find myself stumbling, without a
road-map, or a compass. Jesus wants to walk before us on the
way, to lead us, to prepare the way before us.

I get one chance at life, and it is important that I take it seriously, to the extent that I accept responsibility for how I live it.
Life is a journey, but it is a journey that leads somewhere. If you
don't know where you're going, then any road will bring you
there! Jesus is speaking about bringing us to life. He came that
we should have life, and have it to the full. Our present life is but
a preparation for eternal life. We need to be directed through
this life, to ensure that we are on course for that eternal life.
Without the light of Jesus, we can stumble and fall. Of course,
we can and may fall, but the danger is that we may not be able to
get up again. To stay down is hell. St Augustine says that our
glory consists not in never falling, but in getting up every time
we fall. Jesus is the light of the world. He came into a world in
darkness, a world which lived with the direct results of original
sin. If there was any hope of bettering oneself, it had to be
through meticulous attention to every detail of the law; it had to
be through hard-earned merit and reward. People could never
be sure of this, because there was no way to quantify it. They
could just hope to stumble along, and depend on their own efforts to get them somewhere safe from eternal disaster. For those
who were open to listen, Jesus' message must have been an
extraordinary ray of hope. At long last, the sea had opened out
before them, and they saw a safe and sure way out of slavery.
Jesus himself would be their Moses. He himself would lead
them. All they were asked to do was to follow him.

What exactly does 'follow him' mean? It means listening to what he says, accepting his promises, and trying to live as he tells us to. He gives very clear guidelines. In offering us the Holy Spirit, it is his way of ensuring that we are kept close to the truth, and that we don't wander into the darkness of deceit and lies again. He told us that the Spirit would lead us into all truth, and remind us of everything he had told us. That is surely giving us more than an even chance. Following him means going out there, and doing things his way. Original sin was the result of humans deciding to do things their way, to travel their own way. 'If you love me, you will obey me.' (Jn 14:21) Jesus came to do the Father's will in everything. He did that to perfection. Then he turns to us, and tells us to do what he tells us.

It is worth noting the particular order of words in the last part of this promise. 'You will have the light that leads to life.' This is a statement of fact; it is more than a promise. The gift is ours for the taking. We can, of course, choose to walk in darkness, and in the shadow of death. If we choose to follow him, however, the rest is automatic. It is automatic in that the decision to follow leads on to eternal life. That eternal life begins right now. Our ordinary human existence takes on an eternal value, an eternal dimension. We already experience ourselves as being very much alive. In other words, when we know that we are saved, we begin to look and sound like people who are saved! We just don't settle for arriving anywhere. We have decided that we want to end up with eternal life, we have found the way that leads there, and we are prepared to travel on that way, so that we will never walk in darkness, but will have the light of life.

*If you stay joined to me, and my words remain in you,*
*you may ask anything you like, and it will be granted. (Jn 15:7)*

If I take the latter part of this promise in isolation, and read 'you may ask anything you like, and it will be granted', then I get a fairly clear idea of the core of this promise. There are conditions, of course, but the promise is definite and unambiguous. Quite a lot of our prayers are ones of petition. What we pray for varies from routine to desperate. There is something within us that urges us to try to bribe God, to rattle the cage of heaven, to get immediate attention. Many of our prayers do not brook a refusal. When our prayers are desperate, as for someone dear who is terminally ill, we may try to put God in a position where he cannot possibly refuse us. All of this is perfectly understandable, both to God, and to us mere humans.

This promise gives a clear and direct path of prayer. Jesus is our mediator between God and us. He is the one who bridges the gap between us and the Father, the source of all life. He is the Way, the only Way. That is why he directs us to pray to the Father through him. When I am joined to him, I pray in his name; I do not go it alone. He speaks of us as the branches, and he is the vine and, cut off from him, we can only wither and die. Jesus is the umbilical cord attaching us to the Father, the source of all life. There is no way we can come near to the Father, without crossing the bridge, or the Red Sea, which is Jesus. Jesus has one hand in the Father's, and the other held out to us. He is the one who brings the Father and child together. I kneel at the foot of the cross, as the drops of blood fall to earth, and I know, beyond doubt, that in this is the price for my sins being paid, in this is my salvation. 'The dead arose, and appeared to many.' (Mt 27:52) I arise from death, to live with a whole new life, because Jesus has reconciled me to the Father through his death. 'Apart from me you can do nothing.' (Jn 15:4)

It is not enough that I remain joined to Jesus, but his words must remain in me as well. What exactly does this mean? It means that his words find a home in my heart. When they are heard there, they become flesh, and I begin to live them. When his words are in my heart, I always know exactly what to do to conform to his will for me. His words guide my life. His words become the nourishment for my spirit. 'Not on bread alone do people live, but on every word that comes from the mouth of God.' (Lk 4:4) His words provide me with a map for life, because Jesus is the Way. His words are shot through with his Spirit, who leads me into all truth, and this is the only way in which I will ever arrive at freedom. Jesus speaks of his words remaining in us. We are familiar with the expression 'in one ear, out another.' Jesus is speaking of the very opposite to that here. His words are like a generator within from which we draw power, inspiration, and courage. When others despair, we cling to his promises. His words are all that keep us going, when things get bad. When I come to die, all I'll have to cling to are his promises. His words are what give me any hope for the future.

And now we look at the last part of the promise, the one that many people might respond to first. Like all the promises, there is a condition. There is nothing automatic about God. Pouring water on a baby does not guarantee that the baby will grow up to be a Christian. Kneeling down, and saying lovely words to each other during a wedding ceremony, does not mean that the couple will really come to love each other, until death do them part. There are certain things that must be done, before the Lord can produce the result. I have to sow the seed, before the Lord provides the harvest. I have to buy the Lotto ticket, before I can hope to win the fortune. What this promise tells us is that, if we want to have our prayers answered (providing the answer is for our good), then we must attach ourselves to Jesus, the conduit of the Father's love, and we must keep and practise his word. 'If you love me, you will obey me, and then you can ask the Father for anything in my name …' (Jn 14:21) Jesus loves us too much just to answer our prayers, and leave it at that. In offering to answer our prayers, he is inviting us to come closer to him, to be firmly attached to him, to be nourished by his word, so he can really bless us abundantly beyond our wildest dreams. He is not satisfied just to answer a single prayer, without using that occasion as an opportunity to open the doors of our hearts for many other and greater blessings. Prayers of petition, without any follow-up, can become a very selfish exercise. God would be enabling us to become more and more selfish. God loves us exactly as we are, but he loves us too much to leave us as we are. This promise is about many blessings but, if I meet the conditions of the promise, it will lead to even greater and endless blessings. What a wonderful God we have, and how truly blessed we are!

### *Other promises under the heading: Joined to Jesus.*

Remain in me, and I will remain in you. (Jn 15:4)
If you give up your life for me, you will find true life. (Lk 9:24)
Apart from me you can do nothing. (Jn 15:5)

# Salvation

*I am not asking you to take them out of the world,*
*but to keep them safe from the evil one. (Jn 17:15)*

One of the surest ways of getting to really know another is to eavesdrop on that person's prayers! I don't recommend it, but there are times, in the company of the elderly, when they pray quite audibly and obviously from the heart. In John's gospel, chapter 17, we get to listen in on a long prayer of Jesus to the Father. For those with any interest in just what kind of person Jesus is, how he thought, and what he might be saying to the Father, this is, indeed, a wonderful treasure. It is a chapter that would greatly reward long and prayerful reflection. I have taken the above quote as a promise, because there is a very real promise implied in it. He is speaking to the Father about us. He doesn't ask that any of us should bypass the normal process of living our lives here in this world, but he asks that we be kept safe from all harm during our sojourn here.

In what way do I see this as a promise? I see it as a promise because Jesus is asking the Father for something for us, and I believe the Father would surely answer such a prayer. When Jesus prayed in the Garden he was praying for himself. 'Father, if it is possible, remove this chalice from me; yet not my will, but yours be done.' (Lk 22:42) In this case he asked the Father for what was best, and what was according to his will. Events showed that Jesus had to die to complete the work of redemption. When he prayed at the tomb of Lazarus, or before he multiplied the loaves and fishes, however, he was praying for someone else, and he very definitely expected these prayers to be answered. He even said, 'Father, I thank you that you have heard me.' (Jn 6:11) He knew already that the Father was going to do exactly as Jesus asked. I think of the prayer under review as being another such prayer. He is praying for us, and the fact that we are allowed listen in on that prayer, and know what Jesus is asking for us, I have no hesitation in looking upon this as a sure and certain promise. Jesus tells us that, if we ask the Father for anything in his name, we will receive. (Jn 16:23) How much more certain, then, can we be when it is Jesus himself who is offering the prayer?

From our point of view, what we are promised here is to be kept safe from the evil one. Jesus came, among other things, to end the reign of Satan in this world. He called Satan 'the prince of this world', and we are told that Satan offered Jesus the kingdoms of the world if Jesus would adore him. Before Jesus came, these kingdoms were Satan's to offer. When Adam and Eve fell for the lie in the Garden they came under new management. Jesus came to establish the Kingdom of God. 'Seek ye first the kingdom of God, and its righteousness, and all things will be added onto you.' (Mt 6:33) The very real problem we mere humans have is that Satan is so much more intelligent than we are. He is extremely cunning, and very patient. St Peter tells us to 'be sober and alert because your enemy the devil prowls about like a roaring lion, seeking someone to devour'. (1 Pet 2:8) It is obviously very important to Jesus that we are kept safe from the clutches of Satan. He gives us full authority over 'all the power of the evil one'. He assures us that he has overcome Satan and, in the quote under review, he even prays that we might be kept safe. He obviously sees us as very vulnerable. This vulnerability comes from two sources. Firstly, of ourselves, we just do not have what it takes to protect ourselves from evil. Because of Original Sin we are fundamentally flawed, and we can even be attracted to evil. The second source of our vulnerability comes from our own foolhardiness, and our pride. Jesus tells us to 'watch and pray'. In life, we walk through landmine country, and, if we are stupid enough not to live under the protection of the Lord, then we are sure to end up in disaster. Jesus loves us too much, and has done too much for us to allow this to happen. It would be wonderful to be conscious of the protection that is offered us, and to avail of that protection at all times.

*Anyone who believes and is baptised, will be saved. (Mk 16:16)*

When Jesus was sending his disciples out to preach the good news, and to baptise in his name, he made this promise. This would be the result of their apostolate. That promise holds as good today as it did back then. St Paul tells us, 'God makes us holy by means of faith in Jesus Christ, and this is applied to all who believe, without distinction of persons.' (Rom 3:22) Another translation tells us that our salvation is brought about by Christ's blood, and our faith. Jesus has completed his part of the equation, and it then depends on whether we are willing to accept that or not. Belief in Jesus and what he has done for us opens us up to accepting the fullness of his love. The fullness of that love is salvation, which guarantees us eternal love. The greatest way of thanking Jesus for what he has done for us, is to accept, with gratitude, all the graces and blessings that come from that.

I am not taking it for granted that we all have an equal understanding of what belief really is. It is so much more than just knowing something to be a fact. When I accept that fact as true and, because I know it is true, I can safely act on it, I am beginning to translate the knowledge into faith. Knowledge is in my head, faith is in my heart, and it often expresses itself in my feet, when I step out and do something. Without wishing to over-dwell on this, I wish to make a distinction between knowledge, belief, and faith. Knowledge is gaining facts and information about something. Belief is accepting those facts and that information as being true. Faith is a reliance and trust on the dependability of those facts, and of that information, that enables me step out and act, knowing that I will not be let down, or disappointed. The disciples were to tell the people about Jesus. This included facts about him, and what he taught. The Spirit working in them would give conviction to their words, and the listeners would know that what they are being told was true. The response of the listeners, then, was to come forward, accept what had been said, and follow through on this with a request to be baptised as followers of this Jesus of whom they had been told. When they believed and were baptised, their feet were set on the way of salvation, and their names were registered as citizens of heaven. Through believing, and being baptised, they had met their part of the bargain, and there is never any doubt that Jesus will always meet his promises in all such cases.

Living the Christian life is living with a definite set of beliefs. These beliefs, these convictions, these truths, are what guide my

behaviour in every dimension of my life. When I make a decision to follow Jesus, I refuse all other options on offer. 'Decision'
comes from the French word *decider*, or the Latin *decidere*, which
means to lop or cut off. All other options are gone. As Jesus says,
there is only One Way, and that way is the only one that leads to
salvation. To accept that truth, and to decide to take Jesus seriously, is another way of saying 'anyone who believes, and is
baptised'. From my own experience, it is important to constantly
check exactly what I mean when I speak of 'believing' in something. I have already made a few distinctions between knowing,
believing, accepting, acting, etc. One very important point, however, is the role of God's Spirit in all of this. I know that faith is a
virtue, which is something I can exercise and develop. The kind
of faith which interests me, however, is entire gift. It is one of the
gifts of the Spirit. The apostles knew Jesus on a certain level.
They knew what he looked like, what his voice sounded like.
They saw him work wonderful miracles, and give inspiring
teaching. Yet, when push came to pull, they deserted him, ran
away, and denied him. There was something lacking, and that
would only be supplied when the Spirit came upon them at
Pentecost. With the Spirit came the gifts of the Spirit. One of
those gifts was faith and, with that gift, they would follow Jesus
all the way to a martyr's death. Nothing would ever be the same
away. Their baptism was now complete, and so was their faith.

> *When everything is ready, I will come and get you,*
> *so that where I am, you also will be. (Jn 14:3)*

I am trying to approach this promise as if it were the very first
time I heard it. I read the context in which it was spoken. Jesus
was taking his leave of his apostles. They were sad because he
was leaving them, but he was endeavouring to reassure them. It
was *au revoir*, but not goodbye. It was understandable that the
apostles would be totally mystified, and very afraid. What was
going to happen to him? Where was he going? What is going to
happen to us? How long will we have to wait until he comes to
bring us with him? On the other hand, Jesus knew exactly what
he meant, and his promise was sincere and serious. One of the
problems, at the time, is that the apostles would have to wait till

the Spirit came, when they would receive wisdom, understanding, and faith, and the full implication of this promise would become clear to them. It is an historical fact that the apostles were
expecting Jesus to return very soon. St Paul's Letters refer to this
several times. 'The Lord is coming soon.' (Phil 4:5) This phrase 'I
am coming soon' is repeated in the visions of St John, as recorded
in the Book of Revelations. (Rev 3:11, 22:7, 22:12, 22:20) It is significant that the very last words in the Bible are 'Come, Lord
Jesus.' (Rev 22:20)

There are four long sermons in the early part of the Acts of
the Apostles. They show a very important part of early church
teaching. The sermons are similar, in that they stress the same
points. The Messiah has come, and his name is Jesus. You rejected
him, and you killed him. He rose again from the dead, just as he
said he would. He will return again at the end of time. All of this
was presented as good news. The fact that Jesus was coming
again was wonderful good news for the early believers. The
Jesus of which they spoke, and whom many of them had known
personally, was someone who would always be a friend; someone who would always do what was best for them. The Spirit of
Pentecost had driven all fear out of their hearts. They were filled
with a 'sure and certain hope'. (Heb 11:1) Hope is not something
I can see; it is something I expect to happen. It has more to do
with the future than the present. The hope of the early church
caused them to look forward to the second coming of Jesus.

For most of us, this promise has to do with us being called
home in death. I accept this as a valid interpretation, and it
makes great and good sense to me. I hear Jesus assuring me that,
one day, he will come for me, so that, where he is, I also will be.
(Jn 14:2) This is a promise of great hope. I don't pretend to understand the 'when-everything-is-ready' part, because, in our
human experience, death seldom comes at the right time. For
some, it comes too soon, as with cot deaths. For others, it is long
overdue, as they continue to linger into ageing senility. I don't
feel, however, that I want or need to understand this. God
knows what he's doing, and that's OK by me. I sometimes fanta-
sise what vision I will have, from heaven, as I look back down
through the corridor of my life. It is possible that I may see that
much of what happened in my life was for my good, even if I

failed to see this at the time. This may also include seeing that the timing of my death was part of a plan, and that 'everything was ready' when he called me home. Where this thought begins to limp is when I reflect on violent deaths, genocide, or death from hunger. Rilke, the philosopher, says that, 'Life is a journey from the certainties of callow youth, to a point where I find myself living with questions. I learn to live with the questions, and I come to love the questions, knowing that, at some future date, I will come into possession of all the answers.'

This promise is a source of great hope for me. Of course, I depend totally on the Spirit to impress this deeply within my heart. As I reflect on this, and other promises, I am becoming more and more aware of the role of the Spirit in all of this. 'The Spirit will teach you, and remind you of everything I have said to you.' (Jn 16:13) When I reflect on the promises of Jesus, I become more and more convinced that, when push comes to pull, I have nothing else to cling to. If the *truth* behind the promise now under review makes its way from my head down into my heart, it can have a profound effect on how I see, and think of the future.

Jesus guards us with total jealousy. He is sometimes referred to as a 'jealous God'. This is not our ordinary and usual interpretation of the word 'jealousy'. In this context, it means that, because of his great love for us, he wants us totally for himself. This is all for our good, because it is only in belonging totally to Jesus that we will ever find peace. 'You have made us for yourself, O Lord, and our hearts can never be at rest until they rest in you.' (St Augustine) In this promise, Jesus commits himself to bring to completion the plan he put in motion when he came to save us. He will not be at peace, and we certainly won't be at peace, until we have joined him in eternal glory in his kingdom.

> *I have come to save the world, and not to judge it.*
> *(Jn 12:47)*

It may seem simplistic, but I consider the Lord's dealings with us under three headings. Firstly, in Creation, God opened up an era of infinite love for us. We rejected that so, in Jesus' coming among us, he opened up an era of infinite mercy and forgiveness. If we reject this, I believe we will come face to face with a

God of infinite justice. Jesus came to save us, not to judge us. The gospels present us with many instances of how he dealt with sinners, how he befriended them, and how he showed a special preference for them. We are all sinners, of course, but we depend on the Spirit 'to convict us of sin'. (Jn 16:8) Jesus speaks of the Spirit as a Spirit of truth who will 'lead us into all truth, and the truth will set you free.' (Jn 8:32) Part of the problem with sin is best understood in reference to alcoholism. Alcoholism is one of the few diseases known to medicine, where part of the problem is that it denies its own existence. Everybody knows that John is an alcoholic, but it is only when he can see that, accept it, and understand it, that his recovery can begin. 'If we say that we have no sin, the truth is not in us, because God says that we are sinners.' (1 Jn 1:8)

It is very difficult to speak about a Saviour to those who are not convinced that they are sinners. When the angel appeared to the shepherds that first Christmas night, they were told, 'I am here to give you good news, great joy for all the people. Today a Saviour has been born to you.' (Lk 2:10-11) The shepherds must have had some sense of needing *something*, because they accepted the news, and headed off to Bethlehem to 'see this for themselves'. (Lk 2:15-16) It is ironic that this good news was first announced to shepherds. In those days, shepherds were not highly rated when it came to truth about what they heard and saw! If your work has you all alone throughout the watches of the night, in an open area, or in a cave, then you begin to hear sounds, and to see things that may not have much reality! In general, nobody took too seriously a story told by a shepherd. On this occasion, however, they walked the walk, rather than talked the talk. They were prepared to verify for themselves what they had seen and heard. The infant that they found didn't look too much like a judge. They could identify with weakness and powerlessness. I would like to imagine that, having visited with Mary, Joseph, and the child, they received the added grace of knowing, without understanding, that this was, indeed, good news.

In these days, one can enter a card shop and view rows and rows of greeting cards, each with some different way of saying, 'I love you.' Sending Jesus to us was the Father's way of telling us that he loved us. I could fill a book with quotes from St Paul about this central message of why Jesus came, but I will just give a few examples. 'Love does not keep a record of wrong ... Love never gives up.' (1 Cor 13:5-7) 'Long ago, even before he made the world, God loved us ... His unchanging plan has always been to adopt us into his own family, by bringing us to himself through Jesus Christ.' (Eph 1:4-5) 'May our Lord Jesus Christ and God our Father, who loved us, and in his special favour gave us everlasting comfort and good hope, comfort your hearts, and give you strength in every good thing you do and say.' (2 Thess 2:16) Jesus said that he never did anything except what the Father told him. He was sent to save us, and that is what he did, and it was of this that he spoke. At the end of time, he will come as Judge. For *now*, which is the only real time that exists, he is among us as Saviour. What a joy awaits us when we come to him as sinners, accept this wonderful promise, and experience this gift of salvation.

When we speak of Jesus, we usually use words like Saviour, Lord, or God. We don't often speak of Jesus as Judge. God leaves all judgement to Judgement Day, and we are asked to do the same. 'If today you hear his voice, harden not your hearts.' (Ps 95:8) 'They would not be guilty if I had not come and spoken to them.' (Jn 15:22) Jesus came to save us. He offers us salvation again and again. Salvation is not something we get when we die; rather it is the grace to start again any day we want to. If, after all of that, we still refuse to listen and to respond to his call, then we will bring judgement on ourselves. 'Today I am giving you a choice between prosperity and disaster, between life and death.' (Deut 30:15) If I accept him as Saviour, I won't ever have to meet him as Judge.

> *I will see again; then you will rejoice,*
> *and no one can rob you of that joy. (Jn 16:22)*

As I write these reflections, I am very conscious of a deep sense of joy. Jesus' promises are so powerful, abundant, and uplifting. One thing that really gives life to a meaningful human relationship is that it will have a 'tomorrow'. It is easier to deal with *au revoir*, than with *goodbye*. When Jesus returned to the Father, he sent the Holy Spirit 'to complete his work on earth' (Eucharistic Prayer IV). He himself will come in glory to claim what is his, to end the kingdom of the world, to eternally bind the kingdom of Satan, and to proclaim the victory of his eternal kingdom. His return will be a triumphant one, and will be a time of wondrous joy for all his followers. In the Acts of the Apostles, Peter speaks very powerfully about what has happened, and what is yet to come. For example, in Acts 3:17-21, he speaks about how the Jews had got it wrong, through ignorance, when they crucified Jesus. He speaks of his resurrection, and of sending the Holy Spirit. He concludes by telling them, 'God will send Jesus your Messiah to you again. For he must remain in heaven until the time for the restoration of all things, as God promised long ago through the prophets.' In other words, Jesus' coming again is seen as *good news* for his faithful followers. This belief created such a longing in them that some of them believed he would return to them during their lifetime. St Paul makes frequent references to the fact that Jesus is returning soon. The only point I wish to stress here is that the return of Jesus was something that they all longed for. It is significant that the final word in the whole Bible is *Maranatha*, which means 'Come, Lord Jesus.' (Rev 22:20)

They had many reasons to reflect on this promise with great joy, not least that Jesus told them that 'you will rejoice, and no one can rob you of that joy'. When Jesus used the word 'joy' on a previous occasion, he said, 'My joy will be in you, and your joy will be complete.' (Jn 15:11) After the resurrection, we are told that 'the disciples were filled with joy when they saw the Lord.' (Jn 20:20) In the promise under review, he assures them that no one will ever be able to rob them of that joy. I have no doubt that the apostles clung to this promise when things got difficult, and they longed for his coming again. When Jesus first came on earth, his birth was announced by the angels in a chorus of great joy. It is the Christian belief that his second coming will be an occasion of much greater joy. His work will have been completed. The kingdom of this world will have ended, with all its violence and injustice. The kingdom of Satan will be permanently sealed in a world of darkness, despair, and defeat. The reign of Jesus, as Lord of the kingdom of God, will be proclaimed and confirmed for all eternity.

Throughout these reflections it is often stated that the only real sin for the Christian is not to have hope. This is a promise that inspires and instills hope. As we struggle along on our earthly journey, we have constant need of this hope. It is just such a promise that enables us keep going at times. Hope is something that colours my view of the *future*. It is something to be longed for, something that is worth waiting for. With Jesus, hope is not some sort of pie in the sky, some sort of Utopian dream. Jesus tells us 'I will see you again.' He leaves us in no doubt that this will happen. Under different circumstances, these words could be a serious threat. Not so in this case, when Jesus goes on to tell us that this will cause us to rejoice, with a joy that no one will ever be able to take away from us.

There is an ominous tension in today's world, and there is good reason to be concerned about what the future holds. On a human level, it is difficult to maintain one's hope, either within the church, or within the world in general. This is where the Christian is tested. It is promises like the one under review that sustain our hope. In the final analysis, there is no peace apart from Jesus. 'Apart from me you can do nothing'. (Jn 15:5) I began this particular reflection by referring to the joy that promises like this can give us. I end on the same note, with a deep sense of gratitude for the certainty and reliability of all his promises.

*You will know the truth, and the truth will set you free.*
*(Jn 8:32)*

Original sin was a lie. When Adam and Eve fell for the lie, they came under new management. They hid, because 'they were afraid.' (Gen 2:8) This is the first time fear is mentioned in scripture. I believe that if Adam and Eve had approached God, and confessed to him what they had done, he would have forgiven them, and life for them would have continued. What happened, though, is that Adam blamed Eve, and Eve blamed the devil! In many ways we all can continue more of the same. Jesus called himself 'the truth'. (Jn 14:6) Again and again he begins his teaching with 'I am telling you the truth', which is usually read as 'Amen, amen, I say to you …' When he spoke to Pilate, Jesus was asked 'What is truth?' (Jn 18:38) Unfortunately, we are told that Pilate turned away, without waiting for the answer. The truth can upset, if I don't want to hear it. On the other hand, I will know exactly what God has to say to me, if I am willing to hear the truth.

Over the years, the Spirit of God has had many titles, from Paraclete, Holy Ghost, to Holy Spirit. It is easier to understand how Jesus saw the role of the Spirit when he referred to him as the Spirit of Truth. The Spirit is the antidote, the antibiotic for the poison of the original lie. Part of the legacy of that sin is that we are blinded to its reality. It disguises and justifies itself in many ways. I can rationalise my behaviour, and convince myself that what I am doing is perfectly OK. Any one of us can identify with the story in the Bible where Eve was tempted by the serpent. We ourselves are often in that situation, when the voice is coming from within, justifying something that we were told often enough was morally or ethically wrong. We can develop a sort of 'situation ethic', where we change the rules to fit a particular situation. One day something is wrong but, another day, because of different circumstances, we see it as alright. If God wanted to have a permissive society, he would have given us Ten Suggestions instead of Ten Commandments!

Notice that Jesus says, 'you will know the truth'. He leaves us in no doubt here. If I want to know the truth, then I will hear it. If I am prepared to follow the truth, I will get the grace to follow that path. With the invitation comes the grace to follow that invitation. Quite often, we know the truth, but we rationalise that this is not the time to act on it. This prevents or delays the second effect of this promise, 'and the truth will set you free'. When I know the truth, I must act on it, before I experience the freedom it can bring me. It takes courage to be open to the truth. Like Pilate, we too can turn away, and not wait for the answer. The truth will lay claims on us, and we will not be free until we follow the word of truth. In fact, knowing the truth, and not following it, makes us more culpable. 'They will have no excuse for their sins', says Jesus. (Jn 15:22)

'The truth will set you free.' The freedom that comes from truth is very liberating. Ask any recovering alcoholic how it feels to have accepted the truth, and to have acted on it. It's a whole

new life; it's like living in a different skin. Such a person probably lived in denial for so long, that it seemed impossible to ever
be free. Something happened. The pain was too great, and the
person was sick and tired of being sick and tired. The time came
when the key of truth was accepted, that unlocked the prison
doors, and allowed the person walk out into freedom. Jesus
prefaces this promise with the words, 'If you obey me, you will
be my disciples, and you will know the truth ...' In another
place, he says, 'If you love me, you will obey me, and then you
can ask the Father for anything in my name, and he will give it to
you.' (Jn 16:23) The offer is there, but the promise cannot be fulfilled until we meet the requirements. We are handed the key to
freedom, and it is the hope and longing of Jesus that we be humble enough to accept the gift, and reap the benefits of everything
he is offering us.

### *I will live again, and you will live too.*
### *(Jn 14:19)*

This is a simple, direct, and very profound statement. Hope is
something that belongs to the future. Most of our fears are coming at us from the future. The most universal fear is fear of death.
We have this gift of life, and there is some ingrained fear of having to surrender this, and pass on into the unknown. This is a
great mystery, and no human mind can fully comprehend the
extent of it. Jesus is only too aware of our fears. He knows us
through and through. He came to lead us all the way back home
to Abba. He is our Moses, who divides the Red Sea of death, so
that we can cross over dry-shod into the Promised Land. 'I will
not abandon you in the storm.' (Jn 14:18) On the morning of
Pentecost, Peter preached to the crowds about Jesus, and what
had happened to him. 'With the help of lawless Gentiles, you
nailed him to the cross and murdered him. However, God released him from the horrors of death, and raised him back to life
again, for death could not keep him in its grip.' (Acts 2:23-24)
Peter then goes on to quote what David had said about Jesus
(and, in light of this promise, to us): 'I know the Lord is always
with me. I will not be shaken for he is right beside me ... My
body rests in hope. For you will not leave my soul among the
dead, or allow your holy one to rot in the grave'. (Acts 2:27)

Even the most solemn of our promises are limited by time. In the wedding ceremony, John takes Mary as his wife for better, for worse, for richer, for poorer, in sickness and in health, all the days of their life, until death does them part. I can go so far, but no farther. With Jesus it is entirely different. He passed through death, and he went to extraordinary lengths after Easter to assure them that he was alive and well. Death is the final enemy. To overcome death is to achieve the ultimate and eternal victory. The grace made available to us Christians is that we are offered a *full* share in that victory, and this is pure gift. 'Dying, you destroyed *our* death; rising, you restored *our* life …' 'Lord, by your cross and resurrection you have set *us* free …' The promise now under review is more a statement than a promise. Jesus leads the way and, because he will live again, so will we. It is not possible for us to comprehend the vastness of his commitment to us. He is with us all the way, through thick and through thin, right out to the end, and beyond. In his prayer to the Father at the Last Supper, he prays that 'those you have given me may be with me, so that they may see my glory … and your love may be in them, and I in them'. (Jn 17:24, 26)

Human life is sacred. It is becoming more difficult to experience this in practice, when human life seems to be coming more and more expendable. Once human life begins, at conception, it never ends, as it passes through the three stages of womb-life, womb-of-God life, into the fullness of life. It is only when I die that I will become everything that God created me to be. All of my human limitations will fall away, like the surrounds of a space shuttle as it begins blast off into the atmosphere. I will never go into a coffin. The body which I now inhabit will become uninhabitable, and I will have to change residence, and go to live elsewhere. On more than one occasion Jesus assures us that this 'elsewhere' will be where he is; it will be with him. 'Because he lives, I can face tomorrow …' is a popular hymn. This includes all of my tomorrows.

I remember a popular movie from some years back called *Sunshine*. At the beginning of the movie, a young woman dies of cancer. The film then returns to the beginning, and tells the story up till then. The point is that we knew how the story would end as we watched it. This promise gives us such an inside advantage on life. Our hope is in the future. In Hebrews (11:1), we read 'What is faith? It is the confident assurance that what we hope for is going to happen.' We thank God for his promises, so clearly spelt out for us in Jesus.

### *Other promises under the heading: Salvation*

When I am raised to life again, you will know that I am in my Father, and you are in me, and I am in you. (Jn 14:20)

They will never be condemned for their sins, but have already passed from death into life. (Jn 5:24)

# Disciple

*All those who want to be my disciples must follow me;*
*and, if they do, my Father will honour them. (Jn 12:26)*

The word *disciple* is defined as 'follower, adherent, of any leader of thought, art, etc.'. We distinguish between apostles and disciples, in that Jesus had twelve apostles, and anyone else who followed him were known as his disciples. In the early church they were known as 'followers of the Way' and, in Antioch, they came to be called Christians. We use the word *discipline* to mean being committed to some sort of order, and conforming to expected ways of behaviour. Jesus came 'to do and to teach'. (Acts 1:1) He washed feet, and he told the apostles to do likewise. He fed the hungry, and he asked his followers to do the same. If I want to be his disciple, I must be prepared to follow the example of his life, and to live as he did. A very important part of that living is much more than just behaviour. It points very clearly to the source of all power to be able to live that life. This is the power of the Spirit. We are told that the Spirit came upon Jesus, as he came up out of the waters of the Jordan, at his baptism. (Lk 3:22) When he entered the temple, he announced that 'the Spirit of the Lord has been given me'. (Lk 4:19) He was 'led by the Spirit into the desert'. (Lk 4:1) Jesus was 'filled with the joy of the Holy Spirit'. (Lk 10:21) Again and again throughout the gospel accounts, it is made abundantly clear where the source of his power is. It is obvious, then, that if I want to follow him, I must begin by opening my heart to the fullness of his Spirit. Just as the Spirit came upon Mary, and Jesus was formed within her, it is through the coming of the Spirit that Jesus takes flesh within us. To become a disciple of Jesus is to develop a family resemblance.

The word 'follow' is important. It implies that Jesus is leading the way; in other words, he is not asking us to do anything that he hasn't done, or to go anywhere that he hasn't gone. He opens up the way before us. It is fascinating to watch a flock of geese in full flight. They fly in a V form, with one out front, taking the brunt of the oncoming wind, and the others follow, somewhat sheltered, in two lines behind. After a while, another goose takes over as leader, and this continues in rotation. Jesus is our leader all the way through life. If we follow him, he will lead us home.

Jesus goes much further in the second part of this promise, when he assures us that those who follow him will be honoured by his Father. This is a loving promise, made in love, and will only strike a chord in a heart where there's love. God is love, and he has no other way of loving us than showing or expressing his love in many different ways. Following Jesus is a path that brings us more and more into love. Becoming disciples of Jesus is becoming part of the family of God. 'Who is my mother? Who are my brothers? ... Anyone who does the will of my Father in heaven is my brother and sister and mother.' (Mt 12:48, 50) To become part of God family is a signal honour indeed. There are two little words in this promise that are worth drawing attention to. The first is 'want'; we have to want to be one of his disciples. I don't think the Spirit would put such a thought in one's mind, or such a longing in one's heart, without providing what it takes to act on it. The second word is 'if'. There is nothing automatic about God. The only limits to all he can do for us are the ones we set. God is always on standby, more than willing to move in, and fill us with his Spirit, once we open the door. I could replace the word 'promises' in this writing with the word 'offers', or 'possibilities'. It's all ours for the taking. Our divine destiny is to end up within the heart of the Trinity for all eternity. Jesus leads us to the Father, and the Spirit gives what it takes to enable us to be led. This is not an empty promise, but what a tragedy it would be if it ended up with no response. It is a powerful grace-filled promise, and it comes from the heart of Jesus. It is his hope that it enters into our hearts, and evokes a positive response from there.

*If you love me, you will obey me.*
*(Jn 14:23)*

Original sin was one of disobedience. It was a refusal to submit the human mind to the will of the Creator. It was pride and self-will run riot, and was frightfully destructive. Jesus came to undo the harm of original sin. He would undo it through obedience, 'even to death on a cross'. (Phil 2:8) He said that he came to do the will of him who sent him. (Jn 6:38) In another place he said, 'My meat is to do the will of him who sent me.' (Jn 4:34) He also said that, if we loved him, we would obey him as a sign of our love. The word obedience comes from the word *obedientia*, meaning holding one's ear against, which implies a committed form of listening. We have to learn to listen, if we are to listen and learn. Listening is at the heart of real prayer. Prayer is more God speaking to us, than us speaking to him. If I am to obey Jesus, I have to listen to his instructions. This goes so much beyond the message of the gospel, while it comes directly from that. In our everyday activities, we need to 'check in' to discover what he wants me to do at any particular time. Jesus will certainly let us know what he wants us to do, if we are prepared to listen to the Spirit's promptings. To 'learn to live and to walk in the Spirit' (Rom 8:5), is one sure way of obeying Jesus, because Jesus told us that the Spirit would tell us all about him. (Jn 16:14) Much depends on our willingness to know the will of Jesus. If we have that goodwill, we need never worry about what he wants us to do at any time.

Love always calls for a response, because it is creative. Sometimes that response can be negative, but 'No' is also an answer. Jesus has spelt out very clearly how much he loves us, and he leaves us to decide how we choose to respond to that love. His actions, as well as his words, spoke a language of love. He told us that we would show the world that we were his disciples by the way we loved one another. (Jn 13:35) 'I command you to love one another just as I have loved you.' (Jn 10:12) Jesus asks that our love for him be carried out through our actions.

To love Jesus is to make a decision, and to live out that decision. In involves clearing our hearts of other 'loves' that are not of him. His love is always calling us to an on-going conversion, a purifying of the heart. All impurities can be burned up in his love. In a good sense, he is a jealous God. He wants us for himself, because it is only in and through him that we can discover peace, happiness, and eternal life. 'I came that you should have life, and have it to the full.' (Jn 10:10) Obeying him is to be attached to him, the source of eternal life. This faces us with the challenge of other attachments that may not be life-giving. When Jesus speaks about loving him, we are faced with other loves, and we have to make some decisions. 'You are either for me or against me. No one can serve two masters.' (Lk 16:13) When we fail to obey him, we are obeying some other voice, whether that comes from another, from the evil one, or from within ourselves. Obeying him is a perfect way of preserving us from the lures of the evil one. When we obey him, we are under his protection. We know what we should do, and his Spirit will always give us the grace to do what is right, what is within the will of Jesus for us. Like the vine and the branches, obedience to Jesus is a sure and certain way of being attached to Jesus, because 'apart from me you can do nothing'. (Jn 15:5)

### My prayer for them is that they will be one.
### (Jn 17:21)

This is one of the saddest statements in the gospel, because, within the context of this statement, Jesus implies that his very credibility is at stake. The evidence that we are one is proof that the Father sent him. It can pull at the heart strings of those who love Jesus, to think of him depending on the evidence of our lives as a confirmation of his authenticity. When I listen in on another's prayer, I get a much better chance to understand the mind and heart of that person. In chapter 17 of John's gospel, we have the privilege of eavesdropping on one of Jesus' long prayers. In this prayer, he is pouring out his heart to the Father. It is a beautiful love poem, in which he expresses his love for the Father and for us, and the Father's love for him, and for us. He wants only the best for us, in this life and in the next. He is going to send the Holy Spirit, and the work of that Spirit will be to unite us in a loving worshipping community. The Spirit will become flesh within the unity of the church. This promise is sad in another way, i.e., through the constant divisions, debates, and disagreements so evident among his followers in different churches. This is a complete betrayal of everything he hoped for, of everything he prayed for. His body was broken on the cross, and his Body continues to be broken within his Christian followers. In the early Christian church, the onlookers could not fail to notice, and to remark 'See how these Christians love one another.'

If this is Jesus' prayer, then it must be capable of becoming a reality. If he prayed for this, then he must surely be ready and willing to supply all it takes to bring that to fulfillment. If I am to personally take this on board, there is only one place I can begin. We often hear references to others as being 'All over the place', 'Awfully scattered', 'Badly in need of getting themselves together'. The opposite to this is togetherness, wholeness, or holiness. Holiness can be so abstract a concept for some people. Sanctity can be equally elusive. If we examine the word 'sanctity', however, and translate it as 'something/someone that is sanctioned', we can get a much clearer idea of the meaning behind it. For example, I look at one of my actions, and I ask myself, 'Would Jesus sanction what I have just done? Would it meet with his approval?' The same applies to my words, and even my thoughts. Before going on some sort of Don Quixote crusade, to bring all of Jesus' followers together in unity, and to bind them in love, I have to begin with my own heart. Only a person of peace can make peace. 'Let there be peace on earth, and let it begin with me.'

I am every person in the gospel. I could be split right down the middle, with the Prodigal son on one side, and his self-righteous brother on the other. The Martha in me might have serious problems with the contemplative Mary. When my heart holds resentments, unforgiveness, self-condemnation, etc., then I am more on the side of the problem than being part of the solution. Jesus is praying that I might make friends with my shadow. It is his wish and prayer that I allow his Spirit to bring all of me together in wholeness, in holiness. There are sins to be forgiven, hurts to be healed, and brokenness to be repaired, and empowered. When I turn my will and my life over to the power of his Spirit, then this prayer begins to be answered for me. Jesus could rephrase this prayer to read, 'My prayer for you is that you might become one.' At the moment of death, I will stand totally naked before God, without a hiding place, an excuse, a denial, or a pretence. It would be a great pity, however, if I waited till that time to do this, when I can stand before him any day of my life in this way. This final encounter can be rehearsed every single day of my life. I spread out the canvas of my life, right out to the edges. I stand before him with all my brokenness, sin, and failures. I ask for his forgiveness, his healing, and the anointing of his Spirit. I volunteer to be one person who is ready to supply part of the answer to the prayer that Jesus prayed. When his Spirit is then poured out in abundance upon me, I, in turn, am ready to be a channel of his peace, love, and actual presence among those immediately around me. May his prayer be answered, and may you and I be part of the answer.

### They who endure to the end will be saved.
### (Mt 10:22)

I am not a race-goer, but I spend one day a year at a race festival not far from where I live. I know nothing about horses, and I just pick one here and there, because I like the name, the colours, or the jockey. I will never be a gambler, nor will I ever make a fortune on the ponies! I know one thing, however, and that is that the horse that falls, or pulls up, and doesn't complete the race, will not be reckoned among the winners. I've picked a few of these in my day, and once I see my 'favourite' take a tumble at a fence, I just tear up my ticket and check the runners in the next race. That is exactly what Jesus is speaking about in this promise. 'Not those who say "Lord, Lord" will enter the Kingdom of heaven.' (Mt 7:21) Calling him Lord does not mean that he ever is accepted as Lord. The call is to follow him, and to stay with him, all the way back home to Abba.

Notice the word 'endure'. We all like variety, and occasional excitement. For those who don't understand, living the Christian life, day after day, might seem repetitious and uneventful. This is often expressed by someone who has no idea about the purpose and end of Monastic Contemplative Life. In this particular case, it is the very repetition that produces the discipline, the dying to self, the total giving and living that the life calls for. There are people who are constant 'starters'. They join anything that's going ... for a while. They are always starting a new hobby, a new diet, a new night class. Many of these come to nothing, if the person is not prepared to see it through. I was speaking to a friend recently who was nearing the end of a series of night classes. As it happened, after a class or two, she discovered that she just couldn't warm to the subject; indeed, it was quite boring for her. She is not a quitter, however, and she wouldn't think of dropping out. She completed the classes, sat the exam, and got the diploma. Imagine a group of people setting out to climb a mountain. By the time they reach the foot of the mountain, one third of the group decide not to travel any further. They would have a BBQ at the bottom, while waiting on the others to come down again. Half-way up the side of the mountain, the scene was breath-taking, and yet another group decide to call a halt, abandon the climb, and enjoy the scenery from where they were. The remaining group, however, had left home this morning to climb this mountain, and that is exactly what they're going to do. There are three groups in any parish, or grouping: a small group that cause things to happen; a larger group who watch things happening; and the vast majority who haven't a clue what's happening.

The gospel is a call to action, and the call does not cease until the action is complete. It is becoming more difficult today to accept this concept of living a calling out to the end. I know it is only different use of words, and I don't pretend to think that everything is immutable, unchanging. Some marriages don't last too long anymore. I have known priests who discovered they were 'in the wrong shop' within a year of ordination. I am not passing judgement on any of these, because that is not what is under review here. This promise is about following Jesus right out to the end of my life, no matter what change I make in the form, expression, or circumstances of that following. It has always been part of our traditional prayer-life to pray for a happy death. We ask Mary again and again to 'pray for us sinners now, and at the hour of our death'. It is considered that Satan may well make one last attempt to steal our hope, to shatter our faith, or to destroy our love. 'As you live, so shall you die' is very true indeed. I remember a long prayer for perseverance, attributed to Alphonsus Ligouri, which was part of the stock-in-trade of every prayer book. Even if the words are no longer available, it would be something very special to pray for, because to end my earthly journey with the names of Jesus and Mary on my lips, is to put a seal on a life well lived.

*No one can serve two masters.*
*You cannot serve God and money. (Lk 16:13)*

I often imagine what would happen if Jesus appeared in the middle of a gathering of people, and began to chat with them. Is it possible that the group would end up being split down the middle? His message often has that effect on people, as it had right from the very start. His words were clear and unambiguous, and they called for a decision. If I could not decide for him, I would be forced to decide against him. (Mt 12:30) I have chosen this as a promise, because a promise is implied, even if not specific. We are brought back to the First Commandment. There is only one God, and it's not money. Once we have established clearly that there is only one God, then we can turn our attention to him fully, and not get diverted into worshipping at other shrines. Jesus tells us that we cannot serve God and money. He could also say that we cannot serve God and ourselves. It can be so easy for any of us to play God from time to time.

There is a vast difference between being rich, and being wealthy. I was blessed in growing up in a family that was really rich, while we didn't have much money. Later in life I met, and worked with families who were really wealthy, and I felt they had nothing of what we had as I grew up. Money is a very tough task-master. It can create an insatiable appetite that all the money in the world cannot satisfy. 'What do you give a person who has everything? *More!*' When money becomes a god, it imposes its own commandments. My life becomes controlled by Stock Exchanges, exchange rates, and every possible form of wheeling and dealing that helps accumulate more and more of something that I see as necessary for making my life worthwhile. Instead of owning the money, it takes over, and begins to own me. I can become its slave, and I consider my personal worth in terms of how much money I control. Once I have tasted the nectar of wealth, I generate a fear of ever returning to the 'bad old days'. People become pawns in the game of life, and I find myself living in a bubble, where real love and friendship become commodities that have no price tags, and therefore of no practical value.

When I come to the end of the day, I can take stock of how I lived it by checking how I spent my time and money that day. Where did God figure in my time, and my use of money? There is no suggestion that money is not important. It is all a question of relationship. There is no problem that is not a relationship one, in some way, i.e. I'm not getting on too well with myself, God, or others. Alcohol is a good, but if I cannot relate to it properly, it can become a tyrant that will destroy all that is good in my life. It is the same with money. Its benefits are so limited and, as is often said, there are no pockets in the shroud when I am laid out in death. Certainly, if money were to replace God in anyone's life, that person's soul is taken over, and all personal freedom to live life is gone. The words of Jesus under review are spoken out of a concern for our welfare; for our earthly and eternal welfare. Jesus tells us to lay up treasures in heaven, where they are safe from the vagaries of the world. (Mt 6:20) The human heart can never find fulfillment apart from God. That is why I chose to treat this quote as a promise, because it is a truth that will withstand all human or earthly attempts to convince us otherwise.

*You cannot be my disciple if you do not carry your own cross, and follow me. (Lk 14:27)*

The cross is often not too well understood. We speak of somebody losing a job, getting a stroke, or burdened with care, as people who have a heavy cross to bear. These are not crosses, in the Christian meaning of that word. The cross is always redemptive, it always brings good, and is always accompanied by the grace and strength to shoulder it. The other situations could well be disasters, and there is little possibility of any good coming out of them. My cross is made up of all the little myriad things I just have to do, resulting directly from my decision to follow Jesus. Once I make that decision, I have eliminated the options. I am now bound to forgiveness, love, peace, prayer, service, etc. This is where my cross comes in. It will seldom be heavy at any particular time, because I usually receive it splinter by splinter. Note the words 'carry your own cross'. Each of us has our own combination of weaknesses. What is a cross for one person is sheer joy for another. What is powerfully tempting to one is disgustingly abhorrent to another. There are horses for courses.

There are certain crosses we all share in common. We all have a human nature to deal with, and we have a will that can swing from being conciliatory and docile to being blind and stubborn. We have good days and bad days, and some days are more difficult to tolerate than others. Our Christianity, however, is not measured by our output at work, or in the service of others. This would rule out all those who, because of age or ability, would be considered as non-productive. The yardstick for our Christian living is our willingness. Like Abraham, who became willing to sacrifice his own son, if God asked him, we are often 'let off the hook', as it were, and the impending cross was much lighter than we had expected. The core of the issue is our willingness, rather than perfection. 'Peace on earth to those of good will.' (Lk 2:14) I can turn my will and my life over to the care of God. Notice that I used the word 'care' rather than 'control'. Our God is a God of love, and he does not deliberately inflict pain and suffering on his children. To opt for the cross is to opt for our own good, to decide in favour of the truth. It is to opt for life.

Dying is what a Christian can do during his life-time. Death is like a pile of sand at the end of one's life, which we can take, and sprinkle a little every day, so that, when we reach the end, there's nothing left; our death will have taken place long ago. 'Greater love than this no one has, that a person should lay down a life for a friend.' (Jn 15:13) When was the last time I ever died for someone? That was the last time I really loved someone. To live the Christian life is to face up to death (cross) right now, in every instance of every day. I will be called on to die to my selfishness, my curiosity, my pride, my possessions, or my bigotry, in the course of loving others as Jesus asks me. That is what is involved in taking up his cross. He then tells us that we are to follow him. It is in this way that we prove that we are his disciples. To be a disciple of Jesus is to be bound by his discipline, to live as he wants us to live. Only people of service are life-giving people. Jesus came that we should have life in abundance, and his disciples must also transmit his life and love to others. Jesus took on the cross of our broken humanity, and that was something extraordinary. When I realise what my own struggle is like, with the weaknesses with which I have to contend, I couldn't imagine life, if I took on all of human weaknesses, and had to deal with them, one by one.

The quotation under reflection is an invitation to us from Jesus, to become his disciples, and to do this through accepting the burden that service of others and living in truth will impose on us. His own life, especially his own facing up to the cross, give ample proof of the merits of such an undertaking. I depend completely on the Holy Spirit, if I have any hope of responding to this invitation. Again and again, I can repeat my mantra: 'Holy Spirit, please help me.' Only time will show me how powerful this prayer can be, when said with whatever goodwill I can muster.

*You are Peter, and on this rock I will build my church,*
*and all the powers of hell will not conquer it. (Mt 16:18)*

Never before, in my lifetime, have I needed this promise so much. I'm sure, at the time Jesus spoke these words, no one of his listeners would have had an idea of what would happen to his church in the years and centuries ahead. There are three things we ought to keep in mind, i.e. Jesus, the gospels, the church. Jesus is the same yesterday, today, and forever. (Heb 13:8) Not one word of the gospel has changed. The church, on the other hand, is made up of people like you and me and, therefore, is always in need of renewal. The church has wandered off the straight and narrow many and many a time. It may be highly significant that Peter was the one Jesus chose to be the first pope! Jesus called Peter a rock, meaning a solid person, incapable of being moved. That, of course, was only after the Spirit came upon him at Pentecost. It is interesting that Peter was chosen before events had shown him, and those around him, that, of himself, he just didn't have what it takes to take responsibility, or be a leader for others.

Jesus did what he came to do and, when this was completed, he returned to the Father. He then sent his Spirit to complete his work. Those of us who make ourselves available to that Spirit, by providing the hands, feet, voice, etc., are formed into a family, something we call church. It is the Spirit who unites us, because the Spirit is given to the church, and not to the individual. When Jesus speaks to Peter, he says, 'I will build my church …' In other words, he's not asking Peter to build a church. As the Spirit completes the work of Jesus, once again, as in Mary, the Body of Christ is formed, and this is not something that is within the remit of any human power. In his ascension, Jesus brought his human body with him but, through the work and actions of his Spirit, we are united and joined, with a common mission, and we become the Body of Christ. Jesus told us that the Spirit would never leave us. It is in this second part of the promise that our hope rests. The Spirit is with the church, and the Spirit will never leave the church.

At the time of writing, the church is going through a turbu-lent time, to such an extent that many people believe that it can-not recover. The value of history is that we can learn from other people's mistakes. In the case of the church, we may not have learned a great deal from the mistakes of the past. The problem is that the church is made up of guys like me, and it's nothing new to me to repeat some serious mistakes. While not confess-ing insanity, I have to hold my hand up and admit to insane be-haviour on occasions. This is defined as 'to keep repeating the same thing, and expecting different results each time'. What goes round, comes round and, like me, the church was here many times before. Each time this happened, the Lord sent a prophetic voice to awaken the people, and to lead them out of exile, back to the Promised Land. Francis of Assisi, Ignatius, Dominic, Padre Pio, and John XXIII were among such prophets. When Francis of Assisi heard the Lord calling him to rebuild his church, he understood this to mean rebuilding an old church that lay in ruins in the locality. When he came to understand what the Lord was asking from him, he headed off to Rome, to share this with the pope. Teresa of Avila and John of the Cross found themselves called to renew the Carmelite Order and, through that, to bring renewal to the whole church. John XXIII prayed for a 'new Pentecost of love and understanding'. He got a new Pentecost, and we are now living in the Acts of the Apostles of that Second Pentecost. At the moment, the church is on Calvary, but by standing with Mary, I share her hope that Easter is just around the corner.

The last part of this promise is powerful. There is no equivoc-ation here. This is a straight up-front guarantee. When all the present-day tabloid scribes, and chat-show hosts are dead and gone, the church will continue until the end of time. I am not saying, nor do I desire that the church would remain unchanged. The church, like any of its members, will always be in need of renewal. At the moment, we are witnessing enormous renewal, and one hopes that this continues. At long last, the vision of Vatican II may become a reality. I myself believe that the effects of this Second Pentecost have only begun to show themselves in the last few years. The Spirit is very active in the church and, I often think, he is most effective when we're not sure what he's up to! It is a wonderful time to be part of the church, and it is a very necessary time to reflect on, and take to heart the guarantee that this promise gives us about the future of the church.

### *Other promises under the heading: Disciple*

If you give up your life, you will find true life. (Mt 16:25)

Father, I want those whom you've given me to be with me, so that they may see my glory. (Jn 24)

# Come to Me

*Come to me all you who are weary, and carry heavy burdens,*
*and I will give you rest. (Mt 11:28)*

Most invitations have an RSVP added at the end. This invitation is no exception. It is a personal invitation, and I accept it as being offered to me now. Life can be difficult, and it is so easy for us to become weary, discouraged, and down-hearted. At all times, but especially at such times, Jesus issues this invitation. It is a very definite promise: *I will give you rest.* This is one of those gems in the gospel where I can actually 'come and see this for myself'. (Lk 2:15) There are times when I may not be broken enough to heed this call. Original sin is alive and well, in many different forms. There is some sort of stubborn pride within the human heart that convinces us that we can fix things, that we can solve problems, that we can overcome obstacles. Spirituality is about surrender. It is about letting God take over and do what God does best. In this invitation, or promise, we are asked to hand over the things that burden us, and Jesus will sort them out.

This is a promise that is better prayed over than reflected on. I can come to Jesus exactly as I am at any one time, and I can hand over to him anything that is bothering me. It is in doing this that I can come to believe that this does work. I can come to him with the simple problems and, discovering how he cares for those, will encourage me to come to him when my situation is beyond my control. The third Step of a Twelve-Step programme reads: 'Made a decision to turn our will and our lives over to the care of God, as we understood Him.' Notice the last three words, which are vitally important. Our understanding of God can change with the years. If I was reared with a God of fear, it may take me a long time to discover a God of love. All the promises in this book are spoken by a down-to-earth God of love. We are all familiar with small children who run up to one person, and run away from another. There are several stories in the gospel of Jesus taking children by the hand, hugging them, and sitting them on his knee. They knew they were safe, because everything about him exuded love and peace. It makes all the difference in the world to experience a personal love-relationship with Jesus. There are times when I need a hug, or I need to feel my hand in his. 'I am with you always.' (Jn 12:8) 'I will not abandon you, or leave you in the storm. I will come to you.' (Jn 14:8) The apostles experienced this when they were tossed around in a storm on the open sea. (Jn 6:18-19) Jesus came towards them, walking on the water. As soon as he got into the boat, the storm abated, and, as the account finishes, 'soon they reached where they were going'. (Jn 6:20)

Many of us become sick and tired of being sick and tired. We can choose to remain that way if that is our choice. This promise is an invitation, and an offer. Some people have much heavier burdens to carry in life than others. 'Somebody else had a heavier cross than the one I bear today, and the load were far too much for me had not somebody led the way.' What a change it would make in our lives if we responded wholeheartedly to this invitation, and reaped the benefits of this promise. The only limits to what he can do for us are the ones we set. Quite often, what we seek and need is nothing less than a miracle, and only Jesus can work miracles. We read in the gospels of many people who experienced freedom from blindness, from bondage, and even from death, through his touch. Some of them came to him, begging for a healing. Others were brought to him, and he himself travelled to where others were, as in the case of Jairus' daughter, Lazarus, or Peter's mother-in-law. This promise is entrusted to each one of us. We will benefit enormously, and Jesus will be really pleased, when we take him up on it. I pray that the time might be now.

*I assure you, today you will be with me in paradise.*
*(Lk 23:43)*

This is a message of great hope. Here we have a man who may not have said a prayer in his life. He obviously had not lived life well, and was about to die. At that moment, he turned to Jesus, asked for help, and was offered heaven that day. *It's Never Too Late For God* is the name of a beautiful book. This must surely give hope to all of us. Whatever is happening in our lives now, no matter how low down the ladder we consider ourselves, all that is needed is to turn to Jesus for help, and all will become different. 'Lord, remember me …' In human terms, Jesus himself was at an all-time low on Calvary. He was dying, his friends had deserted him, and everything for which he had worked just seemed to have come apart. This was not a successful end to a life of love and service for others. The power of his miracles, the authority of his words, and the obvious certainty of his trust in the Father, now seemed to be in shreds. However, it is also true to say that he was most powerful when he was nailed to a cross, and could do nothing, because that is exactly where the Father wanted him to be. 'He became obedient even on to death, death on a cross.' (Phil 2:8) It is in this total submission and surrender that God's power emerges. Spirituality is about surrender. This is what the 'good thief' did as well. He let go of all his own needs to control, and have his way. He asked for help, and he was ready to receive it. Readiness to receive is the key to the treasuries of heaven.

There are two immutable or unchanging facts. The first is my own brokenness and powerlessness. I own nothing; everything I have is on loan. One heart attack, and it's all over. The other immutable fact is the infinite Power of God. 'There is nothing impossible for God.' (Lk 1:37) The link that joins these two is willingness. 'Peace on earth to those of goodwill.' (Lk 2:14) When I am unwilling to bridge that gap at times, it may be because I'm not broken enough yet. When you're on the broad of your back, there is only one way to look, and that's up. The words of Jesus are simple and direct. 'I assure you … you *will* be with me …' It is highly significant that this event happened just as they both were about to die. This highlights the whole mission of Jesus' life. He had come to save sinners, and he was prepared to do so right up to his last breath. Through the work of his Spirit, he still continues his mission up to this very moment.

When I was growing up, we had many prayers about having 'a holy and a happy death'. The idea of having a 'happy' death never phased me, even if I never considered death as being something 'happy'! In the writings of St Thérèse and of St Faustina, they speak animatedly about the joy of their approaching deaths. I accepted this freely, coming from such as they, but I never considered this in terms of myself, or those around me. I always had the idea of Satan making one final push at that last moment, and the possibility of his succeeding always frightened me. I no longer have those fears, thank God. I celebrate eucharist each morning with a group of very elderly people in a Retirement Home. Quite frequently, I refer to the fact of standing before God, at the moment of death. No hiding, no denying, no excuses anymore. The canvas is opened out fully to the end. I stand before God exactly as I am, exactly as he sees me. I suggest that we should not wait till the moment of death to come before God in that way, because we can do this every single day we choose. I can rehearse that moment thousands of times before it actually happens. I am confident that this is an excellent preparation for that Great Encounter. The man on the other cross on Calvary got one last chance, and he took it. This is offered to each and all of us, except that we don't have to wait till the last minute to link up with Jesus. We have the privilege of knowing him now, something that was denied this man all his life. He was truly blessed, however, because, like the labourers in the vineyard (Mt 20:1-16), the very last to be called is given the same wages as those who worked there all day long. This is God's prodigal way of doing things, because his love and forgiveness knows no bounds.

*Those the Father has given me will come to me,*
*and I will never reject them. (Jn 6:37)*

Jesus speaks of people who are given him by the Father. It is difficult to understand this, but at least we can examine it, to see what it might mean. Jesus had said that the Father would surely give the Spirit to those who asked him. (Jn 11:13) This is an offer, and we are free to accept or reject it. I imagine that those who choose to respond are those who are chosen. The initiative, or call, comes from God. I then am faced with a choice. If I choose for Jesus, I become a chosen one. This offer is for everyone, but not everyone accepts. 'Many are called, but few are chosen.' (Mt 22:14) The onus is on each of us to be among the chosen ones. By accepting the Spirit, we become part of God's family and, there-

fore, are entrusted to Jesus, the Good Shepherd, by the Father. 'I
have called you by name; you are mine.' Those who accept the
gift of God's Spirit must surely come to Jesus, because that is
part of the work of the Spirit. In fact, because of the action of the
Spirit within our hearts, it is made possible for Jesus to come to
us, and to set up his kingdom within our hearts.

I can come to Jesus in many ways, but I believe it is easier and
surer to allow myself be led to him by the Holy Spirit. When I
learn to live and to walk in the Spirit, I will discover that Jesus is
coming more and more alive within my heart. It becomes a kind
of 'growing into him', as it were, 'until Christ is formed within
you'. (Gal 4:19) It is known that children who are adopted into a
family, develop a family resemblance over the years. In baptism,
I was adopted into the family of God, and it is hoped that, over
the years, some kind of family resemblance might begin to
emerge.

From everything we know of Jesus, it is not possible to imagine him rejecting anything or any person entrusted to him by his
Father. His whole life was devoted to obeying the Father, and he
never did or said anything unless the Father told him. (Jn 6:40)
When I come to Jesus, I can be absolutely sure that he will never
walk away. It is always within my power to turn my back on
him, because there is some sort of insane streak within human
nature that can lead to self-destruction. Jesus didn't want Judas
to go out to hang himself, but he wouldn't/couldn't stop him.
He is extraordinarily sensitive not to intrude on our free will,
and anything that comes from us must be our own personal decision. In his lifetime on earth, Jesus experienced much and
many rejections. He cried as he overlooked Jerusalem, saying,
'How often I have wanted to gather your children together as a
hen protects her chicks beneath her wings, but you would not let
me.' (Mt 23:37) When he returned to Nazareth he could not
work any miracles there, and he was amazed at their lack of
faith. (Mk 6:6) It's a bit scary to think that I can render Jesus
powerless, if I refuse to open the door and allow him enter my
heart. There is no handle on the outside, and he cannot come in
unless I invite him. The people referred to in this promise are
those who accepted the Father's gift of the Spirit and, thus, became members of the family of God. Jesus tells us that if we

deny him before others that he will deny us before his Father in heaven. (Mt 10:33) On the other hand, if we acknowledge him before others, he will acknowledge us before his Father in heaven. In this promise he goes on to say that he will never reject them. Such people can come face to face with Jesus in death, and be sure of a warm and welcoming hug. How many times does he have to say, 'Oh, why did you doubt, oh you of little faith?'(Lk 12:28) A living faith is the response to a living and loving promise. 'The sin of this world is unbelief in me.' (Jn 16:9) One thing that continues to strike me, as I write these reflections on the gospel promises, is the urgency about responding and accepting them now. We are all familiar with ads which tell us 'This offer is for a limited time only.' Jesus' offer is for all time, but, because of the frailty of our mortality, all the limitations are on our side.

*If you are thirsty, come to me.*
*If you believe in me, come and drink. (Jn 7:37)*

Once again, Jesus is inviting us to come to him. He understands only too well our human hungers and thirsts, and how we try to sate or quench those in harmful and destructive ways. The word 'if' is repeated in this promise, even though we all know that we are thirsty and I would like to think that we do believe in him. There is a hole within the heart of every person which can only be filled by God. Any attempt to fill it in any other way will lead us down the road of addiction, compulsion, and death. Jesus came that we should have life, and have it to the full. (Jn 10:10) The human spirit is like a deep deep well, with a spring of gurgling water at the base. Unfortunately, the well can become choked up with the garbage and wreckage of life, and the water cannot reach the surface. Beneath the driest desert there is plenty of water, but the oasis is a rare and special place, where the water comes to the top, and is a source of life to people, animals, and nature. There are people like that, thank God, and it is very edifying to witness their lives. Jesus spoke of the Spirit as being a fountain of living water, rising up from within the human heart. It is with this in mind that he speaks of thirst in this promise.

When Jesus meets the woman at the well (Jn 4:1-42), he speaks at great length about the water of life that he is offering. It is obvious from the passage that this woman had tried to fill the hole in her heart by searching for love and belonging where it was not to be found. This was a very interesting meeting. The woman had come to draw water from the well in the middle of the day when, because of the heat, there would be few if any others around. The apostles had gone, so Jesus was alone, as the woman approached. His introduction was very casual. 'Give me a drink.' He probably was thirsty, but he had something else in mind. There was a wide chasm between them. A man, a woman, a Jew, a Samaritan, all alone at high-noon. He had come with salvation for such as she, and he was holding out a hand to her. She stayed in her head long enough to argue all accepted suppositions about the well, its history, and her own understanding of if. Jesus was gentle, and his words had a quiet, but definite power in them. He spoke of a real thirst, and he spoke of living water. In her head, she could never comprehend the meaning of what he was saying. His words must have touched her heart, however, because she remained to listen. This man seemed to know her through and through. It now was her turn to ask 'Give me some of that water ...' Without knowing it, she had said a prayer. Jesus proceeded to blow away some of the myths about where and how God should be worshipped. He told her that it was more important to worship God in spirit and in truth, than in any particular place. Everything moved fast from then on. The apostles returned, the woman left her bucket, and headed back to the village. For someone who had slipped along in the 'dead' of the day to avoid meeting anyone, she now ran around telling everyone that she had found the Messiah. She told them what he had said, and how she believed he was somebody special. Her message was so real that many of them followed her back to the well, to meet the man of whom she spoke. They, too, listened, and their closing comment, while being true, is somewhat catty: 'Now we believe because we have heard him ourselves, and not just because you told us.' (Jn 4:42)

I remained with this gospel incident for some length, because it puts in clear context the promise under review. If you are thirsty, come to me; if you believe, come and drink. There are two stages to the process. We begin with our thirst, or our desire for something that appears to elude us. When we come to Jesus, looking for that, we then have to decide if we really believe he can supply our needs. The offer is there; the invitation is issued. Like the people from the Samaritan village, it is now up to us to come and find out for ourselves.

*When I am lifted up on the cross,*
*I will draw all people to myself. (Jn 12:32)*

The cross is the sign of our salvation. Quite often, a cross hanging round a person's neck might look little more than an ornament, although it often does say what it signifies: 'I am a Christian.' We are all familiar with symbols, whether it be a wedding ring on a finger, or a hammer and sickle on a flag. Signs and symbols can be either powerful or meaningless. A sign or symbol, of itself, doesn't do anything. A 30-mile-an-hour sign does not, of itself, slow all drivers to within that speed limit. The sign must be seen, be recognised, and be acted on. The cross is a truly wonderful and meaningful sign of completeness, of love, of hope, of salvation. The vertical bar represents God coming down to us, while the horizontal bar represents God reaching out to all of us. It represents the meeting of God with his people. Jesus was both God and man. Through incarnation, he came among us as a God who had taken on all of humanity, and both were sealed together by the blood of Jesus. The cross is a symbol of a meeting place. The pope came to Dublin in Sept '79, and over a million people turned out in the Phoenix Park to greet him. Some months after the pope had gone, and all the crowds had gone home, a huge cross was erected on the spot to commemorate that meeting.

Jesus was hanging on a cross, between heaven and earth. He was the full and final sacrifice for the forgiveness of sin. He spoke to those who stood around, and he cried out to the Father. This was a supreme moment in history. When he bowed his head in death, the veil of the temple was rent in two, the graves were opened, and 'the dead arose and appeared to many'. (Mt 27:52) Every door was opened at that moment. From that moment, we as sinners can now enter into the Holy of Holies. As the writer of the letter to the Hebrews says, 'Let us come boldly to the throne of our gracious God. There we will receive his mercy, and we will find grace to help us when we need it.' (Heb 4:16) Yes, indeed, when Jesus was lifted up on the cross, he made it possible for all people to meet him. Calvary was a place of dispensation, a place where all sinners could rally, and all refugees find safe refuge. Jesus draws us but, of course, we must allow ourselves to be drawn. 'Dying, he destroyed our death ...' is an exclamation after the Consecration of the Mass. This good news must be proclaimed, it must be told to all the world. How can 'all people' be drawn to Jesus, if many of them have never heard of him, or most of them know very little about him?

Notice the use of the word 'lifted'. Jesus said, 'When I am lifted ...', implying that this is something he does not do himself, but he permits others to do. 'Alleluia, my Father, you gave us your Son ... knowing we would bruise him, and strike him from the earth.' It is significant to read, 'When the captain of the Roman soldiers handling the execution saw what had happened, he praised God, and said "Surely this man was innocent." And when the crowd that came to see the crucifixion saw all that had happened, they went home in deep sorrow.' (Lk 23:47-48) Anyone who comes close enough to Jesus, and looks at a crucifix long enough, will surely be touched. He is raised up that we might be raised up. Through his death he has taken the sting out of death for us. 'Death is swallowed up in victory. O Death, where is your victory? O Death, where is your sting?' (Is 25:8, also quoted by Paul in 1 Cor 15:55) The cross is placed upon the roofs of churches, and on the top of hills. He is held on high, for all the world to see. At the time of writing there is much protest, and gallant efforts are being made to prevent another conflict in Iraq. It is significant to note that many of the protesters carry crosses. Calvary is where conflict can end, and forgiveness begin. It is where we are offered a 'new heaven and a new earth'. (Rev 21:1)

> *Eternal Father, I offer you the body and blood of your dearly beloved Son, our Lord Jesus Christ, in atonement for my sins, and for the sins of the whole world. For the sake of his most sorrowful Passion, have mercy on us, and on the whole world.*
> (*Chaplet of Divine Mercy*)

*Everything that is hidden or secret will eventually*
*be brought to light, and made plain to all. (Lk 8:17)*

Immediately after Adam and Eve disobeyed God in the garden,
we are told that 'they hid'. (Gen 3:8) It is no great exaggeration to
say that we are hiding since. Jesus came as a light to the world,
and he told us that, if we follow him, we will never walk in darkness. (Jn 8:12) He also said that some people like the darkness
more than the light. (Jn 3:19) God could not claim to be a just
God, unless everything within every heart was brought to light,
and justice is seen to be done. Some of the greatest movements
for good in the history of the world are brought about by the
quiet prayers of totally unknown people. (Jean Vanier) On the
other hand, some of the most ferocious and destructive acts have
been brought about by the spiteful word whispered in another's
ear. I can see the need for everything to be brought out in the
open, even though I may not be so fulsome, later in this reflection, when I consider my own particular situation! 'The truth
will out' is something we hear, and this is becoming more and
more the fact in recent times. When there is an explosion of the
highways of communication, and when Big Brother gets to
snoop into every corner, it will become increasingly more difficult to cover-up anymore. We ain't seen nothing yet, when it
comes to that communication highway. I can sit at my desk and
speak to someone in Australia, send a fax to someone in China,
and a photo to someone in the US. Even this is only the beginning, and my mind couldn't get round what things might be like
a generation or two from now. Already we have seen the effect
of this communication upsurge. The spotlight has begun to
enter the back pockets of politicians, the vaults of banks, and the
hidden files of the church. Soon there will be nowhere to hide.
Politicians speak of 'transparency in government', even if this is
just a window-dressing exercise, or a statement of an ideal to be
achieved.

No matter how Adam and Eve tried, they could not hide
from God. God knew what they had done, but he needed them
to admit to this themselves. Adam blamed Eve, and Eve blamed
the devil, and we're doing that since! The Spirit of God is a Spirit
of Truth and, until we face up to the truth, we cannot stand at

ease before the face of God. Coming before God, without excuse, denial, or pretence, is what is called for. It matters not what we have done wrong, as long as we are prepared and willing to admit it, and take responsibility for our actions. God loves us because he is good; and this has nothing to do with whether we are good or bad. All he asks for is the truth, because it is only the truth that will set us free. (Jn 8:32) Psalm 139 is a beautiful poem about the omnipresence of God: 'O Lord, you have examined my heart and know everything about me. You know when I sit down or stand up. You know my every thought when far away … You know what I am going to say before I say it … I can never escape from your Spirit. I can never get away from your presence. If I go up to heaven, you are there. If I go down to the place of the dead, you are there. If I ride the wings of the morning, if I dwell by the farthest oceans, even there your hand will guide me, and your strength will support me. I could ask the darkness to hide me, and the light around me to become light, but even in darkness, I cannot hide from you.'

At first reading, this text may come across more as a threat than a promise. This, of course, depends totally on where I'm coming from. I may have something to hide, and I fear exposure. On the other hand, I may have been struggling, doing my best, and never convinced that my best was good enough. It is only right and just that such people should get the recognition that their fidelity has merited. We are speaking of a God of justice here. Justice is more important than charity. Charity means that I am giving you something that is mine, while justice means that I am giving you something that is yours by right. To the children of God, this is a *promise*. God leaves all judgements to Judgement Day, and we are asked to do the same.

### *Other promises under the heading: Come to Me*

The water I give will take away thirst forever. (Jn 4:14)

Your joy will overflow. (Jn 15:11)

# Prayer

*Ask, using my name, and you will receive,*
*and you will have abundant joy. (Jn 16:24)*

Jesus came to find us where we are, and to bring us back to the garden. There is no other way back. 'No one comes to the Father except through me.' (Jn 14:6) It was through and in Jesus that God came among us; it is in and through Jesus that we can return to God. Jesus is the one who has won the victory, and anything we receive is simply part of that victory. He is the one who has climbed the summit, and any 'pull-up' I need must come from him. We are familiar with a situation where a family member has a post within a certain prestigious environment, e.g. White House, Vatican, Buckingham Palace, etc. Because of the family connection, family members are given access, and may even meet up with some of the more important people who live there. They themselves didn't earn this privilege, but they have someone on the 'inside', and everything is taken care of. That's exactly what Jesus is telling us in this promise.

He is now with the Father. He is restored to his rightful place, where he shares equally the life of the Trinity. 'All authority has been given me in heaven and on earth ...'(Mt 28:18) He is the one who dispenses the credit cards. He is the one who is still entrusted with our eternal salvation. He took on that task, and he will see it through. Let me put it this way: A young lad is left a fortune in a will. He himself is living in fairly straightened circumstances, so this is going to make all the difference in the world to his lifestyle. Well, not exactly! You see, he's not 'of age' yet, and he must wait until he reaches his twenty-first birthday before he can get his hands on all that money. In the meantime, however, there is an interim arrangement made. For all the things he needs (not wants), the person looking after the money will supply what is required. You and I are not 'of age' yet, in that we must pass through the rites of passage in death, before we can come into our full inheritance. In the meantime, however, Jesus is the guardian of that inheritance, and if there's anything

112

we need (not want), then all we have to do is come directly to him, or ask the Father in his name. It's as simple as that.

Jesus promises us abundant joy, and surely this access to the treasuries of heaven is a source of abundant joy. It is the wish of Jesus that we act on this promise, that we take him up on it. I met a man last Sunday and his greeting was, 'Ok, I will take you up on your offer.' I had to pause to remember what the offer had been! The last occasion on which I met him, my parting words were, 'I'll buy you a cup of coffee the next time we meet.' I was pleased that he felt free enough to take me up on my offer, and I was delighted to be able to be true to my word. It would have been unreal, indeed crazy, if he had come to me demanding a cup of coffee, or trying to get around me, in the hope of getting a cup of coffee. I had made a promise and, like the person he is, he walked up to me and took me up on my offer. This is a very important attitude to bring to our prayers. God doesn't want us groveling, moaning, bargaining, or trying to manipulate. Jesus has made an offer, he has offered a promise, and all he asks is that we take him up on that promise. When I turn on the computer here in the morning, it asks for a password before allowing me continue. Jesus tells us that his name is the password for entry into the treasuries of heaven. When I enter my password I expect the computer to give me access, and allow me freedom to open what file I need at this time. It is the very same with Jesus. Ask in his name, and you will receive. The realisation of how true and how faithful this promise is, is what gives us abundant joy. We are truly blessed indeed.

*If two of you agree down on earth concerning anything you ask, my Father in heaven will do it for you. (Mt 18:19)*

A Christian community is like a mirror I take off a wall, smash it, and hand one of the pieces to every single person in the community. Each piece reflects some aspect of God. If we can put all the pieces together, we will reflect the face of God. Each person is uniquely gifted. Each piece needs every one of the other pieces to complete the picture. On its own, a small piece of broken glass is meaningless. It doesn't belong on its own; it has no meaning on its own. It was made to be part of a greater picture. God has

instilled within the heart of each of us a great desire for belonging. I can feel very alone amidst the city throngs. The most basic
human need we all have is, that my life and my work are worth
something to somebody. 'No man/woman is an island.' We are
all part of the mainland. When I'm in a plane that is coming in to
land, I always like to have a window seat. I can see the many little islands down below and I know that they belonged to the
mainland one time. Long years of being battered by stormy and
angry seas had taken their toll, and parts of the land became separated from the mainland. This process continues in different
parts of the world right now.

Jesus asks us to come together in prayer, to pray as a community, as a worshipping church. There is a place for private prayer,
of course, but even this must not be me talking about me all the
time! Let us look at some of the miracles in the gospels for a moment. On occasions we have someone calling to Jesus to heal his
blindness, or to remove his leprosy. On many occasions we have
people coming to Jesus on behalf of someone else, whether that
be a daughter, a servant, or a mother-in-law. We have many incidents where people brought others to Jesus, even to the extent
of having to lower a man through a roof, to ensure that the meeting did take place. We are told that 'Jesus marvelled at their
faith'. (Mt 9:2) He also must have rejoiced at their love. This was
exactly what he had asked them to do. Join with someone else to
do good for somebody else. Stop flying solo, even in your attempts to be good. The individual effort, the private prayer, all
have a place, but we must not become trapped in that place. The
apostles in the Upper Room were quite a disparate group of
people. One had denied, one had remained, the others had run.
What held them together, however, was Mary, whose main concern for always for others, whether that be Elizabeth, Simeon,
the folks in Cana, or Jesus on Calvary. Because of her, the apostles were able to 'pray with one mind and heart'. (Acts 1:14) It is
the power of the group that gives unity to the prayer. The Spirit
is given to the group, rather than the individual, and the more
involved in community I am, the more open my heart becomes
for the Spirit.

We speak of the Real Presence as Jesus in the tabernacle, and
that is correct. He is, indeed, truly and really present there. He is

also present in the worshipping community as well and, in ways, this presence is more real. It is more real in that I can touch him, hug him, hit him, hear him, or ignore him there. I myself always choose to begin Mass, homily, talk, service of any kind with a prayer to the Holy Spirit and to Mary. I want unity to be there amongst those of us who gather; I want us to be of one mind, and one heart, as we pray. It is the unique role of the Spirit to bind us together as a community, to form the Body of Christ. It was the Spirit coming upon Mary at the annunciation that brought Jesus among us in the first place. Prayer can be really powerful if we listen to what Jesus has to say about it, and act on his advice. The apostles saw Jesus walk on water, raise the dead, calm the storm, and cleanse the leper. Yet, while alone with him, the one thing the apostles asked was 'Lord, teach us to pray.' (Lk 11:1) They saw that prayer was very central to his life, and they saw it as a source of his power. They had failed to drive the demons out of one man, because, Jesus said, 'these things are only done by prayer'. (Mk 9:29)

This concept of the power dwelling within the Christian community is being discovered more and more through Prayer Groups, Bible Study Groups, and Faith Sharing workshops. Only now are we wakening up to what Jesus said all those years ago. It's never too late, of course, and today is as good a day as any to begin to pray as closely as possible to the model of prayer taught us by Jesus. At the heart of this promise is the fact that prayer is the link between us on earth and the Father in heaven.

### With God everything is possible.
### (Mt 19:26)

There are two definites in life that we should remember. The first is that, of myself, I am powerless, I own nothing, and anything I do, as a mortal, will die, just as I will. The second certainty is that God can do all things. The link that joins those two extremes is my willingness. Everything I have is on loan; one heart attack, and it's all over. The axis of original sin is that it was an attempt to become like God. The first step on the road to conversion is that I stop playing God. God becomes God in my life the very moment I stop playing God. Napoleon is quoted as saying

'Impossible is a word that is found in the dictionary of a fool.'
Unfortunately, for him, life faced him with many impossibilities.
I am not an historian, but I hope that life brought him to accept
the fact that he wasn't God after all, and that he surrendered to a
Power greater than himself. I saw an advertisement one time
that stated, 'The difficult may take some time, and the impossible may take a little longer.' When Mary asked the Archangel
Gabriel how she possibly could fulfill the vocation entrusted to
her, she was told that the Holy Spirit would make all this possible, because 'nothing is impossible with God'. (Lk 1:37) Humility
is about knowing my place before God, and in relation to him.
Mary *magnified* the Lord which, in ordinary language, means
that she made God bigger and bigger, as it were. The bigger my
God, the smaller my problems. Some people have very big problems, because their God is too small.

I can read this promise, and it may never become more than a
concept. It's something I accept, without any great import. I may
feel totally unattached to the consequences for me of such a
statement. This promise can have profound effects in my life.
There is a much better chance of this happening, if I am convinced enough of my own powerlessness and brokenness. If I
am honest enough to accept and acknowledge the very serious
limitations of my own nature, and if life has brought me to the
point of experiencing my own powerlessness, then there is some
possibility that the idea of an all-powerful God might provoke
more than just a passing interest. Indeed, it may well cause me
to utter prayers of 'quiet desperation'! It is not possible for a
human being to fall on her/his knees, cry out to God, and not be
heard.

Thomas Aquinas says that when we speak of God, there is
only one thing we are sure of: we are wrong! No matter what we
might think about God, or say about God, we know that God is
much much more than that. The God who created us is quite capable of changing us, of healing us, of saving us. The only limits
to what God can do in our lives are the ones we set. God's love is
boundless, and unconditional. An important question I must
ask myself is 'What kind of God do I have?' I inherited an Irish
Catholic Male God, and I didn't trust him at all! It took me years
to get rid of him, and to discover the Father of the gospels; the

God who cares for the birds of the air, and the lilies of the field. The gospels can be summed up in one sentence: God loves me, and in one word: Abba/Father. There is no other God. 'They who see me, see the Father. They who hear me, hear the Father. The Father and I are one.' (Jn 12:45) There is no hidden agenda, nothing that has not been said. Jesus laid it all out before us, and he wants us to trust him on this one, as on any one of the many other promises he made about the Father.

I would not recommend it, but it would be interesting to make a list of all the things in my life that I see as being impossible. As I study these, I select those things that I really need, and that are necessary for me to live my life to the full. All that is needed to live life to the full, comes with the gift of creation. Unfortunately, human nature steps in, with greed, violence, aggression, and injustice, and half the world suffers from deprivation and injustice of one kind or another. In human terms, it seems impossible to redress this wrong. It is only God who can set this right. In this is a real test of our faith in a God for whom everything is possible. Where do we start? The obvious place is within my own heart. I cannot pray for justice and toleration in the world while there are prejudices, resentments, and unforgiveness within my own heart. I made my own decision of willingness to be part of the solution, rather than remaining part of the problem. This, in itself, can require a miracle. I finish this reflection where I began. The link between my own brokenness and powerlessness, and the power of an almighty God is willingness. 'I can do all things through him who gives me strength.' (Phil 4:13)

*If you believe, you will receive whatever you ask for in prayer.*
*(Mt 21:22)*

There are certain words that jump out at me as I look at this promise. If you believe ... Jesus is setting the boundaries here. Belief/faith is a response to love. Please don't ask me to trust God until you have convinced me that he really loves me, and has my best interests at heart. Becoming familiar with Jesus, his actions, and his words, is one sure way to do this. It is obvious that Jesus is anxious to pour his love in every way into the hearts of those who are open to him. If I believe ... 'I believe, Lord, help my unbelief.' (Jn 9:38) 'Lord, increase my faith.' (Mk 9:34) We have incidents in the gospels where we are told that Jesus marvelled at the faith of someone, e.g. the story of the centurion (Mt 8:10), when Jesus remarked, 'I have not found faith like this in Israel.' To many who came to him, pleading for his help, he replied, 'Your faith has healed you.' (Mt 9:22) At other times Jesus was disappointed with the lack of faith that others showed. 'How little faith you have.' (Mt 8:26) 'Have you still no faith?' (4:40) Faith on our part is the door that allows him enter with his healing and help.

Another phrase that jumps out at me is 'you will receive whatever you ask for'. Jesus sets no limits to the power of faith, and he doesn't want us to do that either. I often think that, when I die, and these eyes I now use are closed, and the eyes of my soul are fully opened, I will stand and stare in amazement for all eternity at all that was available to me throughout life, and how my lack of faith held most of that at bay. The road to heaven is heaven, and there is nothing I receive then that is not offered to me now. I know it is difficult for the human mind to comprehend the wonder of this but, on the other hand, this is entirely the work of the Spirit. There is a *virtue* of faith, and a *gift* of faith. I practise the virtue, and become better at exercising it over a period of time. It grows from a tiny seed into a huge mustard tree. (Lk 13:19) Jesus speaks of the mustard tree providing shelter for the birds of the air. In other words, as my faith grows, others come to me, asking for my prayers, and thus my faith is providing a safe place for them to seek help. The *gift* of faith is one of the gifts of the Spirit. This is pure gift and, like all charismatic gifts, it is given to me for others. We know of people whom the Lord uses to dispense his gift of healing, discerning, and speaking. When this speaking involves interpreting the present, or presenting the word of God, it is called the gift of prophecy. Whether we speak of virtue or gift, we are speaking about the Holy Spirit, who makes all of this possible.

I said earlier that I can practise and develop the virtue of faith. This faith grows, as I turn over to God's care all those things, great and small, that I just cannot handle. I am powerless over persons, places, and things. I cannot change yesterday, nor can I change another human being. 'Lord, give me the serenity to accept the things I cannot change, courage to change the things I can, and the wisdom to know the difference.' 'Holy Spirit, please help me' can become my mantra, as I gradually, one after another, hand over those things, behaviours, relationships, addictions, etc., that are getting the better of me, or are getting beyond me. This virtue of faith is somewhat akin to surrender. I can't, he can; I ask. I learn to trust by trusting. My faith grows every time I put it in action. God does want to answer prayers. The problem comes from our side, when the petition is lukewarm, lacking conviction, and with little or no expectation of being answered. This promise is very specific. If you believe, you will receive whatever you ask for in prayer. The onus is obviously on us after that.

*Keep on asking, and you will be given what you ask for.*
*(Mt 7:7)*

This promise has to do with perseverance in prayer. Jesus tells a story about a widow who came to a judge, seeking redress for some injustice. (Lk 18:2-4) The judge feared neither God nor man. He obviously was a tough character, who was difficult to influence. The widow, however, just kept pestering him until, at last, he yielded to her entreaties and gave her what she asked. Jesus is setting this story against the idea of praying to a loving and caring God. God always answers prayers, and will give us what we ask, unless, of course, he has something better to give. If I am serious about what I'm seeking, then I won't just mention it once, and forget all about it. It will be obvious to God that I am serious in making my petition, and that I know that he can grant it. The organ that God gave me with which to pray is my heart. When I speak from the heart, I speak to the heart. A prayer from the heart goes straight to the heart of God, who is a God of mercy and compassion.

This promise is selected from a threefold promise Jesus made: 'Ask, and you will receive; seek, and you will find; knock, and the door will be opened to you.' All three sections imply the possibility of waiting for a response, which is sure to come. We are all familiar with knocking on a door, or ringing a doorbell, and having to wait for the door to be opened. At times, we find that we have to knock or ring a few times, before getting a response. And, again, we are familiar with looking for something we have lost. In most cases, we usually find what we lost, but it can take quite a while to find the lost object. Our insistence and persistence in the search is one way of understanding the kind of prayer to which Jesus refers here.

There is an expression I hear, and use, from time to time, regarding persistence in prayer. It is spoken of as 'shaking the gates of heaven'. This is bound to get attention! While it is not stubbornness, it must come from a deep-held belief that God can do what I ask, and that he will, if it is for my good. 'Do you believe I can do this?' (Mt 9:28) is a question Jesus sometimes asked those who came to him for help or healing. If I believe he can do it, then, I should check on the nature of my request, and ask myself, 'Do I believe that he would really want to answer this prayer?' It is said that if God were cruel and sadistic, he would give us everything we ask and would then have a good laugh. However, of course, God is not like that, but there are times when he sees that what we seek would not be good for us. 'Be careful what you ask for in prayer, because you might get it' is another comment we hear from time to time. I could ask myself some of the following questions: 'Why am I looking for this? Do I need it, or simply want it? Will anyone else benefit, if God gives me what I ask for?' Quite often, thankfully, many of our prayers are for other people, e.g. a sick family member or neighbour. There is a wonderful story in the gospel of a woman who came to Jesus asking him to heal her daughter. It is a strange story, in so far as it is difficult to know why Jesus played 'hard-to-get' so much with her, before finally granting her request. (Mt 15:21-28) We are actually told that, when she asked him, he didn't say a word, and continued to walk. The woman persisted, however, to such an extent that the apostles asked Jesus to send her away, because she was a nuisance with all her begging. When Jesus did speak, his words seemed offensive, if not downright insulting. I like to think that Jesus knew the woman's background, and the circumstances that led to her daughter being possessed by a demon. He certainly was putting her to the test. Nothing he said could persuade her to give up on her request,

so, finally, Jesus' heart was touched, and he spoke those wonderful words, 'Woman, your faith is great. Your request is granted.' What an example of the 'keep on asking' mentioned in the
promise now under reflection. This woman wouldn't take 'no'
for an answer, because her prayer came from a heart that was
filled with love for her daughter. It was as if she knew that Jesus
couldn't refuse such a prayer, even if he did hold out on her for a
while.

I sometimes think that I could be praying for something,
which God intends giving me at a certain time, but, long before
that time, I give up the prayer, and no longer bother asking for
it. Could this be another way of giving up on God? I certainly
know people who just hung in there, and kept up the prayer,
day after day, and, eventually, the prayer was answered.
Sometimes the desperate nature of the situation gives one the
energy and determination to continue the prayer. It can also be
greatly helped when we realise that what we seek is away beyond our own ability to reach, or to achieve. Prayer that flows
out of powerlessness must surely touch the heart of God. I can
hardly imagine someone falling on her/his knees, crying to
God, and not being heard.

### *Ask anything in my name, and I will do it.*
### *(Jn 14:14)*

Once again, we have a simple, direct, uncomplicated statement
or promise. This is one that Jesus himself stands over, and takes
full responsibility for keeping this promise. It is a generous
promise, in that we are told to ask for anything. This 'anything',
of course, would have to be within the ambit of what would be
pleasing to God. Asking in his name is the key to the treasuries
of heaven. Jesus came to us, to find us, to redeem us, and to
bring us back to the Father. Before Jesus came, it was as if the
gates of heaven, like the veil in the Jewish Temple, was closed
against us. When Jesus was baptised in the Jordon river, we are
told that 'the heavens were opened, the Father spoke, and the
Spirit was seen to descend on him'. (Lk 3:21-22) When he bowed
his head in death on Calvary, the gospels tell us that, among
many signs and wonders, 'the veil of the Temple was rent in

two'. (Mt 27:51) These were very powerful and significant moments. The Red Sea had, once again, been divided, making it
possible for us to go directly into the presence of God. St Paul
tells us that we are no longer slaves, but children of God, and we
can come right into his presence without fear. (Gal 4:7)

In many ways Jesus speaks of himself being the Way, the
only Way back to the Father. He is the gate of the sheepfold, and
nobody can enter in any other way. (Jn 10:7) Because I spend
some time working with a computer, I notice that I have little
pieces of paper stuck on the side. Each piece of paper has the
phone number of some helpline, for when the computer acts up,
and I need to cry out for help! Any one of these numbers will
give me direct access to a technician, who already possesses details of computer, printer, e-mail service, or whatever compo-
nent that is causing me problems. Jesus is more than a helpline
in an emergency! He tells me that I can go straight to him, and I
will receive his personal attention. My generation grew up with
doctors coming to us, making house calls, rather than us sitting
for long periods in a waiting room in his clinic. Jesus is always
'on call', and we do not have to go back to the gospels for assurance on this. In his messages of Divine Mercy to St Faustina, he
is begging people to come to him, and he is promising his willingness to come to our assistance at any time. It is sad to think
that Jesus has to beg people to come to him, or allow him come
to them. It is difficult for the human mind to comprehend the
word *love* when applied to God. 'God is love' says John. (1 Jn 4:8)
Jesus is God's love in human form, and he came among us to
dispense that love in generous and unconditional ways to those
who are open to it.

I consider this the kind of promise that requires deep reflection. It is the work of the Spirit to translate these words into a
conviction in the heart. I can hear them with my ears, or read
them with my eyes, but the Spirit will write them in my heart,
where the truth they contain becomes a reality, a conviction that
calls for action. This word can, and must become flesh in me, a
word that I live out in my life. 'Heaven and earth will pass away,
but my word will never pass away.' (Mt 24:35) As I said at the
beginning of this reflection, Jesus takes full responsibility for the
promises he makes. He will see to it personally that his word is

kept. It is a great tribute to say about another, 'He is a man of his word.' We have all experienced times when someone let us down, and did not fulfill a promise made to us. Indeed, every one of us can recall a time when we ourselves failed to deliver on a promise made. I myself can recall promises I made without great thought, or without any great intention of keeping that promise. We certainly must see Jesus in a very different light. He is a man of his word, and someone we can take at his word. If acted on, this promise holds the key to many wonderful graces and blessings in our lives. Jesus doesn't *give* me anything, but he *offers* me everything.

### Other promises under the heading: Prayer

Keep on looking, and you will find. (Mt 7:7)

Keep on knocking, and the door will be opened. (Mt 7:7)

# Kingdom of God

*Seek first the kingdom of God,*
*and everything else will be added to you. (Mt 6:33)*

This promise is about priorities, about putting first things first. It is so easy for any of us to become so preoccupied with the urgent that we neglect the important. The kingdom of God is all about getting the priorities right. In the kingdom, Jesus is Lord, and nobody or nothing should get our obedience if this causes us to act against the wishes of Jesus for us. Sometimes words like 'holiness' or 'sanctity' can appear very abstruse and abstract. However, if I interpret 'sanctity' as acting in a way that my words and actions can be sanctioned by God, then I'll get a better idea of what the word implies. Would God sanction what I said to that person this morning? Would God sanction how I behaved towards someone else yesterday afternoon? There are three simple rules involved in kingdom living, and they are not for negotiating: Jesus is Lord, and no false God of money, power, or popularity can replace him; everybody is on this earth with equal right – the most disabled child is on this earth with as much right as the greatest genius that ever lived; the third rule is that the Holy Spirit is the source of power that enables us live in the kingdom.

The kingdom of this world can mess up my priorities, with each ad on the telly presenting something that's so much better than the item they were flogging a few months ago. The computer on which I am now working was in 'hospital' recently for some repairs and, while it was away, I felt like a headless chicken! I spent most of my life without a computer, but now I found I had become dependent on one! My time for private prayer, meditation, or reflection can often come a poor second, if I have something interesting to do on the computer. People with a worldly mind-set are preoccupied with serving one of the many false gods of this world. They act exactly as dictated by the Stock Exchange, the bank rates, opinion polls, or Tam ratings. These facts do their thinking for them, and they are obeyed totally. For the person living in the kingdom of Jesus, whatever Jesus says is the spur for all my actions. He is Lord, and it is my duty and privilege to obey him.

The second condition for kingdom living must be to free myself from all bigotry, biases, racism, intolerance, and resentments of every kind. That's a tall order! Of course, this is impossible for me, on my own, but certainly not impossible when the power of the Spirit is invited to take over. You see, if I stand with a group of multi-ethnic Christians, all colours, all races, and we pray the Lord's Prayer together, I will hear each of them speak to God as their Father also. As I look sideways at them, I must accept that all of these people, through a deliberate plan of God, are actually my brothers and sisters. 'Who is my mother? Who are my brothers? ... These are my mother and brothers. Anyone who does the will of my Father in heaven is my brother, sister, and mother.' (Mt 12:48-49)

The very atmosphere, the very air necessary to sustain life in the kingdom is provided by the Holy Spirit. The kingdom, the power, and the glory are yours ... If I supply some of the power, I will surely claim some of the glory. Before Jesus ascended into heaven, he asked his apostles to stay in Jerusalem, not to leave it, until the Spirit came. One could imagine Jesus saying to himself, 'Because if you do, you'll surely get it all wrong again.' By myself, I am like a tape-recorder with batteries. I can play, but I won't keep playing. On the other hand, when the tape-recorder is plugged into a socket in the wall, it has a much better chance of playing for many days to come. The kingdom is given to me as a gift. 'It has pleased your Father to give you a kingdom.' (Lk 12:32)

The kingdom of God in this world is like the US embassy here in Dublin. It is in Dublin, but it doesn't belong to Dublin. It is American property, and Irish authorities may not enter there uninvited. Over the years, we have read of persecuted individuals or groups entering an Embassy in their own country, seeking refuge, and their own government authorities were unable to follow them into that building. I have no desire to labour this, beyond trying to make it very clear that there are three very specific conditions for kingdom living, and it is only in fulfilling those that we can hope to come into possession of the treasuries of that kingdom, referred to in this promise.

'Everything else will be added to you'. That is quite a generous statement. Another way of putting this would be: If you
choose to live in my kingdom, you won't ever have to ask for
anything again, because being in the kingdom brings with it the
assurance that you will have everything you need. Jesus doesn't
ask us to do anything without providing the means to respond.
With the call comes the power to reply. It is obvious then that to
get the best possible conditions for my relationship with God, is
to live in his kingdom, where Jesus is Lord, everybody is important, and it can be lived only through the power of the Spirit.

*Blessed are the poor in spirit, for theirs is the kingdom of heaven.*
*(Mt 5:3)*

There is one thing that must be made clear at the start. Jesus is
not saying that the poor are blessed, or that it's a good thing to
be poor. Far from it! If that were the case, then the poor people of
this world should be considered the lucky ones, and that's obviously not true. Jesus is speaking about being poor in spirit,
which is another way of describing humility. A person could be
a millionaire several times over, and yet be quite detached and,
in no way does the money own him/her. Our perception of great
wealth, either through the media, or personal observation, tends
to project a lavish lifestyle, where everything is worth mega
bucks, and where money opens every door. This is true, of
course, and there's no denying it. On the other hand, there are
people who have a great deal of money and, while they may
have a lavish lifestyle, they are also very generous towards worthy causes. The 'poor is spirit' referred to here is someone who is
the exact opposite to a miser.

Humility is the 'mother of all the virtues'. If I could get that
one down, I would develop the other virtues so much more easily. Humility is truth, it's about reality, about the way things are.
I own nothing. Everything I have is on loan from God. One heart
attack, and it's all over. God gives me nothing for myself. He
doesn't give me the gift of speech to go around talking to myself!
Everything is gift which the Lord gives, and the Lord can take
away. It is possible to be wealthy and be humble but, as Jesus
says, 'It's more difficult for a rich man to enter heaven than for a

camel to pass through the eye of a needle.'(Lk 18:25) The 'eye of
a needle' is not as we would probably understand it and, therefore, would be one way of saying that the task is impossible. The
eye of a needle was an expression used about one of the many
narrow entrances into the Temple. In other words, it was possible for a camel to pass through such an entrance, but certainly
not with any trappings or burden on him. One of Anthony De
Mello's last books has the catchy title *Unencumbered By Baggage*.
Wealth has a habit of controlling people and their actions, and of
being a very strong influence in all dealings with others. It can
become very demanding, and one can easily become so preoccupied with the urgent that there's no time to attend to the
important.

This promise is not directly a promise of the kingdom, because those who meet the humility of heart, and the poverty of
knowing their own mortality and powerlessness are already
able to pass through this narrow gate into the kingdom. The
kingdom is theirs, rather than something that will happen at
some future date. The kingdom of God now, is what we'll call
heaven later on. The road to heaven is heaven, and there is nothing I'll get when I die that I'm not offered today. I can have the
fullness of the Trinity living within me, and what more can I
possibly receive, or be capable of receiving? The only difference
is that, when I die, the limitations of the body will be removed,
and my soul will be open to eternity and to infinity. Too much of
that now, and my heart would stop!

While I spent some time reflecting on wealth as a possible
stumbling block, I must also remember that possessiveness,
greed, and selfishness can be just as destructive, even if the arti-
cle in dispute is worthless in money terms. This promise speaks
of a freedom of the heart, the ability to let go, and not be possessed by one's possessions. I know this can be a beautiful ideal,
or even a dream, but it is the work of the Spirit to make these
dreams come true. When I am in touch with my real hungers, I
discover that material things don't satisfy the way they used to.
If money brought happiness, then every millionaire would be
deliriously happy. The suicide rate among millionaires doesn't
witness to any great or automatic happiness. There is a difference between being rich and being wealthy. I could be very

wealthy in material things, but completely spiritually bereft and bankrupt in my spirit. On the other hand, I may not have a great deal of the riches of this world, but my life could be filled with love, going from me, and coming back to me. 'Freedom's just another word for nothing left to lose' has more than a grain of truth in it. Let me put it this way. Suppose I hand over to God everything I possess, spiritually, materially, professionally. God accepts my gift, and he then hands it all back to me, with the following instructions: 'Now remember these are all mine, and I am lending them to you, to use them on my behalf. You can entertain the stranger in your house, because it is now my house. You can give a lift to someone seeking this, because the car is mine.' I could go on and on, but I think I have made a point and, hopefully, there is something there worth reflecting on.

*Unless you are born again, you cannot enter the kingdom of God.*
*(Jn 2:3)*

'Born again Christians' is a term not always used in a complimentary way. At the beginning of the church, it was at Antioch that the followers of Jesus were first called 'Christians', and this was intended as a derisory term. In the context of this promise we have Jesus attempting to explain to a very intellectual Jewish leader what 'born again' is all about. It is important that I clarify my own understanding of it, before going any further in this reflection. When I was born, I arrived into a situation where there were parents, brothers, sisters, a home, a family name, a nationality, a religion, etc., etc., all waiting for me. I had no say or choice in any of that. It was like coming into an inheritance; it was all there at my disposal. The nuclear family is but a piece of the jigsaw which makes up the family of God. While I had no say in the situation and circumstances surrounding my birth, I do have a very personal input into whether I choose to be a member of God's family. The decision is mine now; it is totally up to me. I can accept or reject the offer. To fully accept the offer of complete membership within the family of God is to be born again. I can be a born-again Jew, Hindu, Muslim, or Christian. These are just different streams flowing towards the same sea, which is God.

Generally speaking, when a baby is born there is an official record of that birth, with name, date of birth, place of birth, etc. At any time during that person's life a certificate with such details can be obtained, and must be obtained when certain events and undertakings come up. When the baby is baptised, an official record is also made of that, with name, date, parents, godparents, officiating minister, etc. This is where the child is officially signed up as a member of Christ's family, as a brother or sister of Jesus, given the wonderful privilege of being able to speak of God as Father, Abba, Daddy. Some years later, that same child returns to church for confirmation, when what happened at baptism is officially confirmed by a bishop. This is, as it were, a completion of baptism. Now, the core issue I am endeavouring to bring to the fore here is that in most instances all of these things happen at such an early age, that the child cannot have any great appreciation of, or personal input into what's going on. Sooner or later, sometime or other, later in life, that person must accept full and personal responsibility for the obligations committed to, on behalf of the child, by a godparent or sponsor. The result of this personal commitment to Jesus and to his teachings is what I would call 'being born again'. This is a whole new beginning; it is the most crucial point in one's Christian journey. Jesus tells us that unless we are born again, we cannot enter the kingdom of heaven.

In Charismatic Prayer Groups there is a programme called Life In The Spirit Seminars. On the fifth night of this seven-night programme, there is a ceremony where the Holy Spirit is asked to come upon all gathered there in a whole New Pentecost. They accept Jesus as Lord in their lives. They ask for forgiveness for times when he was not Lord, and when they chose to walk in other ways. As in the early church, hands are placed on the head of each, joined with prayers for the release of the Spirit. The participants do not receive anything, because they already have the Holy Spirit since baptism. The problem often is, if I might put it this way, they have the Holy Spirit, but the Holy Spirit may not have them! The Spirit has to be 'released' within them; in other words, to be given the freedom to take over, and work in and through them. This is called *Baptism in the Spirit,* and it is a very fitting title, because it implies a pulling together, and an affirming of our baptism and confirmation. When the power of the Spirit is released within me, and that Spirit comes out in my words and actions, then I can claim to be born again.

This 'being born again' is, as it were, a visa and passport to heaven. I have joined Jesus in the Jordon, and on the cross, and I have witnessed the heavens opening, as I stand under the Niagara of the Father's love.

*I assure you that, when I sit on my throne in the kingdom,*
*you who have followed me will also sit on thrones. (Mt 19:28)*

At the time of writing these words there is widespread international anger, anguish, debate, fear, and sometimes despair, as it appears that the US and Britain are going to begin war with Iraq. 'Might is right', and different voices are coming from different cultures, speaking different languages, while still using English. The bottom line is that nobody really knows what's the best thing to do, and nobody really knows what the result will be of whatever action is undertaken, or suspended. There is an ominous silence amidst the haggle of raised voices. I thought of all this as I read the promise now under review. Jesus came to declare war on Satan, and to overcome sin, sickness, and death. He was sent by the Father, to whom nothing was impossible. Therefore, because of his faith in the Father, Jesus could confidently predict the outcome of the conflict. 'When I sit on my throne ...' leaves one in no doubt as to what Jesus expects. His is not a Mission Impossible. 'The Father loves his Son, and has put everything in his power.' (Jn 3:35) Jesus is assured of victory, and he assures his followers of this fact. In him is our victory, and all he asks is that we be willing to accept the fruits of that victory.

Because Jesus has the final victory, everything will be put under his control, when his kingdom is fully established. There will come a time when the kingdom of this world, with its false gods and wrong priorities, will come to an end. Satan will be completely defeated, and confined to eternal darkness and powerlessness, no longer able to attack any of God's children, or to intrude on the success of the kingdom of God. There will be but one kingdom, where Jesus will be Lord for all eternity. It is then that he will sit on his throne, with all dominions under his feet. It is at this time that those who follow him will share fully in that victory. All of this is a reality right now, even if we have to wait until it is fully and finally revealed. We can already live with this victory, when we trust him to keep us close to him. 'By your cross and resurrection you have set us free. You are the Saviour of the world.' We are already free, if we choose to live with the freedom of the children of God.

When a war has been won, there are trophies for the victors. Unfortunately, in human terms, there are no real winners when it comes to war. To have to go to war in the first place, is itself a failure, because there are ways of overcoming evil, without death, destruction, and devastation. Because there never could be any expectations that even God could negotiate with Satan, Jesus declared war on him, and defeated him. One of the victims of this war was Jesus himself. However, his 'defeat' was turned into victory through his resurrection. 'If Jesus had not risen from the dead, our faith is in vain, and we are still in sin.' (1 Cor 15:17) The wonderful good news is that all of us can share fully in the results of this victory. 'We are made right with God when we believe that Jesus shed his blood, sacrificing his life for us.'(Rom 3:25) Another translation tells us that there are two parts to our salvation: what Jesus has done, and us accepting that. Everything is offered, rather than given. It's up to us whether we accept or not.

Like so many of the promises of Jesus, this is one of great hope. Imagine what it would be like if I knew beforehand which horse was going to win a race! I would be very foolish not to put my money on that horse. In the race of life, we know the results, if we choose to accept them. God doesn't send us anywhere when we die. Rather he eternalises whatever direction we choose to travel in now. The thrones are waiting for us. At an earlier stage of my life I was never too happy to think of Judgement Day! Reflecting on this promise presents a very different viewpoint of what will be a moment of great triumph for those of us who choose to follow Jesus, walk in his Way, and believe in his promises.

*The good news about the Kingdom*
*will be preached throughout the world, so that all nations will*
*hear it, and then, finally, the end will come. (Mt 24:14)*

Jesus came with a message, and it is his desire that this message resounds throughout the world. It is difficult to understand just how this message is ever going to receive a very wide audience. On the face of things, this message is having quite a limited effect for good among the peoples of the world. Speaking in human terms, and examining it with the human mind, would lead one to give up all hope of this message ever making a real breakthrough. All we need do is look at what has already happened. There is a passage often found on Christmas cards, etc., called *One Solitary Life*. It speaks of an unknown carpenter, in an unknown place, with a message that seems to have little to do with the intricacies of everyday living. Then it goes on to say that this man is still spoken of, admired, and followed by millions, thousands of years later. Right now I am actually speaking of things this man said all those many years ago. It is not the great failure that first appears when we look at the question in a superficial way. Calvary was a 'failure' in every human sense of that word. The leader had been killed, and his followers had denied him, sold him, and run away. God's ways are not our ways. St Peter tells us that 'Jesus was put to death physically, but made alive spiritually.' (1 Pet 3:18) This is one of the great paradoxes of Christianity. What in human terms is failure, is seen by God as victory. Despite all the limitations we observe about the spread of the Christian message, we just have to trust the Spirit that 'all is well, and all manner of thing will be well.' (Julian of Norwich)

Notice the words 'so that all nations will hear it'. It is not implied here that all nations will respond to it. That's not very likely. However, Jesus tells us, 'They would not be guilty if I had not come and spoken to them.' (Jn 15:22) In the story about the sower we get a glimpse of the thinking of Jesus. (Lk 8) The sower threw the seed everywhere in prodigal generosity. The response to that gift was so different in different 'soils'. He is even generous in his understanding of 'good soil', because he includes a mere thirty per cent response ('thirtyfold') as being good. In other words, such people made some response, and that cannot be classified as total indifference. The opposite to love is not hatred; it is indifference.

I don't pretend to have any profound insights into the millions of Muslims, Hindus, Buddhists, etc., in the world, and how they are tied in with the message of Jesus. God has no grandchildren; we are all children of God. I hope and expect that the witness of Christian living might be a source of inspiration for many of them, just as the wonderful example of the good lives of so many of them can be a great source of inspiration for us. I believe that we all share in the Divine economy of salvation, and that what Jesus has done is actually reaching them in some mysterious way. God is multi-facial, and no one group can claim a monopoly on God. I am happy to reflect on this promise in so far as it applies to us Christians, and I'm quite prepared to leave the finer print to God.

Jesus finishes this message with the words 'and then, finally, the end will come'. It is almost as if he's saying that he will allow for plenty of time for the good news to be preached, and for people to respond to it. 'There is a time for sowing ... a time for reaping ... and a time for every season under heaven.' (Ecc 3: 1-17) At the time of Creation, God opened up his infinite love to the world. In Jesus, the infinite mercy of God was/is made available. There comes a time, however, when we must face God's infinite justice. 'I have told you everything before that time comes.' (Mk 13:23) 'The time is coming when all the dead will hear his voice.' (Jn 5:28) 'Now is the time for the world to be judged.' (Jn 12:31) These are not threats; rather are they reminders, because it is so easy for us to forget, like the foolish virgins who forgot to get oil for their lamps when the bridegroom arrived. (Mt 25:3) Jesus tells us that the Holy Spirit will remind us of everything he himself had told us. (Jn 16:12-14) May he find us watching when that day comes.

*Blessed are those who suffer for the cause of justice,*
*for theirs is the Kingdom of heaven. (Mt 5:10)*

Probably never before has this promise been so necessary as a source of inspiration and hope. With the explosion of the communication network, we are well informed about events in every corner of the globe. Justice is such a scarce commodity in so many parts of today's world. The poor, the hungry, the marginalised are crying out for justice, are crying out to be heard. 'The harvest is great, but the labourers are few. Ask the Lord of the harvest to send labourers into his vineyard.' (Mt 9:37) Thankfully, we have some wonderful examples of courageous and prophetic people who are out there, doing everything within their power to promote and defend justice. It is not a question of giving people their rights. They have their rights, even if they are not allowed exercise them. Justice is more important than charity. Charity is sharing what is mine; justice is allowing others avail of what is theirs by right. Working for justice in today's world sometimes appears like trying to keep back the tide with a spoon. It is important to stress, however, that as a Christian I must never lose hope. That is the ultimate sin for the Christian. Justice involves restoring people's hope, but I cannot give hope if I myself do not have it. In working to rectify the situation of others, it is important to remember that the helper is blessed more in the giving than the other in the receiving. Truly blessed are those who work for the cause of justice, because the kingdom of God is certainly theirs.

'Prisoners of conscience' is a term that has begun to be highlighted over the past number of years. The heroic dedication of extraordinary human beings has ignited fires of courage and determination within the hearts and minds of so many. Ghandi, Mandela, Romero, Luther King, among many others, are names that resound around the world. Prophets have frequently ended up as martyrs, much the same as Jesus on Calvary. Many of these heroes have paid the ultimate price in their pursuit of justice. 'Greater love than this no one has, that a person should lay down a life for a friend.' (Jn 15:13) This is love that involved the supreme sacrifice. It is literally walking in the footprints of Jesus, all the way to Calvary. Jesus tells us that we can expect to be treated as he was, if we attempt to follow the Way. It doesn't always involve the supreme sacrifice, thankfully, but it certainly makes great demands on those who develop a social conscience, and attempt to be faithful to it. Peace marches are one form of seeking redress, which in most western countries there is little danger of being attacked. In recent years, however, we watched our television screens in amazement, as thousands upon thousands of unarmed men and women marched on the dictators' palaces in Romania, Yugoslavia, or the Philippines. This was people power, and these were people who had said that enough is enough. They knew they would never get justice unless they were prepared to face down the tyrants.

For most of us life is not so dramatic. Not one of us, however, can detach herself or himself from the concerns for justice. Half the world is dying of hunger, while the other half is on a diet, trying to lose weight. The pictures of hungry emaciated faces from Ethiopia, for example, stare out at us from our television screens. We all can do something. And we all can do something *now*. That's the problem! There's nothing more powerful than an idea whose time has come. I can take a stand on issues of justice right in my own backyard. It is possible that some of us could find issues of injustice right within our own families. Becoming a spokesperson for justice, becoming a voice for the voiceless, can lead to one being branded a troublemaker and a nuisance. That's what Jesus has in mind in this promise.

I honestly believe that we should certainly be held accountable for remaining silent in the face of injustice. We have to face up to the moral coward within most of us. It can appear to be so much simpler not to get involved. In the story of the Good Samaritan (Lk 10:30-37) we are told of a priest and a Levite who just didn't want to get involved, and they continued down the road. 'He didn't do anything, because that was the kind of man he was' is a sizzling indictment of a lawyer in a novel by Albert Camus. 'All that's needed for evil people to succeed is that good people should do nothing' is a phrase one often hears. There is a cost in Pentecost, and if I choose to befriend the marginalised, or to speak out on behalf of the repressed and down-trodden, Jesus leaves me in no doubt as to the reception I will get from the world. However, it is to such courageous, honest, and moral souls that the kingdom of heaven belongs.

### Other promises under the heading: Kingdom of God
Those who are considered least here, will be the greatest in the Kingdom of heaven. (Mt 19:30)

Many who are first now will be last then, and many who are last now will be first then. (Mt 20:16)

# Treatment of Others

*If you give even a cup of cold water to one of the least of my followers, you will surely be rewarded. (Mt 10:42)*

Another translation of this promise finishes 'you do it to me'. Jesus identifies so much with the poor, 'the least of my followers', that he accepts everything we do for them as being personally done for him. There is nothing complicated in this promise and, while we could gain much from reflecting on it, there is little need to explain it. Any one of us can build up the kingdom of God in two very simple ways. Firstly, the many many tiny acts of kindness and of love that we all can do any day of the week. Secondly, these acts are of such a nature that hardly anybody knows anything about them. 'Some of the greatest movements for good in the history of the world have been brought about by the quiet prayers of totally unknown people' (Jean Vanier). One of the saddest phrases in the gospels is the comment of one of the apostles, as he looked at the thousands of hungry people, and the few loaves he held in his hand. 'What are these among so many? '(Jn 6:9) It is important to know that, as far as God is concerned, whatever you have is enough. At Cana, they only had water, but they gave that to Jesus and the miracle happened. The apostles had only a few loaves and a few fish but, once again, these were given to Jesus and the thousands were fed. I'm sure if I won the Lotto I'd give some of that money to charity. Jesus would think much more of the few pennies I give out of my bus money to a homeless person downtown.

I have the privilege of celebrating eucharist every morning with a group of very elderly folks in a Retirement Home. Many of them are in wheelchairs, and are not able to do much for themselves. I continue to remind them, however, that even from their wheelchairs, they can touch the hearts of thousands, and be a strong influence for good in the world through their quiet prayers and aspirations.

Jesus tells us that, on the Day of Judgement, many will be surprised that he took note of the good things they did. (Mt

25:37-40) These are people of good heart who, acting out of the kindness of their heart, always do the right thing, without fanfare or trumpet. They are just generous souls who are always willing to lend a helping hand where needed, and would never think of walking by when there is someone is need. They are not looking for plaudits or earthly acclaim. They are kingdom people, and the Spirit within has sensitised them to the needs of those around them. A cup of cold water, in Jesus' name, may not be considered as anything major, yet even this is accepted and rewarded. Such people are the leaven in society; they are the ones who continue the work of Jesus among his people. I know some people who are continually organising coffee mornings or other fund-raising events in aid of some charity or deserving cause. They inspire others through their example, and they involve others who themselves might not have taken the initiative or become involved in the endeavour in the first place.

In the gospel, we are told of an incident where Jesus watched a poor widow put her few coins into a collection in the Temple. He turned to his disciples, and said, 'Truly I say to you, this poor widow put in more than those who gave offerings. For all of them gave of their plenty, but she gave from her poverty, and put in everything she had, her living.' (Mk 12:42-44) Jesus takes note of even the smallest act of charity, because he is aware of the generosity of spirit in the giving, rather than the amount given.

### Do not judge others, and you will not be judged.
### (Mt 7:1)

Jesus had a wonderful way of putting a point across in simple uncomplicated language. Nothing could be easier than the words he now uses. Live and let live, is another way of putting it. God leaves all judgements to Judgement Day, and we are asked to do the same. Obviously, this does not include the judgements one must make in hiring or firing staff, or administering justice in a court of law. The very role entrusted to me may place a responsibility on me to make judgements, and to act on them. This is not what is meant in this phrase. Jesus is speaking of the way we can judge, condemn, slander, backbite, or gossip about others in those things that have nothing to do with us, and are none of our business. The surest sign that the Spirit of God is living within a person's heart is the facility that person has to affirm others, and make them feel worthwhile. Those who continually 'knock' others, and make a career out of pulling people down, are reflecting more of what is going on within themselves than the persons under attack. If John and Mary are passing judgements on Pat, their conversation may very well reveal more about the two of them, than it does about Pat.

Once again, the tendency to judge is the direct result of pride. Once I begin to pass judgements on others, it is the result of my own personal verdict that I am superior to these people in some way, and I have a right to tell others what my opinions of them are. We are familiar with the phrase 'looking down on others', implying that I am on some sort of superior level, from which vantage point I have a right to pontificate on what I observe in those lesser mortals. This is a very destructive and dangerous defect of character. Once again, I say that it tells more about the pride and arrogance of the 'judge' than of the weaknesses and failures of the 'accused'. We speak a great deal today about intolerance, prejudice, racism, and other forms of injustice closely aligned. Prejudice means 'pre-judging'; in other words it's coming in with a verdict before the evidence is presented. This flies in the face of all natural justice, and it certainly is well outside the remit of Christian living. In the early church, most people weren't sure what these followers of a crucified leader were up to, or what they intended to do. Were they some sort of radical force, determined to undermine all lawful authority? Were they just dreamers, driven by nostalgia, desperately trying to hold on to something that had died on Calvary? Whatever their opinions were, they began to notice something that these people seem to have in common. 'See how these people love one another.' This was the very thing that Jesus had told them. 'By this shall everybody know that you are my disciples if you love one another.' (Jn 13:35) When we listen carefully to the words of Jesus, and become familiar with his thinking, and get an inner sense of his heart, then we just have to see how unChristian it is to pass judgements on others out of our pride and arrogance. Jesus asks us to love one another as he loves us. One of the most gripping incidents in the gospels, that reveals the heart of Jesus more than most, is his encounter with the woman about to be stoned to death for adultery. (Jn 8:3-11) She was about to receive the official penalty meted out by the law for such conduct, and most of those onlookers were there to see that 'justice' was done. Like public executions in some countries even today, this may well have been a regular spectacle in the town square. Jesus looked at her accusers in the eye, and he asked one simple question: 'If there is any one of you without sin, let that person throw the first stone.' Wow! One could imagine the silence! This was really a show-stopper. In a way it is humorous to watch what happened next. Slowly, one by one, beginning with the oldest, they turned and walked away. It was as if they were saying that the older they were, the bigger sinners they were! And there can be some truth in this. Not only had they more years in which to accumulate sin but, because of the wisdom that can come with age, they may have been more conscious of their own sinfulness. The story ended that that beautiful line, as Jesus turned to the woman, and said, 'And neither do I condemn you; go in peace …' He told us very clearly about his own mission. 'I came to save the world, not judge it.' (Jn 12:47) If we are asked to love others as Jesus loves us, then we must purge our hearts of any tendency to judge. What a beautiful, consoling promise! If I can overcome my instinct to judge, I myself will not have to be judged.

> *Whatever measure you use in giving,*
> *will be used to measure what is given back to you. (Lk 6:38)*

Once again, we are offered a simple, common-sense promise that allows for no prevarication or 'nit-picking'. As forgiveness, love, compassion, or assistance goes out from me to others, so in like manner will that be poured into my heart by the Spirit. God sets no limits to what he wants to do for us. The choice is ours, and we can avail of it with openness and generosity. The more understanding, tolerance, and compassion I give to those in need, the more of that will I receive. In the Twelve-Step programme of Alcoholics Anonymous, there is great stress placed on the simple principle: it is by helping others to become sober than I myself will continue to be sober. It never ceases to amaze me, as I reflect on these promises, just how much the responsibility is placed fairly and squarely on our shoulders. The 'measure' is in our hands. 'Whatever measure you use in giving ...'

Again and again I find myself coming back to the central role the Spirit plays in all of this. By myself, I can practise generosity, but because of the limited boundaries of the human heart, my generosity will always be limited. It is very human to expect a return for what we do for others, and the plaudits and recognition we receive for this can become our reward. 'Why should God reward you if you love only those who love you?' (Mt 6:46) 'You have received without pay, so you should give without pay.' (Mt 10:8) Generosity certainly belongs as a Gift of the Spirit. It is also a Fruit of the Spirit. The Spirit sows it in our hearts, and we are led along the road towards an open and generous spirit. This is part of being formed in the image and likeness of Jesus. In the accounts of the miracle at Cana, or with the loaves and fishes, one cannot but be struck to read that much more than was needed was provided, when Jesus worked the miracle. No penny-pinching. Jesus speaks of his joy being poured out upon us, overflowing into our laps. (Jn 15:11) There is a certain insecurity within the hearts of most people. We speak of giving till it hurts, or giving till it's gone. It is difficult to do either, because of a natural instinctual prudence and caution that can tighten the purse strings of our riches, and remind us of the 'rainy day' that's just around the corner. Actually, money is not at the centre of this promise, because it applies equally to all, be they rich or poor. It is here where the Spirit comes in, with discernment, wisdom, and, yes, generosity. Time can be a wonderful gift, when I choose to give it to others. Listening is another gift that can help many a hurting soul.

There is a sadness in a soul that is miserly, and once again I am not referring to money here. One of the most precious gifts I may have is time. The happiest people on earth are those who are involved in giving to others. There can be wonderful joy and happiness in the giving, and there can be greater blessings for the giver than the receiver. At the core of all giving must be the Spirit of God. I can speak words of consolation, and they may be no more than thoughts and ideas I gleaned from my reading. On the other hand, I can ask the Spirit to be in the words I use, and I can be sure that my words will help, even if they are devoid of any great philosophies, theories, or ideas. By involving the Spirit more and more in my giving, I know that my generosity will continue to grow and expand. I will gradually begin to give like Jesus gives. All the love of the Father was poured out on Jesus, and we are told that 'he was filled with the joy of the Spirit.' (Lk 10:21) No wonder he himself could pour out so much love, compassion, forgiveness, and joy on those who came to him. He is our Role Model. In himself he displays the core message of this promise under review. He 'came to do and to teach'. (Acts 1:1) He showed love, kindness, service, and generosity, before telling us to do the same. To walk in his way is to be open to acting as he did.

*I, the Son of Man, will come in the glory of my Father,*
*with his angels, and will judge all people according to their deeds.*
*(Mt 16:27)*

In an earlier reflection I was dealing with the whole area of judgement. I said that God holds back all judgements until Judgement Day. In this promise, Jesus speaks of that day. Without our Christian hope and faith, this could be interpreted more as a threat than a promise. That is why we need to look at it from a Christian perspective. At the very core of human life is the struggle against the forces within us, and around us, that keep throwing obstacles, trials, temptations, and failures in our path. It can be difficult, at times, to hold to the hope that is in us. 'Always have an explanation to give to those who ask you the reason for the hope that you have.' (1 Pet 3:15) In today's world there is a growing sense of foreboding and gloom, as the world titters on the brink of war. Voices of reason are being drowned out by voices of arrogance and self-righteousness. It's at a time like this that I truly rejoice at the good news of the gospels. This promise epitomises the central issue, that at the end of the day we will all have to come before a God of justice, where all wrongs will be made right, and 'the poor will inherit the land'. I don't mean this in the sense that I might say to the oppressed and marginalised 'Live horse, and you'll get grass'. It is so much more than that. I have often heard the debate about reincarnation, where we would return, after death, in some other body, animal or human, with absolutely no memory of our first trip. While I may not have met many people who actually believe that, I have often heard it said that it would be a wonderful form of retribution, if it meant that the oppressed, second time around, would enjoy total freedom, while those who made gods out of wealth, power, and control would be reduced to a level of absolute simple living, having to earn their bread by the sweat of their brow.

Jesus experienced the very depths of failure, rejection, and suffering. Everything he worked for seemed to come apart. Those with whom he gave so much of his love, time, and teaching deserted him when the going got tough. He put himself, and everything he had on the line, and he was rejected and suffered a horrendous death as a consequence. In human terms, this was not a success. Yet, even at the darkest moments, he trusted the Father's promise that evil would be defeated and love would triumph. To contemplate his agony in the garden, or his cries from the cross, one would think he was very close to 'losing it'. This is what is called, in spirituality, *The Dark Night of the Soul*. St. Thérèse, St Pio, and so many other wonderful mystics experienced this, when in human terms it seemed as if God had deserted them. Thérèse prayed in the darkest hours, even when she sometimes wondered 'Is there anybody out there?' Despite the darkness, and the total absence of any consolation whatsoever, these heroic souls continued to believe, and to hold on to the hope they used have before the darkness came. What I'm trying to bring out here is the simple and single truth: Goodness, love, Jesus, and all that he stands for, is *now*, and for *always*. 'Jesus is the same yesterday, today, and always.' (Heb 13:8) Our hope is in the future, and Jesus holds the future. Everything we have ever heard, said, or believed about Jesus is on the line, when it comes to really trusting him on this promise. Jesus coming in glory, with his angels, should thrill the heart of all his followers. We are not saints. None of us has ever been able to live out the gospel and to remain faithful to our promises throughout our lives. The important thing is that we tried. When we fell, and fall we did, we got up and began again. 'Our glory consists not in never falling, but in getting up everytime we fall.' (Augustine)

The final word in the whole Bible is 'Maranatha! Come, Lord Jesus.' (Rev 22:20) For the early Christians, the coming of Jesus in his glory was the one thing they longed for more than anything else. Do you think we may have watered down this hope somewhat?

*If you give, you will receive.*
*(Lk 6:38)*

This is one of the shortest and simplest promises in the whole gospel. Any reflection I share need not include any explanation. Note the two words *if* and *will*, and how they are balanced one against the other. I *will* receive *if* I give. It matters little from which direction I read it, because the simple truth remains the same. The symbol of the cross can be powerfully significant, if I look at the two beams separately, and then put them back together again. There is the vertical, representing what comes from God to me. The horizontal represents what goes out sideways to others around me. The secret of a healthy Christian life is to get the balance right between the two. What comes from God to me must go sideways to other people. Think of the saints, for example. It is not possible to assess the gifts given to a Thérèse, a Pio, or a Faustina; but then, again, it is equally impossible to assess all the gifts and blessings that poured through them to others, something that continues to this very moment. God gave them special graces and blessings and, like the talents, they were held responsible for how they invested, and what return they could show. With the privilege comes the responsibility. 'You will receive power from on high, and (then) you will be my witnesses to the ends of the earth.' (Acts 1:8) I know that God's gifts are free, but it is only right that we should have to take responsibility for them, and for how we use them. They are 'charismatic' gifts, in that they are given for others. Life itself is a gift that is given to be used in the service of others. Everything God gives me can be used for the benefit of others. Yes, health, money, time, talents, etc.; everything can be for the benefit of others. I really believe that I have not 'invested' wisely whatever I keep for myself. Oh, yes, of course, I need time for myself, etc., but am I the only one who will benefit from that, when I return to the community more refreshed, relaxed, and life-giving? Of course not. I know I'm repeating myself, but I cannot overstress this simple fact: Everything in life can be used for the good of others.

Let me take one of the worst possible scenarios, where that last sentence could be severely tested. I was called to a home where a son had died by suicide. (I do not like the expression 'committed suicide', because the word 'committed' implies some sort of crime.) Anyhow, I was with the parents for a very short while, before I realised that I needed some help. I told them I'd be back shortly, and I headed to a home on the other side of the city, and collected a mam and dad who, two years previously, had a son who died in similar circumstances. I brought them over, into the house, and came away. They were the most 'qualified' people I knew to provide proper support at that time, to those particular people. The point I am making is that, even a tragedy can be turned into a good for someone else, because of the empathy and understanding I will have gained from it. This process is central to Twelve Step Programmes, where, for example, it is only an alcoholic who can really under-stand and help another alcoholic. The 'helper' in this case is the one who benefits most from the helping, because it is only through being of service to other alcoholics that a recovering al-coholic can remain sober. Once again, we have the words of Jesus, 'If you give, you will receive.'

One of the most universally known stories of Charles Dickens is the story of Scrooge. In simple words, it's a clear veri-fication of the words of Jesus. When Scrooge was a miser, he was miserable, two words which are closely connected! When he began to give, he experienced a complete transformation, and those around him were transformed through him. One of the points of this story that always struck me was a sense of pity for those people who are not 'givers'. Their lives must be very lonely, because complete selfishness is to live in solitary confinement, where there is nobody in my life but myself. These words of Jesus are so simple, and they are also so very wise.

*Stop criticising others, and you will not be criticised.*
*(Lk 6:37)*

Once again, we are presented with one of those simple choices, which, if acted on, will bring us the blessings we give to others. 'Treat others as would like them to treat you.' (Lk 6:31) 'In the measure you give, so shall you receive, and still more will be given to you.' (Mk 4:24) It is important to remember that Jesus has arranged things in such a way that the onus is on us, the choice is ours. He entrusts our own destiny to us. God will not send me anywhere when I die; rather will he eternalise whatever direction I choose to travel in the now. That is why I will have to answer for what I did with the freedom entrusted to me. He gives me a responsibility, and he expects me to be responsible, to respond to that gift.

The tendency to criticise is so human, and it's a trap that any of us can so easily fall into. However, there is a way to look at criticism that can be a real eye-opener. Generally, the day I feel good about me, I think you're OK too! On the other hand, if I am not having a good day myself, the other person might easily receive some of the anger, resentment, or discontent that's going on within me. I can so easily forget that, when I point a finger at another, there are three fingers pointing back at me. Usually, criticising others reflects more on the disposition of the 'critic' than on the people being criticised. I could deal with all of this on a very human level, at the level of 'pop-psychology', and analyse a situation, as if I was speaking to a patient on a psychiatrist's couch. There are real issues of poor self image, self condemnation, and general inner turmoil, that come out sideways, as it were, and I am in the mood to find fault with everybody around me. I can spend a lot of time looking for my problems, or the source of them, outside myself. In life, the miles stretch ahead of me, but the things that mess up my life are inside.

The reason I wish to move away from the pop-psychology route is that this would by-pass the centrality of the Holy Spirit in the life of a Christian. If I forget the presence of the Spirit, then of course I will criticise, and I will have no control over the moods and dispositions that bring this about. The Spirit, however, provides the Gifts, which in turn produce the Fruits within my

soul. Charity, joy, peace, and patience are among the more significant fruits, when it comes to my dealings with others. Of myself, I just don't have what it takes to have the patience of Job, or
the wisdom of Solomon. The whole purpose and mission of the
Spirit is to complete the work of Jesus in us, and through us.
Only God can do a God thing, and it is only when we surrender
to the power and work of the Spirit that we can possibly live as
Jesus asks us to. There is a gentleness about the work of the
Spirit, and it even becomes evident to those around us. The
surest sign that I have the Spirit of God within my heart, is when
I find that it comes easy to me to confirm others. I cannot give
confirmation, if I don't have the Spirit. The absence of the Spirit
becomes clearly evident when I display a tendency to 'knock'
others at every chance I get.

Another way of presenting this promise would be something
like this: If you allow the Spirit work within your heart, you will
display a great facility to confirm others, and because of this you
yourself will receive much confirmation. Nothing could be simpler, and nothing could be more beneficial to ourselves, and to
those around us. There is a disease in animals called BSE; unfortunately, it can be found in humans when it becomes Blame
Someone Else!

*I assure you, whatever you do to the least of my brothers and
sisters, I will take as done for me. (Mt 25:40)*

This is one of those profound promises, with far-reaching implications, but it is something that, given the limitations of human
insight and intelligence, can be so difficult to grasp fully. Jesus
rejoiced that the Father had given a message so simple that the
intellectual and the worldly-wise would not be able to comprehend it. (Lk 10:21) It's an extraordinary fact that I can be too intellectual to grasp a very simple concept, while I couldn't be too
stupid! Jesus has directly and deliberately identified himself
with the poor, the marginalised, the outcast, and the 'disabled'.
On the human level, people can become very dispensable, because they are often categorised in terms of usefulness, output,
and social standing. People can become quite relative, when
they are placed on the weighing scales of expediency or eco-

nomics. Life can become so cheap, ranging from the unborn to the elderly. The vulnerable members of society find life a real struggle for survival, and they find themselves among the voiceless and the defenceless. That is why Jesus comes out so strongly on their behalf. That is exactly what he did, and how he behaved, when he walked the roads of Galilee. Touching lepers, eating with the 'dregs' of society, or defending the public sinner didn't exactly ingratiate him with the self-righteous religious leaders of his day. He paid the ultimate price for the option he made, and for the way he showed everyone what his real values were, and what he wished others to accept and promote.

At the time of writing, the Gulf War, Part II, is in full swing. Propaganda, once again, is playing a big part in all reports coming from what is euphemistically termed 'the theatre of war'. At the core of the invading forces is the argument that they have come to liberate an oppressed people. Any signal from the civilian population in Iraq that presents them as welcoming their 'saviours' is given constant exposure on television. For the cause of the invading forces to appear justified, it is necessary to portray something of a great welcome from the people whom they have come to liberate. When Jesus came on earth, it is significant that the oppressed, the lame, the blind, the lepers, etc., were to the forefront in welcoming him, and in availing of his ministrations. They welcomed a Saviour, because the circumstances of their lives left them in no doubt of their need to be saved. Not so with the religious leaders, who were highly indignant that anyone should suggest that they had any need of being rescued, when their situation was one of legalistic perfection, without any need to change. It is the hungry who respond faster to the offer of food. The 'least of these, my brothers and sisters', were very dear to the heart of Jesus. He treated them with dignity, he raised them up, and restored to them their rights. In this promise, he is asking us to do the same, and he presents this promise in such a way that it is impossible to avail of his approval and blessing, by attempting to side-step the conditions he lays down.

Jesus wants us to respond to his offer of salvation, redemption, and eternal life, by coming to him through our treatment of others. 'By this will all people know that you are my disciples, if you have love one for another.' (Jn 13:35) The term 'option for the poor', and 'preferential option for the poor' has become part of the mission statement of Religious Life, for some years now. There has been a swing away from a time when the church aligned itself with earthly and political powers in many countries, South America being a good example. Archbishop Romero was 'promoted' as a candidate for such a role by the government of the day in San Salvador. No sooner was he appointed archbishop, however, than he began to draw the ire and opposition of the ruling class, because of the stance he took on issues of justice, poverty, and corruption. His fate was sealed and, for those in the know, his murder was inevitable. Mahatma Ghandi, Martin Luther King, Steve Biko, to mention just a few, paid with their lives because they dared to provide a voice for the voiceless. However, there is no getting around this statement of Jesus, because he meant it literally, and should we choose to ignore it, he takes that as ignoring him. On the other hand, of course, just think of the privilege that is ours to actually minister to Jesus himself through our ministry to 'the least of these'.

# Sheep

*I am the good shepherd.*
*The good shepherd lays down his life for his sheep. (Jn 10:11)*

Jesus was a brilliant teacher because, among other things, the role of the teacher is to bring others from the known to the unknown. As he spoke, there were probably sheep a short distance away, and he may well have had some shepherds among the listeners. The role of the shepherd was well understood and identified within the Jewish tradition, and stories of the heroics of shepherds were part of their folklore. In the Gulf War, which is raging at the moment, there are, of course, some casualties from time to time, among the US or British forces. Having said the usual words of sympathy, and expressed the gratitude of a nation for their bravery, we are then reminded that this is part of being a soldier. When he takes his place on the battlefield, he does so, in the sure and certain knowledge that this could cost him everything. This was how the role of the shepherd was seen. He was responsible for his sheep twenty-four hours a day. He stood guard all day, to protect them from being attacked by marauding wolves. At night-time, the sheep were corralled into a cave, and the shepherd slept at the entrance to the cave, so that the attacker got to the sheep only over his dead body. He was someone whose mandate included being willing to lay down his life for his sheep.

Jesus calls himself a good shepherd, because there was a distinction. While a shepherd might guard his sheep with his life, he might have no problem helping himself to some of his neighbours' sheep, that might be in the vicinity. 'Sheep stealing' was punishable by death in countries like Australia not so long ago. Proselytising, as in 'converting' members of other Christian churches to join your church, is often referred to as 'sheep-stealing', and there is something very unhealthy about this, unless the person expresses a genuine desire to move to another Christian church. Jesus is telling us that he has no vested interest in us, beyond everything that is for our good, our salvation, and our eternal life. He is a good shepherd in that he is faithful, reliable, and utterly trustworthy. There were two levels of loyalty among shepherds and their flocks. The shepherd was completely loyal to his flock, and was willing to lay down his life for them, if needed. On the other hand, the sheep themselves developed a great loyalty to the shepherd, and they would follow him no matter where he went. The shepherd just walked on ahead, and the sheep dutifully followed on in single file behind. This is a very clear and sharp image of the relationship Jesus speaks of between himself and ourselves.

The corollary between Jesus and ourselves, and a shepherd and his sheep, becomes starker when Jesus speaks about laying down his life for us, because that is exactly what he did. I said at the beginning of this reflection that Jesus would have been able to point to sheep as he spoke these words. In fact, to fully understand many of the nuances of Jesus' words, it would be necessary to go back to those times, and look at life through the eyes of a Jew at that time. When Jesus spoke of sheep, fig trees, fish, birds of the air, etc., all the people had to do was look up, or look around, and there Jesus' words were illustrated. In today's language, it would be like a documentary. For us, today, we depend on the Spirit within our hearts to convince us of the truth of what Jesus is saying. Like a tiny grain of mustard seed, our faith continues to grow, and to become stronger with each new day. It is for us to provide the best soil, or living/growing conditions we can. Is it reasonable to expect that the word of God will grow strong in soil that is frozen, undernourished, or polluted?

### I am the gate for the sheep.
### (Jn 10:7)

A very simple sentence, and one that we might not consider in terms of it being a promise. I consider it a promise for one simple reason: I want to belong to the fold of Jesus, and he tells me very simply how I can do so. There is only one entrance, one gate. Jesus goes further in a later teaching, when he says that he is the only way to the Father, and no one comes to the Father, except through him. (Jn 14:6) In life, if you're not sure where you're going, you've no problem, because any road will get you there! On the other hand, if you know where you're going, there is only one road that will get you there. People follow 'roads' all the time, not just as routes, but with diets, alcohol or substance recovery; there is a certain path to travel, very definite things to do, and things that must be avoided at all costs. Jesus is telling us that, if we wish to become members of his flock, then there is only one way to get in.

I wrote in that last reflection how sheep follow the shepherd wherever he goes. A goat herd doesn't have it so easy. Goats cannot be led; they have to be driven. When the goats are mixed in with the sheep they tend to tag along, because they are hugely outnumbered, and they tend 'to follow the crowd'. Take them away from the sheep, and the trouble starts! That is what Jesus means about Judgement Day, when he 'will separate the sheep from the goats'. (Mt 25:32) The sheep represent those who followed him freely, and willingly. The goats, on the other hand, represent those who had to be driven, who never did anything willingly, and who had no idea of obedience or docility. Jesus has no intention of driving us into his fold. He opens the gate, and he awaits our decision that leads to our entering in. This gives him great joy, of course, because 'I came for the lost sheep of the House of Israel.' (Mt 10:6) It gives some insight into the extraordinary composite of human nature. Here is Jesus offering us security, and eternal happiness; yet we may feel we need more time to think about! I think of St Paul in Athens. He gave a powerful sermon to a large gathering and, after all that, they said to one another, 'We must hear him again some time.' (Acts 17:32) After Paul had left, they probably had a prolonged and profound debate on all they had heard! Jesus doesn't want discussions, he wants decisions. The gate to the sheepfold swings both ways; we can walk in freely, and we can walk back out again, if we so choose. Jesus will never impinge on our freewill.

Knowing what they knew about the literal meaning of Jesus' words, I know it would have needed the Holy Spirit to reveal to Jesus' listeners the meaning behind the words he used. When Peter declared Jesus as 'the Christ, the one who has come into the world', Jesus replied, 'You are blessed, Simon Bar Jona, because flesh and blood has not revealed this to you, but my Father who is in heaven.' (Mt 16:17) Genius is the ability to discern the obvious. Sometimes a concept might be so simple that the intellectual mind cannot grasp it. In these seven words, Jesus offers us the keys to his kingdom. The choice is ours. The gate is open right now; all it needs is a gentle push, and it will yield. In today's world, it is necessary to find security, safety, and peace. Jesus offers us that, and he remains on 'standby', as it were, awaiting our reply.

*Those who come in through me will be saved.*
*(Jn 10:9)*

Joining the fold, in itself, will not be sufficient for salvation. It's like, during a bombing raid, even some of the enemy in civilian clothes could join the others in the shelters. Coming in through Jesus is the only valid passport and visa. Of course, I can be a member of a church, and even an active member, but God, who sees the heart, may not be too pleased with what he sees and being in church may not impress him at all. In a way, it's not really what I do, so much as *why I do it*. I could visit someone in hospital today, because I am concerned about that person, and I would like to convey those concerns and a promise of prayers. On the other hand, I could visit someone in hospital because I have longed for the day to see that very person in hospital, with tubes and drips hanging out of him! I could do the exact same thing for two completely different reasons. Christianity is about a person, Jesus Christ, and it is accepting him as Saviour, Lord, and God that opens the gate of the sheepfold to me. I begin where I am, which is a sinner, in need of salvation. I accept Jesus as my Saviour, and I allow him save me. The next step is to allow him become Lord in my life. As Saviour, I entrust him with my past. As Lord, he is given control of the future. Then I accept him as God, to whom nothing is impossible. In effect, all of this implies surrender, when I give up all attempts at playing God, and trying to run the show myself.

In this promise, it is as if Jesus lays greater stress on the method of entrance than on being within the fold. Jesus speaks of sheep in wolves' clothing. (Mt 7:15) He speaks of the man at the wedding who was there under false pretences, because he was not properly dressed for such an occasion. (Mt 22:11) It is possible that, when I get to heaven, I may have a few surprises. I may be surprised at some of the people I will see there. I may also be surprised at some of the people who are not there. And my biggest surprise of all will be to find myself there! Christianity is about a person, Jesus Christ. All references to sheep, folds, etc., are but the tools of a brilliant teacher to use imagery and everyday things to explain things beyond the experience of his listeners. As far as language was concerned, they understood exactly what he said, while many of them may have failed to grasp the idea behind the words. As future events would show, many of them, including the apostles, did not seem to fully grasp exactly what Jesus meant. When the pressure came, they failed him badly. They were not prepared to die for anybody, let alone a flock of sheep.

For those of us who have God's Spirit living within our hearts, it becomes clear exactly what Jesus meant by this statement. We come to him, we accept his message, we believe his promise, and we offer him our will and our lives. By doing that we become 'enrolled', as it were, in that unique and blessed group known as 'children of the kingdom', or members of his flock. We go to Jesus first, and we leave it to him to take it from there. Jesus is the beginning and the end of our salvation. He is our good shepherd, and once we entrust ourselves to his care, we can be absolutely sure and certain that he will take total care of us. Like the apostles on Thabor, once we know that we are in his flock, we too can say, 'Lord, it's good for us to be here.' (Lk 9:33)

*I will give them eternal life, and they will never perish.*
*(Jn 10:28)*

Once again, we have a simple and solemn promise. No 'ifs' or 'buts' in the promises of Jesus. All of that is on our side. Jesus offers, but we have to accept. Remember these promises are made within the context of Jesus speaking to us as a Good Shepherd, and he is calling us to follow him, and to belong to his flock. The 'them' referred are those who decide to follow him, to make a decision for him, to become one of his disciples. From the first moment Jesus arrived on this earth, there were few people to welcome him. Even before he was born, his parents sought in vain for an appropriate place in which his birth might take place. As soon as he was born, a king marshaled his soldiers in a desperate attempt to kill him. He spent most of his life in relative obscurity, as if waiting for detailed and final instructions from his Father. When he did go public, he became a marked man. His very presence among people caused them to polarise, either for him, or against him. You could not stand in his presence and be indifferent. You had to make a decision, one way or the other. Hatred is not the opposite to love; indifference is. 'You are either for me, or against me,' he said. (Mt 12:30) 'Let your "yes" be "yes", and your "no" be "no".' (Mt 5:37) He is single-minded in his commitment to us, and he leaves us in no doubt about how seriously he takes all his promises to us.

Jesus, in a way, is always on stand-by, awaiting our response to his offer, or his promise. The second part of the equation is whether or not we respond to the offer he makes. In this promise, we are told that if we decide to follow him eternal life is ours, and we will never perish. I had the wonderful privilege recently of spending some time with a very special and committed Christian on his death-bed. He was full of joy, and the promises of Jesus were sure and certain for him. It was so edifying to see all this in practice. Everything I ever learned in school or in church told me that this is how things would work out, would end up. I haven't experienced a great deal of that, on the same level, because this case was truly unique. It did wonders for my own faith, and I envied his family the 'legacy' of the memory he was leaving them. He had been a wonderful role model in life, and now he was being an extraordinary role model in death.

'Perish' can allow of several interpretations, to going rotten, to dying, to being demolished. Those who choose to follow Jesus will never perish; they will not go bad, die, or be destroyed. There is a balance implied in most of the promises of Jesus. In simple English, 'if you give me this, I will give you that'. If I give him my 'yes', he will give me his eternal *yes*. If I give him my heart, he will fill it with his life and his Spirit. As I said earlier Jesus is on standby and, as it were, his hands are tied until we open our hands, our hearts, or our minds. 'I stand at the door and knock. If you hear me calling, and open the door, I will come in, and we will share a meal as friends.' (Rev 3:20) The problem, of course, is that there's no handle on the outside of the door, and Jesus cannot/will not enter unless we open the door, and invite him in. In a way, that's frightening, because the onus is so much on us. On the other hand, this is how it must be, because of the sacredness of our freewill, and the respect in which God holds that. In another place, Jesus goes so far as to say that those who leave everything to follow him, will have one hundred per cent on this earth, and eternal glory in the next (Mt19:29) How truly blessed we are ...

*No one will snatch them from me,*
*for the Father has given them to me. (Jn 28:29)*

All of the promises of Jesus are very reassuring. When he speaks of eternal life, he speaks of a life that will never end. In this promise he speaks of those given to him by the Father, and that, to him, is something that will never be taken away from him again. In our human language and experience, we use words which time and events can alter, water down, or change the original meaning. Many of our decisions, promises, commitments, etc., can be made at a moment of great enthusiasm and genuine sincerity. There are times when I could promise the sun, moon, and stars. Unfortunately, however, human feelings and emotions can have a very short shelf-life. Without being aware, we can often be working out of false, if sincere, premises here. Love is not a feeling. Feelings have no morality; they're neither good nor bad. It's what we do with them determines what they are. I could feel angry with you, and there's absolutely nothing wrong with that. I could lift an ashtray and hit you with it! That is wrong! How I express the feeling can make it wrong. I cannot control feelings. I could be very angry with you, slam the door, and walk out to my car. By the time I reach the car, however, I have begun to settle down, and begin to regret my outburst. I return to you, and apologise. What I'm saying here is that a feeling may last for less than a minute.

A decision, on the other hand, is something over which I do have control, and over which I can exercise control. When I consider love as a decision, then I can renew that decision first thing each morning. I cannot live today on a decision of yesterday. Jesus obviously has made a serious decision to love us. It is not an emotional outburst, at a moment of closeness. God's love was declared from the first moment of creation, and the coming of Jesus was to be a public, down-to-earth, and human expression of that love. If the Father has entrusted us to Jesus, then you can be sure that Jesus will take complete and total care of us.

Jesus' listeners understood exactly what he meant, because of the language he used. They were all familiar with shepherds; indeed, some of his listeners may, themselves, have been shepherds. An important part of the shepherd's duty was to guard the sheep against being snatched by wolves or other wild animals. If a sheep gets injured, the shepherd will place that sheep around his shoulders, and carry it. Because of the injury, that sheep would be particularly vulnerable, and could easily be snatched. Once we are entrusted to our Good Shepherd, we are reassured that we are completely safe, and no harm can come to us. One point that must be stressed from time to time. I must read the promises with the mind of Jesus, who spoke them. When he speaks, he says what he means and he means what he says. There is absolutely no room for compromise, uncertainties, or double-talk. Jesus called himself the Truth, and his Spirit, the Spirit of Truth. He is someone in whom we can have absolute trust and confidence.

To experience faith in Jesus is to be aware of having one's hand in his, as we journey in life. He said he would never leave us. (Mt 28:18) Thomas wasn't sure about the way so, in simple words, Jesus told him, 'Thomas, I am the Way.' (Jn 14:6) 'Those who follow me will not walk in darkness, but will have the light of life.' (Jn 8:12) Jesus paid for us with his life, so he is not very likely to allow us get lost again. His part of the covenant is completed, but, through the action of his Spirit, he will continue to open our hearts to everything he has gained for us. His Spirit is entrusted with the task of completing his work in us, and that work will not be complete until we join him in eternal glory.

*I have other sheep too. I must bring them also,*
*and they will listen to my voice, and there will be one flock,*
*and one shepherd. (Jn 10:16)*

Jesus came to save the world. He came to 'bring good news to
the poor, to set prisoners free, to give sight to the blind, and to
free the downtrodden from their oppressors.' (Lk 4:18) He came
for all of God's people, and his final commission to his disciples
was to 'preach the word to all the world'. (Mk 16:15) As his arms
were fully outstretched on the cross, he embraced all of God's
people, even praying for those who were killing him. His love
has no boundaries, and it is as real today as it was then. As the
Good Shepherd (Jn 10:11), he will not be at peace until all his
sheep hear his voice, and respond to it. Responding to his voice
does not necessarily mean following him, because 'No' is also an
answer. 'Many are called, but few are chosen.' (Mt 22:14) Many
are called, but few may decide to answer the call. The X factor in
the whole story of salvation is our willingness to accept the gift.

Jesus' listeners would have been very familiar with sheep,
and all that attached to being a shepherd. Under normal circumstances, the sheep will follow the shepherd, wherever he leads.
There are occasions, however, when one sheep will wander off
on its own, and this is one that the shepherd considers to be very
sick, disorientated, and confused. I am not implying that everyone who does not follow Jesus can be described in those terms.
There are millions of people who know nothing about Jesus, and
there are millions of others whose religion of birth places Jesus
very much outside what their religion teaches. While I don't pretend to understand the full implications of this promise under
review, I am happy enough to deal with it as it concerns those of
us who have heard his message, and have been called to respond. One of the responsibilities that is placed on the shoulders
of a Christian is to spread the good news. St Francis of Assisi
says that we should always preach the gospel and, if we have to,
we should use words. As Jesus spoke the words of this promise,
he had a limited number of listeners. Since that time, his flock
has multiplied many million-fold. There are many others, however, who still have to come to know and accept him. The
gospels are in between two phrases, 'Come and see,' (Jn 1:39),

and 'Go and tell.' (Mk 16:15) I cannot go and tell if I myself have not come and seen. If I am not involved in evangelising others, it simply means that I myself have never been evangelised.

As I said earlier, I cannot pretend to fully understand exactly what Jesus had in mind when he spoke these. In a realistic way, it cannot mean that everybody is going to become a Christian and a disciple of Jesus. There is one possibility that I am willing to accept. Jesus said that he was the only way to the Father, and no one could come to the Father except through him. (Jn 14:9) Allowing for all other religions on this earth, most of them having excellent credentials, and obviously being a source of much blessing to many people, is it possible that, at the moment of death, every single person, of all faiths and none, will come face to face with Jesus, and be presented with a clear opportunity to say 'Yes'? Obviously, I don't know the answer to this question, but it would not be a negation of other faiths because, in a direct way, they were the means of bringing people to God in the first place. If that face to face meeting ever did occur, these people would not be at a loss. At that moment, free from the limitations imposed by the human body, relative to understanding and sensory abilities, it would surely appear clear that Jesus was the Way, and there was no other. This would not be a question of 'trick-conversion', because it would be a logical follow-on to what went before. For example, Jesus himself was a very committed Jew, even if was prepared to deviate from the law when the welfare of a human being called for that. As I write, I am reminded of a very significant parable about the owner of the vineyard who hired workers to work there. (Mt 20:1-7) He called the men at different times of the day, morning, noon, afternoon, and evening. When he came to pay them, they all got exactly the same wages. This upset those who had been working since morning, so the owner explained that he had agreed a certain amount with them that morning, which they received. Because of the kind of person he was, he also decided that everyone who joined the work-force, at whatever hour, would receive exactly the same wages. He did this, he told them, because he was free to do this, and this is how he did things. If I apply that story to what I have been reflecting on up till now, I would have no problem with Jesus offering full salvation to anyone who accepts it, even if only at the very last moment.

Anyhow, for us Christians, we can accept this promise with gratitude, and trust Jesus to work out everything in the way that he sees best.

### I came that you should have life, and have it in abundance.
### (Jn 10:10)

I particularly love this promise. I love it especially because I apply it more to this life than to the next. Everybody dies, but not everybody lives. Some people settle for existing, and there is never must life before death. I am not speaking of those with disabilities of any kind here. All of these are fully human, and fully alive and, for those who love them and care for them, there is a huge void when these people die, and are no longer around to be life-givers to them. To be a life-giving person, one has to be fully alive oneself. Sin brought death, and Jesus came to overcome that evil, and to restore life to us. 'You were spiritually dead because of your disobedience and sins.' (Eph 2:1) Jesus took on our damaged humanity; he lived within, and through his obedience onto death, he transformed us into new beings with potential for eternal life. Let me put that another way, and in smaller segments. Something in us died at the time of original sin. The spark was extinguished, the inner soul was in darkness. There was nothing, absolutely nothing, that any of us could do that could change that situation in any way. (If Jesus hadn't done what he did, it would be sadly amusing today to see the multiplicities of self-help and do-it-yourself groups that would be all over the place!) Anyhow, thank God, Jesus came. He came to take over the situation in person. He could have loved us from a distance and, indeed, redeemed us from a distance. Because he came in love, however, he just had to come to us exactly as we are, exactly where we are.

He took on the brokenness of our nature. 'He was like us in all things, tempted like us in all things, but without sinning.' (Heb 4:15) He experienced every possible human weakness but, through the power of the Spirit within him, he overcame each weakness, one by one. If I had a human weakness that Jesus

himself did not wrestle with and overcome, then I would still be
outside the scope of his salvation. The last and final enemy was
death, and Jesus took that on also. He overcame death and, after
much suffering, rejection, temptation, opposition, he finally had
all the enemies under his feet. The Jesus who walked the roads
of Galilee was Saviour. He was not Lord yet, nor could he give
the Spirit. It was when he himself had paid the full price, and
gained the final victory, that he could return in glory to his
Father, where all power and authority in heaven and on earth
was restored to him. (Jn 3:35; Acts 8:10) That is why he came. He
came, as he tells us, that we should have abundant life. It was
important, therefore, that his disciples should be left in no doubt
whatever that he had overcome death. He appeared to them in
many places and in many ways, after his resurrection. He offered to cook breakfast for them. He asked for something to eat,
as evidence that he really was alive. He invited Thomas to touch
him, if he still doubted. They would be commissioned as witnesses to his resurrection throughout the world. It was essential,
therefore, that they should be convicted witnesses.

Paul tells us, 'If Jesus had not risen from the dead, then our
faith is in vain.' (1 Cor 15:17) If death had the victory over Jesus
then, of course, he couldn't give life to anyone, least of all himself. Now, however, he can offer us life in abundance. This abundant life is intended to be lived out on this earth. We have a responsibility to ensure that there's as much life before death as is
possible. Life is a gift from God to be used in the service of others. We take on a serious responsibility when we accept the gift
of life. We also take on enormous potential for all that is good, if
we decide to live that life to the full. This very moment, as I
write, or as you, dear reader, read, is the most important moment in our lives. God is totally a God of now. 'I am who am.'
Let us open our hearts even wider this very moment, so that we
can be filled with ever more abundant life.

# Fear

*Don't be afraid, little flock, for it gives your Father*
*great happiness to give you the kingdom. (Lk 12:32)*

When Adam and Eve fell for the lie in the garden, we are told
that they hid, because they were afraid. This is the first time that
fear is mentioned in the Bible. They were afraid because they
were no longer able to let God look them straight in the face
again. Unlike Moses, they wouldn't have been able to look God
straight in the face anyhow, but if he looked at them, they would
hang their heads in shame. It is significant to note the number of
times Jesus uses the words 'Fear not; be not afraid; oh why did
you fear, oh you of little faith?' Faith is to have the courage to accept the simple truth that God loves me, and I don't have to
hang my head when I stand before him.

There is a beautiful gentleness in this promise. I could just
imagine Jesus whispering it. There seems to be joy all round. His
Father is really happy to give them the kingdom. Jesus is truly
happy to be announcing this good news. And, of course, his disciples are hearing wonderful good news, even if their understanding of all that is implied may be quite limited. As I am writing this, the war in Iraq seems to be coming into its final days,
hopefully. All the talk now is what happens next? There are so
many tribes, and different loyalties within the country, so many
of whom have waged bloody battles against each other in the
past, how is it possible to hold these people together as a nation,
as a democracy? Nobody has come up with the answer to that
one yet but, in general, it is presumed that all of this is going to
take some considerable time. When Jesus looked around the
world of his day, he saw how scattered and fragmented God's
people had become. He compared them to sheep without a
shepherd. (Mt 9:36) He is offering a refuge, a safe haven, where
they can be safe. That haven is what we call the kingdom.

A shepherd with his sheep has to have structures within
which he exists. He must have access to water for himself and
the sheep. There must be food, even if the sheep have to forage

around in the sand to find it. He must also have a cave or covered area, to which he can lead the sheep each night. Normally, this is a cave in the side of a mountain or cliff. When the sheep enter, the shepherd settles down at the mouth of the cave, so the marauding wolf will encounter him first, before getting to the sheep. This is the sort of safe haven that Jesus promises. If we accept his offer, and enter his kingdom, then we are safe from, and immune to, the evils of this world. It's a beautiful insight into a God of love when Jesus tells us that it gives his Father great happiness to be able to give us this kingdom. Jesus uses a simple expression of endearment when he speaks to his followers as 'little flock'. He has the heart of a shepherd for the weakest of his lambs.

I often feel like intervening when, at a graveside, I hear somebody say to one of the bereaved, 'Come on, don't be crying; sure it's happy for him.' No doubt this person means well, even if he is far from being helpful. The bereaved has every reason and right to cry, and they should be allowed plenty of space and time to do this. Better to cry now than scream later. I think it would be more helpful to say, 'It must be really painful, and I know you must still hope that you'll wake up, and discover it was all a dream.' Similarly, there are times when people have every reason to be afraid. I have seen terror in the eyes of Iraqi civilians over the past two weeks. Bombs and buildings are crashing down around them, and I walk over and tell them not to be afraid! How would the words of Jesus hold up in a situation like that? I know this is not a 'normal' situation, but I imagine it would require quite a lengthy period of practice, before I could get to that level of confidence and trust. I have to face up to my fears in the simplest of situations. I have to confront fear wherever I find it. It is a bully, and will back off if confronted. By practising this approach, I can come to a place in my life where fear is no longer a significant part of each day. The recovering alcoholic is afraid of alcohol; the cheat is afraid of the truth; and the nervous are afraid of the dark. We can be stalked by fear, and frozen into inactivity by it. It is in these situations that we should hear these words of Jesus. If I come into his kingdom, like running into an embassy building, the enemy cannot follow in after me. I have found a safe refuge, where 'nothing will harm you.'

(Lk 10:19) What a huge relief it would be for so many fearful and fear-filled people if the truth of this promise seeped down into their hearts, and found a home there. If it found good soil there, in which it could grow more and more, there would come a time when all fear is gone.

> *When you are arrested, don't worry about what to say in your*
> *defence, because you will be given the right words*
> *at the right time. (Mt 10:19)*

To understand this promise better, it would be good to reflect on the situation and circumstances in which it was spoken. Notice Jesus said 'When', not 'if' or 'in case'. Jesus knew that once they went out to spread the good news, not everyone would welcome it and, as often happens, when they don't like the message they often shoot the messenger. His listeners themselves would also have been deeply conscious of just how practical and realistic this promise was for them. At the actual time of hearing these words, the Spirit had not come yet, and nothing serious had happened to Jesus, so they probably didn't attach any great urgency to the message. It might prove useful information on a later occasion. I am speaking of the horse and cart situation here, in which the cart came first, followed by the horse. Jesus gave them a message to deliver, and then he gave them what they needed to be able to do that.

Jesus was being very upfront and honest with his disciples here. He was realistic in letting them know that, like him, they also would be arrested. He knew only too well what fate befalls the prophets, many of whom end up as martyrs. Ghandi, Martin Luther King, Archbishop Romero didn't get a chance to stand trial, when the assassin assumed the role of judge, jury, and executioner. Good, by definition, will always be opposed by evil. If it is not opposed, its value is very suspect. Jesus, however, is referring specifically to what will befall his followers because of him. In other words, it is because they chose to follow him that they're on trial. Therefore, like free legal aid, he is promising them an Advocate, someone who will speak on his behalf. That someone, of course, is the Holy Spirit. Whether heroes or villains, our Irish history is littered with epic and heroic 'speeches from the dock'. Robert Emmet is remembered more for his

powerful speech from the dock, than he is for anything he had
tried to do, and that landed him in the dock in the first. Pearse,
Mitchell, Parnell, the list goes on ... of those whose speeches are
available in every library in the country.

I heard it said one time that, 'If every one of us here was
arrested, brought down to the police station, and charged with
being Christian, how many of us would get off scot-free for lack
of evidence?' I honestly believe that if I do try to live the gospel, I
can be sure of meeting cynicism, sarcasm, and even direct opposition. Quite often that opposition can come from those closest to
me, because the most difficult place to practise the gospel is in
my own kitchen. 'When the world hates you, remember that it
hated me before it hated you. The world would love you if you
belonged to it, but you don't.' (Jn 15:18-19) Simeon spoke of
Jesus as 'a sign of contradiction'. (Lk 2:34) He came for the fall
and for the resurrection of many. His words express values
which the world dismisses as foolish. They dressed him with a
cloak of mockery, and crowned him as a clown-king.

In speaking these words, Jesus is asking for our trust and
confidence. OK, at the time he spoke this to his followers they
did not yet have the Holy Spirit and so would not have what it
takes to accept and act on the promises. After Pentecost, however,
when Jesus had left and the Spirit came upon them, and they
went forth to spread the good news, this promise must have
been very central to their thinking. I'm sure they remembered
Jesus' words, as they stood before their accusers. No expensive
Tribunal barristers at their disposal! However, the irony of the
situation is that they had the very best possible aid at their disposal, and they knew it, because they needed it. Something dramatic had happened at Pentecost, and these frightened men,
who were afraid to mention Jesus' name, went forth in boldness,
confidence, and with a whole new-found courage. They had the
Spirit of Truth in their hearts and among the tasks of the Spirit is
to remind them of everything Jesus had told them. That is why I
am convinced that these words were a very real inspiration to
the early Christians, and to millions of persecuted Christians
since.

*Don't be troubled. You trust God; now trust me.*
*(Jn 14:1)*

To be troubled is to be agitated or disturbed. It is to be in a state of dis-ease, when the inner spirit is highly tensed, and the experience is one of fear. Fear covers many things from shyness to anger. One of the sharpest memories I have as a child are the thunder storms. My mother was terrified of lightening, and there was no way she could possibly disguise her fear. At the first rumble of thunder the curtains were drawn, the candle was lit, and the holy water was flying in all directions. Naturally, she passed this fear to all of us, and I'm sure there are members of my family who still live with that fear. The reason I recall that here is the connection my mind is making between being troubled, and the word 'trust'. 'Oh Sacred Heart of Jesus, I place all my trust in Thee' became the mantra until the storm had well gone. Fear and trust were co-existing, and it would have been difficult to keep the score as to which of them won. Ah, no, that's not right! Trust always won out, because the trust remains for other things, long after the fear was gone. Jesus is appealing to something his followers seemed to possess already. He implies that they trusted God and, no doubt, he had seen evidence of that on occasions. Using that as a base, he invited them to trust him in the same way. St Paul (1 Cor 11:1) is trying to be as clear and specific as he possibly can, as he speaks about Christian living. He uses a step-by-step approach, as he brings them from the known to the unknown. If God is too remote, then, in Jesus, we can see a very real down-to-earth personification of God. Paul goes one step further, because he is obviously speaking to a Christian community in Corinth, who had not actually seen Jesus in person. He tells them that they can look at his life, and, because he is imitating Jesus, they can get a much clearer idea of what Jesus was like, and what he taught. A brave man Paul, but undoubtedly an honest man. Jesus makes a connection between the apostles' trust in God, and the kind of trust that he wanted them to have in him. It must have been relatively easy for them to get the message, even if it were difficult for them to put it into practice.

The apostles had many reasons to trust Jesus. They saw him

calm the storm, raise the dead, and cleanse the leper. They saw his authority over demons, and his healing touch for deaf, blind, or dumb. They saw his wonderful love and compassion in action. Faith is a response to love, so Jesus had every right to ask for their trust. Surely, by now, they must know that he had their welfare at heart. He needed them to trust him, before he could ask them to trust his words, to trust his promises. An honest person speaks honest words, and makes genuine promises. If they were to believe in his word, they had to have great faith in the source of that word. He had told them that heaven and earth would pass away before his word would pass away. (Mt 24:35) I like to think that they believed him, even if, when the pressure came, they failed him badly. God never wastes a thing and I'm sure that experience of their own failures was part of their preparation for ministry. After Judas, Peter had failed very badly indeed, but that did not prevent Jesus appointing him as the leader of the early church. Judas had committed a crime, not by hanging himself, but by losing hope. Peter had failed badly, but he didn't lose hope. Later in one of his letters he would write, 'Always have an explanation to give to those who ask you the reason for the hope that you have.' (1 Pet 3:15)

Jesus made very direct connections between himself and the Father, even if he himself, for most of his life, wasn't completely sure that he was God, something suggested as a possibility by some scholars. This matters little because of his complete trust in the Father, something that is made possible for any one of us. God is my Father, and I can, if the Spirit is allowed to work in and through me, have complete and total trust and confidence in the Father. Jesus identified with the Father when he told his followers that to see him was to see the Father; to hear him was to hear the Father, because he never said anything unless the Father told him. (Jn 14:9) Because of his own alignment with the Father in mind, heart, and spirit, he could stand before his followers and ask them to trust him, because that was the same as trusting his Father. That is why he tells them not to be troubled. He is with them, and will be with them always. (Mt 28:20)

*So don't be afraid. You are more valuable to him*
*than a whole flock of sparrows. (Lk 12:7)*

Once again, we have Jesus allaying the fears of his followers. Being aware of our basic weaknesses, powerlessness, and help-lessness in so many situations, it is so easy for us to be afraid. 'Oh Lord, please help me, because the sea is so vast, and my boat is so small' is a fisherman's prayer. Jesus is trying every method possible to convince his hearers of one simple truth, i.e. God's love and care for them. The whole gospels could be summarised in one sentence: God loves us. If I were to die this moment, it is possible that Jesus might have just one question to put to me: 'Did you come to believe, personally, that my Father loved you?' If I ask why that is important, he could reply, 'That's why I came on earth in the first place.'

At the time of writing it is late spring, the weather is beauti-ful, the flowers are out, and the lambs are at that most endearing time. So often one hears people referring to this as ample proof of the presence of a wonderful caring God. That's exactly what Jesus is saying in this promise. It was obvious to his listeners that God took good care of the birds of the air, and the lilies of the field. If he did this for them, how much more will he do for those who are made in his likeness? Jesus joined us, as one of us, and that, in itself, was an extraordinary act of affirmation. Jesus became one of us, and he established an affinity with us that will never be broken. It is unthinkable to imagine Jesus joining the demons, and becoming one of them. Jesus was prodigally gener-ous when he took ordinary human sustenance, like water, bread, or fish, and multiplied them to feed those in need. By doing this, he was showing what kind of God he represented; a God who cared enough about everything that concerns us. In his own actions, he was clearly demonstrating to his followers that God was capable and willing to care for us in every way. That is why he continually called for faith, as a response to his Father's goodness. The only limits that apply to God's goodness are the ones we set. Mary magnified the Lord; in other words her God was Almighty, 'because there's nothing impossible with God' (Lk 1:37), as the Archangel Gabriel had told her. The bigger my God, the smaller my problems. 'Your God is too small' is the name of a book that was readily available some years ago.

When I look at the small print of what Jesus is saying, I become very aware of how he uses every image he can muster to get his simple message across. He speaks of God as someone who is aware of every hair on our heads. (Mt 10:30) The Psalmist speaks of God knowing us through and through. (Ps 139) We are led to think of God as a loving parent, whose strong desire is for all that is best for his children. Because he created us, he takes full responsibility for our welfare. He gave us the gift of life, and he offers us all that it takes to live that life to the full. That is why it is such a sacrilege that so many of his children are deprived of basic human rights, through the greed or cruelty of others. The most disabled child is on this earth with as much right as the greatest genius that ever lived. How abhorrent it must be to such a loving Father to see the outcome of self-will run riot, in a world where half the people are dying of hunger, while the other half is on a diet, trying to get down the weight. It is only right and just that we should be held accountable for how we have used the gifts he has entrusted to us, and how we respected the rights of others to the gifts that were rightly theirs. I cannot imagine such cruelty and insensitivity among a flock of sparrows.

*I will not abandon you as orphans; I will come to you.*
*(Jn 14:18)*

Jesus said that he would not leave us orphans, and then he offered us his Father, and he offered us his Mother. However, he added that this won't work unless we are willing to become as little children. Rather than leave us orphans, he actually invites us into full membership of his family, as he calls us his brothers and sisters. (Mk 3:34) There is a scene in the gospel that has powerful significance. The apostles are in serious trouble. They are in a boat, out on the sea of Galilee, and are in real danger of sinking. (Jn 6:19) Just then Jesus came towards them, walking on the water. What a beautiful example of Jesus being there when he is really needed. His actions spoke more about his care for them, than any of his words. Actions speak louder than words; that is why 'Jesus came to do and to teach'. (Acts 1:1) He acted first, and then he spoke to them about his care for them, or how he wanted them to care for others. This theme of being there for them runs throughout all his teaching. When he came to leave them at the ascension he was most sensitive. He spoke at length about the Spirit coming as a Comforter (Jn 16:7), and he assured them that the Spirit would continue his work and his presence among them.

Relationships are dynamic; they are never static. In other words, if a relationship is not moving forward, then by itself it will begin to slip backwards. A relationship today has no meaning, if it does not have a tomorrow. Our hope is basically in the future, because we had yesterday, and we have today. To have any kind of worthwhile relationship with Jesus, it is vital that we trust it to continue into the future. How often are the words 'I love you' said today, and never heard again. Love is a decision that involves a commitment. It is a commitment to be there for the other, as they go forward together. 'I'll be there for you', Jesus is telling us. The problem arises when we forget that promise. Jesus can be assigned to our list of Emergency Services, under a 999 number. This is far from what he has in mind, or from what he desires. He wants to be with us in everything we do. He wants us to involve him in decisions, work, loneliness, or worry. A good friend is always interested in everything we do. Such a person wants to know how I got on, after I return from a trip; how some new undertaking is progressing; how I handled a particular situation. It is at such times that love grows and develops.

'I will come to you.' There are many situations in the gospels where this is seen in two different ways. The first one is when he comes into a situation, even though he hadn't been called there. The widow of Naim was at a very low point in her life, when Jesus walked into that situation, and turned it completely around. (Lk 7:12) In a previous paragraph, I referred to Jesus walking on the water towards his apostles, as they battled with the wind and the waves. This kind of thing, when Jesus comes into a situation completely unannounced, and comes to the rescue in an emergency, is found several times in the gospels. The second kind of situation, as when Jesus is asked to come to the assistance of someone in real trouble, is also quite frequent. Examples of this is the story of Jairus (Lk 8:42), or the visit to Peter's mother-in-law. (Lk 4:38) There are other situations where he was stopped, as he passed by, e.g. the little woman in the crowd (Mt 9:20), or Batimaeus, the blind man. (Mk 10:46) It is very evident from reading the gospels, that Jesus was very much there for those who needed him. It was out of this experience that he could assure his disciples that he would always be there for them. In the words of a song: 'You just call out my name, and you know wherever I am, I'll come running to see you again. Summer, Spring, Winter, or Fall, all you've got to do is call, and I'll be there, yes, I will; you've got a friend.'

# Eucharist

*Those who eat my flesh and drink my blood, have eternal life,
and I will raise them up on the last day. (Jn 6:54)*

The word that jumps out at me in this promise is the word *have*.
This is not something that will be fulfilled in the future; it is
something I can have today. Without going into sacramental
theology, transubstantiation, etc., it is sufficient for now to say
that if I accept Jesus into my being then, of course, I have eternal
life. Jesus said that he *was* life (Jn 11:25), and that he came that
we might have life in abundance. (Jn 10:10) He makes a direct
connection between us having eternal life, and being raised up
on the last day. We are guaranteed a full sharing in his victorious resurrection. When I eat ordinary food, that food becomes
part of me, through a process of digestion. For example, when I
cut my finger, the very blood that oozes from the wound has
been made from the food I ate or drank. When I receive Jesus in
eucharist, however, the opposite process happens. It is I who
change and, with each such encounter, I become more and more
that which I consume, namely, the living Lord Jesus himself.
This is food and drink from heaven, to sustain and nourish us on
the journey of life. From their times in exile, and long years in
the desert, the Israelites were very conscious of the importance
of having access to food and drink. To highlight the centrality of
his role in their lives, Jesus spoke of himself as food and drink.
This is food and drink for which I must open my heart, and not
just my mouth.

Because receiving eucharist has a divinising effect on us, our
lives do become different and, slowly but surely, our human
condition begins to change and to take on immortal qualities;
something we never could do by ourselves. This is food and
drink for the journey, and food of such a nature could never be
for just a year or two. With the integration of his Body and
Blood, we are changed, bit by bit, area by area, until Christ is
formed within us. Just as Jesus becomes part of us, each of us becomes part of his Body. That he should become our very food is

a bonding beyond all other possibilities, and it is from this that
the reality of eternal life flows. Mary's body was so directly connected to the body of Christ, through the months of gestation
and moments of birth, that her body was brought, with her soul,
directly into the joys of heaven at the moment of her death.

Eucharist is a definite and eternal bonding of our souls with
Jesus himself, and we share in his divinity. It is in this way that
we become changed in such a way that our lives take on an eternal dimension, and we are assured of resurrection and eternal
life with him. He is the vine, and we are the branches (Jn 15:5),
and it is from him that this eternal life flows. That is why Jesus
tells us that 'apart from me, you can do nothing; you can only
wither and die'. (Jn 15:6) The body and blood of Jesus becomes
part of what we are, and we assume the qualities of his risen
body. This is an eternal bond that will never be broken.
Receiving the body and blood of Jesus is to sit at table with our
heavenly Father, who shares his greatest gift with us. This communion is much more than mere symbolism, because in the
bread and wine we actually consume the Living Word of God
and are nourished by the very life of God.

If I had a fairly large piece of the true cross of Calvary, I
might well be persuaded to share small splinters with my
friends, because I know how interested they would be to receive
one. In eucharist, I can share with them the very body and blood
that gave meaning and importance to that very cross. The splinters of the cross would be quite limited, and I certainly would
have a very limited sharing, no matter how tiny the pieces were.
In eucharist, there are no limits, and we can share the Body and
Blood of Jesus every day of our lives. Jesus has nothing greater
to give than himself, and I can have no greater sharing with
friends than to approach the altar with them. If my mind was
fully able to grasp the full significance and meaning of such a
sharing, I would approach with a sense of awe and wonder, and
a truly profound reverence.

*I am the bread of life.*
*(Jn 6:35)*

Jesus came that we should have life, and have it in abundance. (Jn 10:10) It is interesting to see the balance between bread and life in this promise. As I work at this computer, I am conscious of having what is called 'backup', in case my programme collapses, and I lose everything. God adds backup to everything he offers us. He offers us eternal life, and he also provides what it takes for us to accept and integrate that gift. In other words, spiritually, we are more crippled than we often realise. Our confusion comes in the following way: Of course, by myself, I can do good. This is where the deception can enter the factor. If I were to honestly assess that good, I would discover that it has a very brief shelf-life. In other words, I am mortal; I will die; and everything I do will also die. By myself, I'm like a tape-recorder with batteries, which of course will play but will not last. When the tape-recorder is plugged into a socket, however, and draws from a power not its own, then it will continue to play with the same power everyday. The alcoholic, by himself, can stop drinking. That's easy. The problem is he cannot stay stopped! What I'm saying here is that, of course, there is such a thing as human power, but it is very finite, and it can never do the work of God. Only God can do God-things. The 'backup' to which I referred just now, is best explained in this way: God calls me to do something and, with the call, he gives me all that it takes to answer that call. With the call comes the grace to respond to the call.

Jesus gives us life, and he also presents us with the bread to sustain that life. Without that on-going nourishment, the life would not last. Failure to understand this central truth can present us with many problems. I have confrères working under very difficult conditions in the mission fields of Mozambique, India, Philippines, to mention but a few. As I am now, age-wise, health-wise, etc., I could not do what they are doing. The simple fact is that I am not being called to do that work and, therefore, I don't require those gifts. If I ever felt drawn to work in one of these places, I would expect the good Lord to supply me with all that it takes to work there. As I write here, I could imagine the reaction I would receive should I fax all I have written so far, and ask one of my confrères to finish it! 'There are horses for courses', and each of us is gifted with whatever it takes to live the Christian life where God has planted us.

'I am the bread of life.' This is a simple unambiguous statement. It doesn't specify the amount of bread, or the length of life. I am sent on a journey, and I am given whatever I need to sustain me throughout that journey. I came out of a church late at night in the north of Ireland some years ago, and was prepared for the long drive home in very stormy conditions. As I approached my car, I heard someone call my name, and I looked back to see an elderly lady struggling to run in my direction. She had a walking stick but, such was her hurry, that she had the stick under her arm and was making every effort to reach me before I escaped. I experienced a degree of self-pity, as I imagined that I would have to listen to her story about every family problem, while being conscious that I was anxious to get on the road. Anyhow, when she reached me, she was out of breath. She handed me a small boat-shaped basket of neatly cut egg and onion sandwiches, covered with cling film, as she tried to get enough breath to say, 'You've a long journey before you, father, and I thought you might life to have these to eat as you drive on your way home.' I was both gobsmacked and guilty, as I accepted the sandwiches. They were beautiful, and I still have that little basket in my office here as I write. She had given me 'food for the journey', just as Jesus offers in the promise on which we have reflected.

*Anyone who eats this bread will live forever; this bread is my flesh, offered so the world may live. (Jn 6:51)*

I cannot see how I could possibly be open to the fullness of eucharist if my faith weren't grounded in a deep conviction of God's love. Jesus was condemned because 'he welcomed sinners, and ate with them'. (Lk 15:2) Even at the very first reading, this promise comes from a heart that is pouring out love in great abundance, and certainly wanting all that is best for us. The bread that is offered is not just for *now*, and that is what makes it so precious. I could never be happy in a relationship with someone if I didn't believe that the relationship has a 'tomorrow'.

Love is not like that. It extends beyond the grave, and lasts for eternity. I know a woman who still writes a Valentine's Day card to her husband many years after his death. The love is still there, and, I have no doubt, it is on both sides. 'If you want to feed me today, give me rice. If you want to feed me for all my days, teach me how to grow rice.' Sharing in eucharist is but a foreshadowing of the Eternal Banquet of heaven. Eucharist is a sacrament, and a sacrament is something that happens now, but depends on the future to give it meaning. I can pour water on a baby at baptism, but it's what happens ten, twenty, or thirty years from now that shows whether the person is really a Christian, and whether the sacrament is still alive, and life-giving. A couple can kneel in front of me on their wedding day, and make all sorts of beautiful promises, but their marriage begins after they leave the church. The wedding is for a day, but marriage is for a lifetime.

Eucharist is food for the soul, which never dies. Once life begins, it never ends. It's only the body that grows old; the person inside is always a child, and that is how the Father sees each of us. Eucharist is food for the journey, and that journey, like a river, ends up in the ocean of God's life and love. There is nothing automatic about this, of course, because we all have the freedom to reject God's offer. In St John's gospel (13:26-27, 30), we read, 'So Jesus dipped the bread, and gave it to Judas Iscariot, the son of Simon. And as Judas took the piece of bread, Satan entered into him ... Judas left, as soon as he had eaten the bread. It was night.' A very chilling account that pulls us up sharply. Communication is two-way, or not at all. Love always calls for a response, so it can survive. There is a light over my desk as I write. I can walk away, leave the room, close the door, and find myself in darkness, while the light continues to shine. God's love is always available, even when I put myself outside of that love.

Jesus speaks of his flesh being offered so that the world might live. He was speaking to people who were very familiar with flesh being offered for the forgiveness of sin, whether it be a lamb, an ox, or a goat. He is called the Lamb of God, because he himself becomes our sacrifice, and this sacrifice is so infinite that it replaces all other possible sacrifices, and accomplishes in itself infinitely more than all human sacrifices could possibly achieve. His flesh is offered, freely offered. Once again, we are free to accept or reject the offer. The idea of using bread and wine as a way of offering himself, body and blood, is highly significant because, once again, Jesus the teacher is bringing us from something we know, to something of much greater importance. This is food for the soul, just as ordinary bread is food for the body. Unlike ordinary bread, we need to open our hearts as well as our mouths in order to receive it. There are two references to life in this promise. One refers to living forever, and the other is speaking about living now. It is just as important to ensure that there is full life before death, as to believe that there is eternal life afterwards. This bread is for now, and for the hereafter.

> *All who eat my flesh and drink my blood, remain in me,*
> *and I in them. (Jn 6:56)*

It is obvious that if I remain attached to Jesus, I am in a relationship that never ends. He speaks of that relationship as a branch attached to a vine. (Jn 15:5) The only life the branch possesses is what it draws from the vine and, if it becomes separated from the vine, it can only wither and die. (Jn 15:4) I'm sure, at some time in our lives, each of us found ourselves with the following dilemma: Imagine a circle, with Jesus at the centre. I am on the circumference of the circle, and I dearly desire to come close to Jesus at the centre. My problem is that there are sins and patterns of behaviour in my life that seem to make it impossible for me to get near Jesus. If I could only remove those obstacles, one by one, I would arrive at Jesus in the centre, and he would pin a medal on me, and say 'Well done, good and faithful servant.' This whole scenario is absolutely and completely at variance with what Jesus has in mind, and how we are to come to him. The branch begins at the vine, and grows out from there, not the other way around. The invitation of salvation and redemption is asking us to go directly to the centre of the circle where Jesus is, exactly as we are, and with him we then move out, and all those obstacles are removed one by one. If I could have moved from the outside of the circle towards the centre with my own power, then Jesus need not have come at all! He came because it was evident to God that there was no way we could ever make our own way back to the garden, unless Jesus came to lead us there. This truth is at the heart of the good news.

In this promise we have some very important teachings. My generation grew up with an approach to eucharist that made it very difficult to grasp its real nature. We were always struggling to be worthy enough, and this had us going to confession on Saturday, before we could approach the altar on Sunday. Forgiveness belonged to confession on Saturday, while 'the state of grace' was an essential ingredient for Mass on Sundays. In practice, this meant that many people at Mass on Sunday did not receive communion, because, not having been to confession on Saturday, they were not worthy! My opening sentence in our reflection on the previous promise was: 'I cannot see how I could possibly be open to the fullness of eucharist if my faith weren't grounded in a deep conviction of God's love.'

Let's look at this from another angle. Just think of the variety of people who came to Jesus as he walked the roads of Galilee. They were blind, deaf, dumb, crippled, leprous, outcasts, public sinners, and insane. Do you think that they were worthy enough to come to him, as we considered 'worthy' in my earlier life? Do you believe there was anything they could do to make themselves 'more worthy' of such a unique encounter? They came to him because they fulfilled the criterion of the kind of people Jesus was looking for. It was for such as they that he came, and he made no apologies for his preference for them. (Lk 7:37-48) I think it is sad if we cannot see eucharist as a wonderful time of forgiveness, healing, and experiencing God's love. I am not ruling out confession, but I am not in favour of making a direct connection, making one depend on the other. My own opinion is that, as we cross back over the bridge from a love of law to a law of love, our understanding and celebrating of confession will continue to evolve. To a large extent, individual confession, as in a 'box', is more and more being replaced by public Services of Reconciliation. There is a community dimension to sin, and it is good that the reconciliation take place in a community setting. I believe, even if not in my day, that the Penitential Rite at the beginning of Mass will be restored to its proper place, and it is there that forgiveness will be sought, and received. 'If you bring your gift to the altar, and there remember that your brother / sister has something against you, leave your gift before the altar, go and become reconciled with your brother / sister, and then come to offer your gift.' (Mt 5:23) In other words, this reconciliation, taking place outside and beyond the confines of the church, will be restored to its proper place as the correct preparation for celebrating eucharist.

Eucharist is the surest way we have at our disposal to remain in Jesus, and to have him remain in us. My own favourite prayer after communion goes something like this:

*Thank you, Lord, for coming to me; I welcome you. I ask you to make your home, be at home, and feel at home within my heart. Proclaim your victory there. Put all the enemies there under your feet, as you hoist your flag of victory. Take a whip of cords, and rid the temple of my heart of anything that is not of you. May your presence within me touch the hearts of those I meet today, either through the words I say, the prayers I pray, the life I live, or the very person that I am.*

### No one who comes to me will ever be hungry again.
### (Jn 6:35)

Once again, a very simple, straightforward, and uncomplicated statement. Jesus is either telling me the truth or he's not, and it's up to me to find that out for myself. In this context, I must use the word 'hunger' in its broadest possible sense. We have many appetites, and most of them have little to do with food and drink. Mother (now Blessed) Teresa often said that the greatest hunger on earth was to be loved, to love, and to belong. There is a deep hunger within the human spirit that can only be satisfied by God; a hole in the heart of our inner spirits that can only be filled by God. When Jesus spoke to the woman at the well, he told her that the water he offered meant that she would not thirst again. (Jn 4:13) Our real deep human hungers are like restless spirits within – always in search of something that continues to elude us. There are many possible names for this, but I choose to call it *life*, life in abundance. People often look for this in the very places where it can never be found, e.g. in drugs, money, power, or pleasure. These may satisfy our short-term appetites, but our inner being is still not at peace, and the restlessness continues. There is a sense of being ill-at-ease, not being balanced, fulfilled, or contented. Peace is what I experience when my relationships are the way they ought to be. There is no problem on earth that is not a relationship one. I'm not getting on too well with God, with myself, or with others.

Getting this balance right is often called wholeness, and some people would call it holiness. This is exclusively the work of the Holy Spirit. 'Come, Holy Spirit, *fill* the hearts of your faithful ...' It is only the Spirit who can fill every hole in the heart and in the human spirit. Our egos can get so inflated that we become 'full of ourselves', and there's no room for anything else. Mary was so humble that she was completely emptied of self. Therefore, she could become 'full of grace'; she could be filled with the life and gifts of God. John the Baptist spoke of himself decreasing, so that Jesus could increase. (Lk 3:16) In the promise now under review, Jesus speaks very definitely about being the source, the only source, from which we could be fully and properly nourished. He does not say that everybody should come to him, because he knew they wouldn't. He speaks very definitely, however, about those who do come to him, and his promise and commitment to such people is clear and unequivocal. They will never be hungry again; it's as simple as that.

Any of us who have been around for a while must surely raise our attention level at the mention of this promise. Life can have so many blind alleys, so many disappointments, and empty promises. We are bombarded with ads for everything, and the whole idea behind each advertisement is to convince us that this particular product is exactly what we need, and this will change our lives forever. I smile these days at all the junk mail that arrives on this computer, promising everything from restoration of long-lost hair, to removal of well-established wrinkles. Too late, my friend, too late! All these things are usually consigned to the rubbish heap of good resolutions, election promises, and good intentions. However, as I read this promise, I have a desire to go away somewhere on my own, where I could spend some serious time in prayer, reflection, and listening, until this promise will have made its way deep into my heart. I am thinking of absorption, osmosis, or some such process, something like how I think of the Spirit working within us. The truth behind, or within the words, becomes real for us, and the promise has reached our hearts. These words are spoken from the heart of Jesus, and they are spoken to our hearts. To speak from the heart is to speak to the heart. To come to accept and believe that, by taking Jesus seriously on this one, I will have made the greatest possible discovery of my whole life – and that, indeed, is exciting.

# Father

*The time will come when I will tell you plainly all about the Father. (Jn 16:25)*

Jesus came with a mission. He came to repair the broken relationship between Creator and creature. He would be 'God-among-us'(Emmanuel), and he would lead us back to the garden, and connect us once again with our state of original innocence. He would do this is several ways. Firstly, he never said anything unless the Father told him. (Jn 8:26) In other words, 'they who hear me, hear the Father'. (Jn 8:40) When I was growing up there was some sort of persistence that, no matter what Jesus said, God (Father) was away in the background somewhere, with his own private and personal agenda. From early childhood, I could visit Jesus in the church; I could love him, and know that he loved me. However, there was this other 'God' out there somewhere, with a long white beard, and a mighty big note book! He was watching me; I could do my utmost to please, but was always convinced that this was really impossible. No matter how hard I tried, I was convinced that, should I die right there, my day of reckoning had arrived, and all these pages in that notebook would be opened out before me. He was a sort of 'Gotcha' God, and there was no escape. Thankfully, through the years, this phantom has vanished, and the words and mission of Jesus have gradually made some inroads into my consciousness.

Jesus also came to show us the Father. 'They who see me, see the Father.' (Jn 12:45) Jesus made no apology for his strong preferential love for the outcast, the broken, and the marginalised. He touched the leper, he spoke to the prostitute, and he ate with the tax-collectors. In himself, he was showing what the Father was like, and how the Father thought. He told us about the forgiving father, who waited, longed, and yearned for his erring son to come home, to receive his hug of welcome and his words of forgiveness. When Jesus spoke about the Father, he also spoke about us being his children, and becoming like little children. It would make no sense if the Father-child relationship couldn't become a reality. The Father, the source of our life, is also the on-going preserver and maintainer of our life. He just didn't create us like rag dolls, and then throw us out into outer space, to be at the mercy of every element of his creation. In his lifetime, Jesus went a very long way in giving us a fairly clear image of a very loving and caring Father. His own relationship with the Father was obviously strong, vibrant, real, and sustaining. From his perspective, of course, there was so much more. Getting to know the Father would be something that would go on for all eternity. When Jesus had completed his part of the mission, he handed on that responsibility to the Spirit. The Spirit would take over where Jesus had laid off. The message of Jesus was evident and audible. The work of the Spirit would be silent and interior. The Spirit leads us into all truth (Jn 16:13), and that truth has to do with the nature and action of the Father's love. There is no question that I will ever come to understand God, because of my finite, human mind. However, like a tiny fish in the middle of the Atlantic, I will continue, for all eternity, to make new discoveries about the same God. It would be a very foolish little fish, and a very dead little fish, if it tried to rise above the Atlantic and get an overview from Galway to New York. It wouldn't live too long out of its natural environment.

Jesus speaks here about telling us plainly about the Father. Certainly, in my own case, I have a much more down-to-earth concept of the Father than I had back down the years. I am aware of some sort of on-going revelation in all of this, and I expect this to continue. When I use the word 'Father' I find that I mean that in all its best connotations. It helps me in understanding about becoming as a child when I stand before him. When Jesus preached in the Temple, he said, 'These words are being fulfilled even as I speak.' (Lk 4:21) When I reflect on the promise under review, I can imagine Jesus telling me that this promise is being fulfilled even as I write.

> *You can go directly to the Father, and ask him, and he will grant your request, because you use my name. (Jn 16:23)*

Again and again, in these promises, we are reminded that Jesus has opened up a Way for us to come directly to the Father. He even calls himself 'The Way'. (Jn 14:6) Before the members of the early church became known as Christians in Antioch, they were referred to as 'Followers of the Way'. There are two very significant instances in Jesus' life which refer directly to the opening up of this Way. When he went down into the Jordan to be baptized by John, we are told that 'the heavens were opened'(Lk 3:21), and when he bowed his head in death, we learn that 'the veil of the Temple was torn in two'. (Lk 23:45) In simple words, full communication was restored between God and his creatures. From the Fall, it seemed as if the gates of heaven were closed against God's people. The Holy of Holies was cut off from all public access, and it also was a sign that mere humans could never enter such a sacred place. The life and death of Jesus changed that utterly. St Paul tells us that we are no longer slaves, but we can come boldly into the presence of God. (Eph 3:12) The Berlin Wall has fallen, and there is free access to all who wish to cross over. This is a very bold and deliberate promise of Jesus, but the last few words contain the most important element ... 'because you use my name'. The name of Jesus is the key that opens up to us the vaults and treasuries of heaven. 'No one can come to the Father, except through me.' (Jn 14:6) 'There is no other name given to us under heaven, whereby we can be saved.' (Phil 2:9)

We are all familiar with letters of recommendation, introductions, references, and influence-getters. I advise somebody about where to obtain a book, and I may add that, if there's any problem, ask for a certain person and tell her that I sent you. We do things like this all the time. As I write these very words I can pray quietly, 'Father, Jesus told me that I could come directly to you, because of him, and I would have your full attention ...' Not a bad way to start a prayer! Many of our liturgical prayers end with the words 'We ask you this in Jesus' name' or 'through Christ our Lord'. When Jesus spoke of being the Way, he wasn't speaking of being one of many possible ways. He was offering himself as a direct, sure, safe, and certain path that leads right before the throne of God. It would have been awesome for a Jew to enter the Holy of Holies, even after the veil was torn in two, and I am fairly certain that none of them attempted to do so. In the case of Jesus, the offer is real; there is no snag, no hidden agenda, no catches, no small print. At the moment of death, I imagine that I will stand before God with the canvas of my life wide open before him. No hiding, no denying, no pretending any more. The important thing is, of course, that I can do that right now, right here, just as I am. I don't have to die to stand before the throne of God. I mentioned a few sentences ago about stopping my world right here, right now, and doing exactly what Jesus suggests in this promise. When I actually do that, and do that on a regular basis, I am beginning to take possession of this promise, and to activate it in my life. The possibilities are infinite, and the process could not be simpler. I learn to pray by praying, and to trust by trusting. It must surely cause sadness to the heart of Jesus that some of his most powerful, most effective, and simplest promises may not yet have been accepted, believed, or acted upon. 'The words that I have spoken will be your judge on the last day. If I had not come and spoken, you would have an excuse for your sin.' (Jn 12:48)

*Your Father, who knows what you do in secret, will reward you.*
*(Mt 6:18)*

Jesus came to tell us about the Father. In this promise, he tells us one piece of information that is worth knowing. Our Father has us constantly in his sight. He knows and sees all that we do and say. This is not surveillance, as much as genuine care, concern, and love. He never lets us out of his sight. In recent years, we had had some horrific incidents where young children went missing and, after some time, unfortunately, the bodies of some of them were found in a woodland or bog. It's at times like this that one hears the concerns that parents have about letting their children out of their sight. It is difficult not to get paranoid about this, because some of the more well-known incidents have taken place in the most unlikely places. It is as if there's no safe place anymore. One can feel greatly for the concerns of such parents.

On the other hand, for *Big Brother* watchers on TV, we see another form of being under observation, of being under the spotlight at all times. I'm sure some people obviously find this entertaining in some way or other, and I wouldn't dare comment on that, one way or another. This is voyeurism, which is a step beyond (beneath?) surveillance, and it is hardly a situation that the average punter would feel at ease with. And then again, we have other ways of keeping an eye on others. A young prisoner hangs himself in his cell, and there is an enquiry, because he was checked on every fifteen minutes. There had been concern about his mental state, and he was under observation; and, despite this, the occasional suicide occurs. The exam supervisor moves silently but constantly up and down between the rows of desks. For the nervous pupil, this can be a problem, because such a one could be having a blank moment, and is very conscious of someone approaching, when he/she is obviously doing nothing. I could go on and on about the many and various kinds and forms of supervision, of check-ups, of surveillance, or of voyeurism, but I think I may have made the point I need to stress. In the words of this promise, we are told that the Father knows what we do in secret. This doesn't necessarily mean that he is watching us all the time. God knows all about us; he knows us through and through.

The Psalmist sings (Ps 139): 'O Lord, you know me; you have scrutinised me. You know when I sit and when I rise; from far away you discern my thoughts. You observe my activities and times of rest; you are familiar with all my ways. Before a word is formed in my mouth, you know it entirely, O Lord.' The Psalmist is in no doubt whatever that he is constantly held within the concern of God. God's concern is like a sort of overall care, so that we are never separated from him, either in mind or sight. It is as if we were attached to God, some sort of extension of God. My foot is not free to go down the road for a walk on its own. I cannot act independently of God, even when my actions are directly opposed to what God would want me to do. A mother is walking along a footpath with her three-year old. She will take all reasonable precautions to ensure that he stays on the footpath. If, however, on a whim, he darts out into the passing traffic to retrieve a ball, she cannot stop him. She can dash to his rescue, she can become frantic, but she can also be too late. If she didn't have any kind of harness on him that kept him in restraint, she is powerless, if he decides to do his own thing.

In this promise, Jesus is speaking about positive actions from us. The kingdom of God is built up in two ways: through tiny acts, and most of them are hidden. What this promise is saying is that not one of those acts will go unnoticed, unrecorded. Jesus was probably the only one in the Temple who saw the poor widow put in her few pennies. (Mk 12:42) God is very aware of all such things. Jean Vanier suggests that the most significant events for the good of this world have been brought about by the quiet prayers of totally unknown people. In Matthew's gospel (Chapter 25), Jesus gives us a preview of the general judgement. One line in particular is worth noting. When he commended the good for the kind acts they had done, they were amazed, because they had not attached such importance to what they did. They were the kind of people who were always disposed towards doing the good, and because this had become a way of life for them, as it were, they no longer thought of it as being anything extraordinary. Their kind acts had developed kind attitudes, and they knew no other way of being. I grew up with a God who kept a very strict register of even my smallest failures! In this promise, Jesus assures me that he notices and rewards every good act, every good intention, and every attempt to activate the goodwill that he has placed in our hearts as part of his creation.

*My Father will love them, and we will come, and live with them.*
*(Jn 14:23)*

Jesus begins this promise with the words 'If anyone loves me ...' The rest of the promise above is the result of doing that. Jesus is quite specific in this part of his teaching. He tells that if we love him, we will obey him. In other words, we don't have to be in doubt about what exactly he means by 'loving'. His love for his Father was expressed in his total commitment to doing exactly everything the Father asked him. A child can continue to proclaim a great love for a parent, while at the same time going out and doing exactly the very things the parents have forbidden him/her to do. It is obvious that it is through their actions they can best display their love. 'What you do speaks so clearly that I cannot hear what you are saying.' Jesus speaks of a man who had two sons. (Mt 21:28) He asked one to do some work for him; the son said he would, but he didn't. He asked the other, who said he wouldn't, but changed his mind, and did what he was asked. 'Which of the two sons did what the father wanted?' Jesus asked. The answer is quite obvious, but he wanted to make a point. In another place (Mt 7:21), Jesus says, 'Not all who call me "Lord" will enter the kingdom of heaven.' In other words, calling me Lord, if I'm not Lord, is of no value whatever. 'By their fruits you shall know them.' (Mt 12:33)

I said that Jesus leaves us in no doubt what he means when he speaks of us loving him. He is even more specific when he speaks of his love for us. In this promise, he speaks of the Father loving us, and all Persons of the Trinity coming to make their home in us. This is prodigal love to an infinite degree. If original sin was an attempt of humans to assume divinity, then right here we have this very offer made to us. All three Persons of the Trinity will come and make their home in us. It is not possible for my human mind to grasp anything of the significance of this, but I do know that this is *awe-full*. Every single word in this promise is important. 'We will come and live with them.' They are not coming to dominate us or control us. They want to make their homes within us. What an extraordinary gift and privilege! With all my heart, Lord Jesus, I want to love you, and I want to obey you. I can approach this in one way only. I have no reason to trust myself, so I depend totally on the Spirit to transform my heart to become obedient, submissive, and disciplined, in the terms of being a disciple. By and of myself, I cannot do this, as all my good resolutions of the past have shown me so clearly again and again. I could continue with this prayer, but what I have written may give some directive as to how to approach this whole area. I find myself facing a familiar problem here. There are two sides to every agreement. 'In this is our salvation: his blood, and our faith.' (Rom 3:24) There is nothing automatic about God. Jesus didn't want Judas to go and hang himself, but because of freewill he wouldn't stop him. In our present promise, we are told that the Father will love us, and that the Trinity will come and live in us, *if we love (obey) him*. It is that X factor that causes me concern on a regular basis. St Paul writes that he cannot trust himself at all. (Rom 7) He knows what is right, and he knows what he should do, but there is something deep within him that keeps getting in the way of his attempts at doing the good. He goes on to show that he has every reason for being on the point of despair, when he pulls himself up with the phrase: 'Who will free me from this slavery to my lower nature? Thanks be to God, it has been done through Jesus Christ; he has set us free.' (Rom 7:24-25)

Again and again I find myself returning to this simple fact: any response on my part, any possibility of a response on my part, is completely and entirely the work of the Holy Spirit. Jesus makes an offer, and he offers me the grace to respond to, and to accept that offer. There is absolutely no place whatever for an approach that I would have identified at an earlier stage in my life: I would invite Jesus to take over my life, to half-save me, as it were, and then, when everything was under control, I would thank him very much, and politely tell him that I'll take over and finish the job from here. How often I have seen a child insisting on tying shoe laces, or buttoning a coat, until eventually they have to surrender and allow a patient mother take over and do what she knew would fall to her anyhow. The Lord is surely very patient with us. There is an extraordinary richness of pure solid teaching contained within this simple promise. Even coming to any kind of understanding of it is, in itself, the work of the Holy Spirit.

*Father, I will keep revealing you. I will do this so that your love for me may be in them, and I in them. (Jn 17:26)*

There have been occasions when I have had a very privileged insight into the heart of another. The most significant of these have been those times when I listened as another prayed. Because I've had the privilege of working with senior citizens in a retirement home, and still offer Mass daily in one such place, I often have an opportunity to be by a bedside when a saintly soul of eighty or ninety years pours out her soul to God in prayer. Sometimes the prayers are confused, and recited from rote memory, but there are other times when it is truly a privilege to be present. In this promise, we are eavesdropping, as it were, on Jesus as he is speaking to the Father. This Chapter 14 of St John's gospel gives some beautiful insights into the mind and heart of Jesus. It is such a privilege to listen in as he speaks directly to his Father, and to our Father. There are many words that come to mind when we think of why Jesus came. He came to show us the Father. He came to tell us about the Father. He came to convey the Father's message to us. In this promise, he speaks about revealing the Father. The word 'reveal' implies lifting a veil off something that is already there, something is already almost visible. It implies unwrapping, unfolding, uncovering. At the public gathering, I can see the outline of the statue to be unveiled, but we hold our collective breaths for the moment when the official reaches up, and whips away the cover, to a chorus of a united *wow!* (or sometimes to an ominous silence!). Jesus promises the Father that he will continue revealing him; he will continue lifting the veil, gradually, slowly, and constantly. Revelation is a process of discovery. It is a journey I make with Jesus. As I climb the mountain, the expanse of the valley below becomes vaster in every direction. My walk with Jesus is a journey of revelation. I think of some of the more inspiring tour guides I have followed on various pilgrimages over the years. They had the knack of retaining my attention, and my expectation of what lay around the next corner. All the objects of interest are present, but I need an experienced guide to draw my attention to them because, of myself, I would be totally incapable of grasping the history and the significance of all that surrounds me. Jesus is my guide as I travel the road of life. Prayer is becoming more and more aware of what is happening around me, and within me. Jesus speaks of the spirit continuing this process of revelation.

Jesus goes on to speak of the reason behind such revelation. Through this process of revelation, the love of the Father is revealed to us; we become more and more aware of the vastness of eternity that extends around us in all directions. Jesus is preparing the way for the love of the Trinity to gradually seep into our hearts, calling us to greater awareness, to deeper consciousness, to more spontaneous appreciation and prayer. Jesus is, above all, a teacher. Through the process of information, we are led to formation, into transformation. On this journey of revelation we are brought 'into the secrets of the kingdom'. (Mt 13:11) We are brought beyond parables here, beyond mere ideas and theories. His word becomes alive in us, and evokes a response within our hearts. This response is what we call prayer. Our final destiny is sharing the fullness of the life of the Trinity. Jesus is leading us on this greatest journey of all time, right into the arms of God for all eternity. 'Those who follow me will not walk in darkness, but will have the light of life.' (Jn 8:12)

When these words were spoken, it was at a particular part of an on-going journey, a journey that will continue until the end of time. 'I will keeping revealing you.' Jesus will hand on this task to the Spirit, who will 'complete his work on earth'. Just as Jesus reveals the Father to us, he speaks of the Spirit revealing him to us, and reminding us of everything that he has told us. This process of revelation will be complete when we have arrived home, and come face to face with God for all eternity.

# Obedience

*Anyone who obeys God's laws, and teaches them,*
*will be great in the kingdom of heaven. (Mt 5:19)*

There is a twin-programme involved in this promise. Jesus speaks about obeying God, and teaching others to do the same. There is a direct connection, of course, between both, because if I do not obey, it is very unlikely that I will teach others to obey. This strikes at the very heart of catechesis, homiletics, and evangelisation. If I myself am not obeying, it is unlikely that my attempt at teaching others to do so will bear much fruit. Jesus said about the Pharisees, 'Do what they say, but not what they do.' (Mt 23:3) This direct connection carries over, all across the board. If I obey God's laws, I will be automatically teaching others through my example. St Francis of Assisi said that we should always preach the gospel and, where necessary, we could even use words!

This is an interesting promise from many aspects. Jesus can move so smoothly from restating God's law, to the point of pushing aside a law if it conflicts with practical charity and love. He inherited a very stringent code of law, and this law dominated and influenced every dimension of the life of the people. Law, in itself, is good. Law is there to protect. I cannot drive through my local village at 100 miles an hour, and that law is there to protect every form of life within that village. There is a sign, as I enter the village, which says '30'. That's it. That's what I must obey. On the other hand, I have somebody in the back seat who is in labour, or who is bleeding to death, and it is vital that I get to the hospital with that person as soon as is possible. At this moment that '30' sign becomes irrelevant and the rules are changed. When I was a child it was a sin to eat meat on Fridays. What happened with those hungry people who never saw meat from one end of the year to the next? If good fortune should provide a lamb or a deer for a meal, I don't think God would be very worried what day of the week it was! If God's laws were to be interpreted literally, I can't see any scope for teaching them;

191

memorising them, yes, but there's nothing to teach. Discussion is part of the teaching process, but if everything is written in bronze, then there's no scope for discussion.

Both obeying God's laws, and teaching them to others, is something that should come from a heart of love, from a contrite and humble heart. Respect for God will ensure respect for his law; and respect for the importance of his law will be the motivating factor in wanting me to pass this on to others. It is obvious that those who will be the greatest in the kingdom of heaven will be those who have contributed most to the building of that kingdom. This requires some explanation, because it is important that it be properly understood. Everyone of us is involved in building up God's kingdom. This is done through the simplest acts, most of which are hidden or unseen. The poet speaks of all 'the unremembered acts of kindness and of love'. Imagine a child having a savings booklet in the local post office. Every week she arrives with her few pennies, and lodges them. Her name won't make it to the billboards in the Stock Exchanges rooms. However, that is how the kingdom is built. Jesus drew the attention of the apostles to a simple incident in the gospel, one that probably he alone had seen. 'Jesus sat down opposite the Temple treasury, and watched people dropping money into the treasury box; and many rich people put in large offerings. But a poor widow also came, and dropped in two small coins. Then Jesus called his disciples and said to them: "Truly I say to you, this poor widow put in more than all those who gave offerings. For all of them gave of their plenty, but she gave from her poverty, and put in everything she had, her very living".' (Mk 12:41-44)

In another place Jesus speaks of those who serve as being the greatest in his kingdom, and he washed their feet, as a demonstration of what he saw as real greatness. Many teaching congregations in the church used this promise as part of their motto. They were seriously following Jesus' injunction to teach others, and to pass on to them what he had given them. He went to great lengths in many ways to emphasise that he was not speaking about becoming part of an on-going pharisaic tradition, in which the law became an end in itself. Jesus was interested in the law of love, rather than a love of law. He was speaking about those who themselves had accepted the torch of love and, with that, the responsibility to pass that torch on to others.

*You can receive eternal life if you keep the commandments.*
*(Mt 19:17)*

It could be quite counter-productive to take this promise at its face value, and to interpret it literally. The commandments were there long before Jesus came and, if keeping the commandments were sufficient for salvation, there would have been no great need for Jesus himself to come. After all, through Moses, God had already instructed the people to obey the commandments. The commandments smack of religion, of external performances, of something that we do, and have something to do with control. The Pharisees were into commandments in a big way. If commandments alone could save us, Jesus would be better off to leave the Pharisees alone; indeed, he could have pointed to them as paradigms of virtue, representing in themselves everything he was speaking about. But this was far from the truth. To understand what Jesus means, it is necessary that we understand what he means when he speaks of the commandments. I think of him as seeing them as pointers to goodness, as sign-posts to peace and happiness. They were based on love, and nothing more. They were there to give direction, rather than to effect control. He spoke of them as being summarised into two: love of God and love of neighbour. He saw them as guides to love, to harmony, to balanced and healthy well-being.

Jesus had noticed that the commandments had been turned into laws by the Pharisees. Again and again he began his words, 'The law says onto you; but I say to you …' The law spoke about an eye for an eye, and Jesus spoke of forgiveness, and turning the other cheek. The law emphasised our meticulous observance of all aspects of worship of God, but Jesus gave us a new commandment: to love one another as he loved us. (Jn 15:12) Keeping the commandments was to develop the attitude of a humble heart. It was more about disposition than action. There are many references in Scripture to having a humble and contrite heart; and God makes it clear that this meant more to him than all their sacrifices. 'Wash the evil from your hearts that you may be saved.' (Jer 4:14) 'I will give them a new heart and a new mind. I will remove their stubborn heart of stone, and give them an obedient heart.' (Ez 11:19) Jesus spoke of the people honouring God with their lips, while their hearts were far from him. (Mk 7:6) Of course, there was a place for commandments, but not as something to be superimposed from on high. God created us in such a way that the commandments are written within our hearts. Without being told, I would know that I should not kill, steal, lie, or neglect my parents. We all have that inner voice, called conscience, that lets us know when we have deviated from the path of truth. If I were to write out all the commandments in a list and, then alongside them, to write what each commandment is really about, I might get a clearer idea of the enlightened common sense involved. Because of original sin, I am fundamentally flawed, and I am constantly aware of some kind of inner battle going on between what I want to do, and what I ought to do. A wise old monk spoke about these two wolves, one good, and one evil, and they are battling within us for supremacy. One of his students asked him which of the wolves was more liable to win the battle, and he was told that it would be the one we feed most! When we understand this, we realise that this is more than just keeping rules, and conforming to fixed roles. This surely is a question of the heart, which replaces the tablets of stone on which the original commandments were written.

Jesus summarised all the commandments into two, and they are about love, and nothing else. God is love, and they who live in love, live in God, and God lives in them. (1 Jn 4:15) 'For this is the message we taught you from the beginning: we must love one another ... My dear children, let us love, not only in words and with our lips, but in truth and in deed.' (1 Jn 11, 18) I can rephrase the promise under reflection, in different words, without changing its meaning: 'You can receive eternal life if you love.'

*Anyone who does the will of my Father in heaven
is my brother, and sister, and mother. (Mt 12:50)*

The background to these words gives us a broader view of what
is being said. Jesus was speaking to the crowd, when word was
passed to him that his mother and some of his relatives were out
at the edge of the crowd and would like a word with him. He
must have been in full flow in pouring out the word of God at
the time and, no doubt, the Spirit was powerfully at work
through him. It is almost as if he slid into prophecy here, spoke
the words that came to his heart, without any great reflection on
the full meaning of those very words. In his teaching he was
opening the hearts and minds of his listeners, and he also was
opening up to them the treasuries of heaven and the secrets of
the kingdom. This particular statement, then, was one of great
power, that just flowed out of him like hot lava from a volcano.
His offer was nothing less than full membership within the family of God. He loved his mother very much, and they were very
special to each other. He had brothers and sisters, in the way
such terms were used in those times. It never meant just blood
brothers or sisters, but members of the extended family, like
members of a tribe would consider themselves as brothers and
sisters to each other. In usual human attempts to form closely
built units, recourse is often made to comrade, brother, sister, as
a way of describing a certain level of closeness, and for shared
responsibility for the welfare of the others.

This promise is clear and unequivocal. If we do the will of
our Father in heaven, we qualify, through Jesus, for full membership within his family. It's as clear and as simple as that. I am
only too aware that it's impossible for the human to grasp the
full significance of that, and I don't ever look towards my heart
for reassurance about many issues. I don't think it an accident
that I chose to call this book *Jesus Said It … and I Believe it!* In
other words, any trust I have is in the fact that Jesus said it, and I
honestly do believe that he meant it. There are different ways of
being members of a family, besides being born into that family.
Children can be adopted into a family, and assume the names,
rights, and privileges that any natural-born child in that family
would be entitled to. Children can be fostered within a family,

and what began as a temporary arrangement can continue for a lifetime. Sons become son-in-laws, and mothers become mother-in-laws. There is no end of the permutations and combinations of relationships within the family. In this promise, Jesus brings us directly into the centre of his family. As our society is growing and evolving today, there is more and more emphasis on identity, belonging, and integration. Refugees, asylum seekers, and nomads provide quite a headache to the authorities, who feel that they lose control if they don't have details in files, and identities for inspection. Young people are being asked to have prove-of-age cards for admission to certain forums of entertainment. Passports, visas, and different forms of green or other coloured cards are required to cross many state borders. I could go on and on, but the point I wish to stress here is that Jesus removes all barriers, restrictions, and obstacles, and invites us to walk in off the street and become full members of his family. There is one simple condition, i.e. to do the will of his Father. In another part of the gospel Jesus says, 'This is the will of your heavenly Father that you should know him, the one true God, and Jesus Christ whom he has sent.' (Jn 6:29) The will of the Father is that we should accept his invitation to come back to the garden, where he is waiting with a big hug for us. The will of the Father is that we should listen to Jesus, obey him, and thus return into full membership within the family of God.

> *Anyone who obeys my teaching will never die.*
> *(Jn 8:51)*

The truth involved in this promise has also been contained within several of the promises on which we have already reflected. For a moment I was tempted to omit it but, thankfully, became aware that this would be a mistake. Firstly, I cannot hear the words of Jesus too often and, secondly, the more time I spend with his words the more I come to understand the heart from which those words come. There are three parts to the promise, to get as complete a picture as we can. Jesus speaks about obeying him. He then specifies that this means obeying his teaching, in doing what he tells us to do. He concludes that, by doing this, we will never die. It would be interesting to see just how many times Jesus actually says this in the gospels, in a variety of different ways. He came with a message, which includes a map, a road ahead, that leads back home to the Father. There is no other way so, naturally, it is important that we obey him, in that we walk in the way pointed out by him. We can, of course, walk in any way we choose. If I don't know where I'm going in life, there's no real problem, because any road will get me there. If, however, I have one particular destination in mind, there is only one road that leads to there. The student at college who wishes to graduate into a professional career, and pursue that career with success, has very few options.

The teaching of Jesus has to do with love in every possible expression, situation, and circumstance. It is about forgiveness, compassion, judgement, resentments, tolerance, patience, and all the many other ways in which love can be expressed or thwarted. The love of which he speaks is a life-giving love. That is why he says that those who become channels of such love will never die. I cannot give life to others, and not increase the depth of my own life. Jesus did many things during his lifetime. He raised the dead, calmed the storm, expelled the demons, and restored the senses of sight, speech and hearing to those without them. One of his greatest preoccupations, of course, was teaching. He availed of every opportunity he got to teach the people. He had a message to pass on, and he experienced a very powerful compulsion to give this every ounce of energy he had. 'I have a baptism to complete, and I am in anguish until it is over.' (Lk 12:50) His zeal for the Father's glory kept driving him, and this kept him going up till the end. The onus was on him to begin with it. He could not ask others to obey his teaching until that teaching that been given and instilled. Like many of the reflections in this book, many of the teachings were repeated again and again. Teaching is more than simply transferring knowledge from one head to another – and certainly more than transferring information from a teacher's notebook to a student's notebook, without having passed through the head of either! Jesus was at his best as a teacher when he himself was actually doing the very things he wanted his disciples to learn. He touched the lepers, he embraced the children, he fed the hungry, he defended the outcasts, and he gave hope and health to many who lived in darkness and despair.

What exactly does he mean when he says that such people will never die? Let's suppose that death was a pile of sand at the end of my life. My Christian life allows me to take that sand, fist by fist, and sprinkle it throughout every day, as I journey along the road. To love as a Christian is to die to myself in a thousand ways, again and again and again. I have to die to my pride when I forgive, or to my selfishness when I share. I have to die to my comforts when I entertain or give time to others, and I have to die to my patience when I have to listen to the story of another. This is love. 'Greater love than this no one has that a person should die for a friend.' (Jn 15:13) It is obvious that, through such loving service, the giver is being transformed, and the life of such a person continues to evolve into a quality that is eternal. Thérèse of Lisieux and Padre Pio, for example, were very certain that their real work would begin after they died. A life that is spent in giving, is a life that is fully invested in the bank of heaven, and such a life gives back eternal dividends.

### *Those who obey my commandments are those who love me.* ### *(Jn 14:21)*

Once again, Jesus makes a direct connection between obeying him and loving him. Love can be expressed in a very large variety of ways but, lest there be any confusion, Jesus highlights obedience as the main ingredient in our love for him. 'Does God take as much delight in burnt offerings and sacrifices, as in obedience to his commands? Obedience is better than sacrifice, and submission is better than the fat of rams.' (1 Sam 15:22) From the very beginning, sin was seen as a refusal to obey, from the rebellion of Lucifer, to Adam and Eve in the Garden, to the rebellious Jews throughout their ancient history. The only way back to God is the path of obedience. Obedience is to know my place before God. God is love, and everything that comes from God is some particular expression of love. His will for me is based on pure love, and his relationship with me is nothing but on-going love. His commandments speak of love. Jesus summarised the original Ten Commandments in two: Loving God, and loving neighbour. If I keep these two commandments, all ten will be observed, because this would exclude murder, stealing, lying, fornicating, neglect of others, or not giving due deference to God. The commandments are not intended to be some sort of restrictive harness that restrains us within certain confines and deprive us of liberty or freewill. When I live within the confines of the commandments, I am protected totally from everything that might harm or damage me. Like the rules of the road, or international peace agreements, they are designed to protect the safety and welfare of people. Obeying Jesus is a constant guarantee of happiness, and that is his one and only motive for teaching us these guidelines for living.

Of myself, how could I possibly know how to love God? Because of the weakness of human nature, I could so easily slip into a self-enhancing way of loving, something that would make little demands on me, and that would be self-sculptured to my own needs and inclinations. Children need boundaries, and discipline has to be an external thing, until maturity and formation causes it to become internalised, and my own inner spirit is trained into proper and healthy behaviour. In his own life, Jesus laid great emphasis on his obedience to the Father. He never said anything unless the Father told him. (Jn 10:25; 5:19) His very food was to do the will of him who sent him. (Jn 4:34) 'As the Father sent me, so I am sending you. If you love me, you will obey me.' (Jn 15:10)

Love, by definition, is something that calls for a response. Jesus came to reveal the Father's love to us. Our response to that is to strive to love in return. I have come across many a broken-hearted parent whose love is being rejected by a child. I cannot make someone love me. Love must be freely offered, and freely given. It is not a commodity that can be bartered, sold, or exchanged. Pure love is unconditional, with no price tags attached. In human relationships, we can speak of someone surrendering to love. I accept the love of the other, and I return that love in kind. This is often called 'falling in love' or 'being in love'. It is a condition of being, where one's thoughts, actions, and interests are powerfully influenced by the love given to and received from another. Real love leads to a commitment of one kind or another. Love is a moving forward together; it is a growing in sharing a common vision. Rather than 'falling in love', I can grow into love. It enables us over-ride our own selfish needs, and put the welfare of another before our own. There is a bonding and a unity in love, and this process is unending. This is what Jesus has in mind, because he is offering us something that will never end. Love is an investment in the future. Our love for Jesus is an investment in eternity.

# Children

*Anyone who becomes as humble as this child,*
*is the greatest in the kingdom of heaven. (Mt 18:4)*

Jesus really went to a great deal of trouble to ensure that we understand what he means when he speaks about the kingdom of heaven. On many occasions, he begins with the words 'The kingdom of heaven is like ...' The kingdom of heaven now is what we will call heaven later on. The road to heaven is heaven, and if we follow the rules for kingdom living now, we will surely end up in the fullness of the kingdom later on. The kingdom that Jesus came to proclaim is diametrically opposed to the kingdom of this world, in every possible way. Each is based on a completely different set of values. Greatness in the kingdom of the world involves power, wealth, influence, and aggrandisement. In the kingdom of God, the power is with the little ones, the humble of heart, those who give, rather than those who receive. The kingdom, the power, and the glory are God's. If I supply any of the power, I will be tempted to steal some of the glory. That is why Jesus stresses humility as being a necessary ingredient for kingdom living. 'The greatest in the kingdom are those who serve.' (Lk 22:27) Humility is truth, is stating and accepting things as they are. The mind of a child is unpolluted by manipulation, deceit, or conniving. The child lives with a sense of dependency and trust. Under normal circumstances, the child trusts adults, and accepts that they have his/her welfare at heart. They have a natural tendency and ability to accept love, without feeling that there is any price-tag involved.

For the child, humility is an attitude, not just some thought-out decision. It is natural for the child to trust, to depend, to receive. A child has no problem with free gifts, and is totally uninhibited in reminding the rest of us that a birthday is on the horizon. This ability to accept as gift all that is given is central to our relationship with God. Pride would have us striving to earn or merit God's approval, and we strive to succeed through our own human endeavours. This does not work in God's plan of

Salvation. What God offers is pure free gift, and can never be earned. It requires humility to accept God's love, knowing that I never possibility could earn or merit it. The only limits to what God can do in our lives are the ones we ourselves set. If I receive a gift for my birthday, I will ensure that I remember your birthday, and that the gift I give you is reasonably equivalent in value. The child has no such problems. Jesus told us that he would not leave us orphans, and he then offered us his Father and his Mother. He stipulated, however, that this would not work unless we became like little children.

Humility, in a child, could hardly be called a virtue, as much as a simple reality. It is just a fact of life that the child instinctively depends on elders, and is able to live with many impossible things. If help is not offered, it is sought. Not only is it sought, it is also expected. As the years go on, we can forget one simple truth: the body grows older, but the person inside is always a child. Naturally, as I grow older, I become wiser and more competent. There is one area of my life, however, that never changes. Only God can do a God-thing. I never become so 'grown-up' that I can manage without God. Spiritual wisdom would indicate that dependency on God actually grows stronger, and more evident, as the years go by. To know my place before God, to be fully aware of the relationship between Creator and created – that is humility in practice.

*Anyone who welcomes a little child like this, on my behalf, is welcoming me. (Mt 18:5)*

God could have chosen to come among us in any shape or guise. He was joining us in our humanity, so it is very appropriate that he should come into this world as a new-born baby, just like any of the rest of us. This was the real thing, and not some sort of nativity play, or role-playing drama. He was a helpless, dependent infant, in every single way. 'He was like us in all things but sin.' (Heb 4:15) Even as a helpless baby, he was still God; he was God who had chosen not to cling to his divinity, but to experience human nature in all its weakness and limitations. In this helpless child resided the power of the infinite God. Herod was a powerful king with great earthly powers and, yet, he trembled before the potential of this new-born baby. I remember reading about a very wise old teacher who, upon entering a room to stand before a class, always began with a profound bow towards the pupils; a bow of great reverence and respect. He did this because he was profoundly conscious of the extraordinary potential that resided among that class. No one could know just what genius, or what profound blessings for the future dwelt within the hearts of that group of pupils. When Jesus looks at a child, he sees a soul of infinite beauty, and of infinite potential. That child is like a mirror of his Father to Jesus, a child that has been created in God's image and likeness. That is why he reserves very harsh words for anyone who would scandalise such an innocent one. 'If anyone should cause one of these little ones to stumble and fall, it would be better for him to be thrown into the depths of the sea, with a great millstone around his neck.' (Mt 18:6) Jesus strongly identifies with the sacred frailty of a little child. Because St Thérèse of Lisieux retained the heart of a child throughout her whole adult life, she is one of the most loved and revered saints in the church calendar.

There are two points that must be emphasised if we are to grasp the full implication of this promise. Jesus speaks of welcoming the child, and he adds 'on my behalf'. What do I believe he means by this? Hospitality is a wonderful expression of love. Jesus tells us that, when we welcome another, he takes that as done to him. He has a very definite preference for the weak and the marginalised and, if we develop that same characteristic, we become more and more aligned with the mind of Christ. We come to *see Christ in others*, when we begin to *be Christ to others*. Just imagine the privilege of actually being able to welcome Jesus. I know it can be difficult for the intellectual and the worldly-wise to grasp this simple concept. (Lk 10:21) I can be too intellectual to grasp many of the core messages of the gospels, but I cannot be too stupid. It is a very simple programme for very complicated people. Jesus came 'to do and to teach.' (Acts 1:1) He himself took the little children on his knee, and he hugged them. He must have had a real magnetic personality, because children can be very selective about who they choose to go to, or who they feel at ease with. One person could cause an uproar by approaching a child, if that child experiences some real or imaginary fear. Many of the pictures we see of Jesus with little children have one thing in common: the laughing face of Jesus is so significant. It is easy to imagine him throwing back his head, and really laughing out loud. Time and space set their own limitations on these reflections but, apart from mentioning it, I cannot hope to deal with the abomination of abortion. In saying this, I am not condemning people, because I cannot possibly look out through their eyes, and see things as they see it. What I refer to here is the blasé acceptance and promotion of abortion, without any attempt to treat it as a moral issue, or having anything to do with the attitude of Jesus towards the 'least of the brethren'.

*Let the little children come to me,*
*for the kingdom of heaven belongs to such as these. (Mt 19:14)*

The occasion that prompted Jesus to speak these words is very understandable. Jesus was in great demand, as 'everybody was looking for him'. (Jn 12:19) The apostles had assumed a role of responsibility for marshalling and controlling the crowds. There was much work to be done, and they were going to ensure that nothing got in the way of that work. They were so concerned about the urgent that they overlooked the important. Women and children didn't score very high in the social ladder of those days. To the apostles, they often became an irritant, and took up valuable time that could better be used in more fruitful work. They intervened when a group of mothers brought their babies to Jesus to have them blessed. This was too much for the apostles, and they moved in to prevent this happening. Imagine their surprise, if not their impatience, when Jesus rebuked them, undermined their self-assumed authority, and made it clear to all and sundry how he saw the situation. These children were priceless in his eyes. They were precious drops of love from heaven. They had something sacred, which was unseen by the apostles. In their innocence and dependency, they represented the very qualities he yearned to implant in the hearts of his followers. It appears that some of the children, of their own accord, wanted to come to him. He didn't ask his disciples to bring the children to him. The mothers had done that. There was something about

Jesus that attracted these children and, once they laid eyes on him, they reached out to him. Children have that very special spontaneity, and this must have delighted the heart of Jesus. He defended their right to have free access to him, and his directive to the apostles is unambiguous and direct.

In the kingdom of the world there exists a set of relative values. Not all are born equal, nor do all have equal rights. There is a class system, a caste system, and a very clear order of importance and prestige. In the kingdom of God there is a very definite set of values and priorities. Everybody is on this earth with equal right, and the most disabled person is on this earth with as much right as the greatest genius that ever lived. If there is any preferential treatment, it is reserved for the most deprived and marginalised. A child is as weak as they come. If a child is given priority in the kingdom, then every one of us should look again at our credentials. There is no room for social climbing, or for currying favour through one's own endeavours. Everything in the kingdom is total gift. The only requirement for the child is the very fact of its existence. God created, and God insists on taking personal care of the on-going creation. The whole story is one of the divine initiative, and God does not relinquish that right to any human being, irrespective of class, social standing, or intellect. God is Father, and those who retain the heart of a child are full members of his family. This is in direct contradiction to the values of this world, where political, military, or monetary might can guarantee anybody a larger slice of the cake. It is central to genuine spirituality that we see God's gifts, blessings, and work in us as complete and pure gift. The idea of the child is very powerful, because it represents someone who is incapable of earning or meriting through achievement, accomplishment, or endeavour. The child just has to be, to exist, to qualify for all of God's love, and for a special place within the kingdom. I cannot overstress the importance of accepting God's gifts and love as free and unconditional.

One way of thinking of this statement of Jesus would be something like this: A large group of adults are battling to get in the door of heaven. They have worked hard to get here, and each is laying down some special claim for preference or priority. There is a competitive spirit, as they vie with each other for a special place in the kingdom. 'Then the mother of James and John came to Jesus with her sons, and she knelt down to ask him a favour. Jesus said to her, "What do you want?" And she answered, "Here are my two sons. Grant that they may sit, one at your right and one at your left, when you are in your kingdom"'.' (Mt 20:20-21) In the words under review, Jesus turns such human ambition totally on its head, when he takes an innocent child, and tells his listeners that such a child will always receive priority within the kingdom. It is an ego-deflating statement, and that is exactly what is needed to enter the narrow door of the kingdom. (Lk 13:24) It is almost as if one has to become as small as possible, to stoop, and to unload all the surplus baggage, before entering that narrow door into his kingdom. The child has no such problem, and can enter in with complete ease.

> *Those who exalt themselves will be humbled,*
> *and those who humble themselves will be exalted. (Mt 23:12)*

A very simple, yet profound statement. Exalting oneself is a judgement, and it is a very wrong judgement. Giving myself false credentials, and undue merit is fraught with danger and difficulty. Pride, by its very nature, is highly destructive. All self-promotion is at the expense of others. It is like climbing on the back of others, so that I can have a better view than them. It is meeting my needs at the expense of others. Pride comes before a fall, and the fall is inevitable, sooner or later. The whole premise is based on a lie, and only the facts are friendly. Truth will out eventually, no matter how long I succeed in keeping up the façade. Only real gold lasts, and continues to glitter. The imitation gold watch will rust at the first shower of rain. On every level, there is something very distasteful about arrogance, haughtiness, and disdainful attitudes. Such people are propelling themselves towards a fall, and usually the onlookers are watching and waiting for the inevitable. The day of reckoning comes for all of us, and we cannot live the lie indefinitely. In the words quoted above, there is a road map and, like all maps, it gives me a choice which way to travel. Road signs and traffic signs don't make me do anything. They point a direction, or indicate a choice, and the rest is up to me. I can choose to ignore them, and head straight to destruction and death.

We are presented with two choices here. I can choose to exalt myself; or I can choose to humble myself. The choice is mine. I will choose the positive option as our topic for reflection, because that is the only one that deserves our attention, and our obedience. What does it mean to humble oneself? Humility is truth, and to humble myself is to accept the facts as they are. It is nothing more than accepting and living with reality. I own nothing. Everything I have is a gift, and one heart attack and it's all over. God has no favourites and he has no grandchildren. We are all children of God. God gives me nothing for myself. Every gift I have is for the service of others. He doesn't give me my gift of speech to go around talking to myself! Jesus tells us that 'The greatest in the kingdom are those who serve.' (Mt 20:26) He also speaks about how difficult it is for rich people to enter his kingdom. (Mt 19:23) There is nothing wrong with being rich, and it's no virtue to be poor. The problem with being rich is that such a person can easily assume a more important place among his fellows, and when riches lead us into such mistaken attitudes, they become a very negative influence. The riches can begin to own the owner. Jesus speaks of unburdening, of discarding, of letting go, of dependency, when he speaks of his kingdom. He speaks of a child being the ideal candidate (Mt 18:4), and he speaks of the need to remove all the burdens from a camel's back before it can pass through the narrow door into his kingdom. (Lk 13:24) There is a simplicity in being humble, and a wonderful freedom of living in the truth, and with the truth. When God speaks about having no other gods but him (Lev 23:32), he is certainly not confining himself to gods made of silver or bronze. The most frequent god on display today is some human being, who has assumed or has had bestowed a status away beyond his deserts or his human status. Hero-worshipping is quite a passing phenomenon, and time shows us all as having feet of clay. Humility is made of much sterner stuff.

Humility is a gift, and it's not something I can cultivate. It's not so much my words and actions, as an attitude of heart that expresses itself through my words and actions. This is purely the work of the Holy Spirit. Jesus came to serve (Lk 22:27), and he did not cling to his divinity, but became 'like us in everything but sin'. (Heb 4:15) To come to a deeper understanding of humility, I need look no further than Jesus. He encountered the most abject and rejected elements in his society, and he raised them up and gave them dignity. He caused great shock and scandal to the religious leaders of his days through the company he kept. One can easily imagine the shock in their voices when they said that 'He meets sinners, and even eats with them.' (Mt 9:11) There is a great paradox involved in humility. It requires real greatness to put others before oneself. In his great manifesto (Beatitudes), Jesus presents very clear priorities to his followers. 'Blessed are the poor in spirit, theirs is the kingdom of heaven. Blessed are the gentle; they shall possess the earth.' (Mt 5:3, 5) To pray for, to sincerely desire, to acquire, and to practise humility is the surest road to happiness now, and for all eternity.

### God blesses those whose hearts are pure, for they will see God. (Mt 5:8)

There is grave concern in today's world about the level of pollution that is effecting our planet. The environmentalists must feel that theirs are voices shouting in the wilderness. The greatest concern is the lack of international co-operation to stop the rot. Big business, greed, competition, and marketing are the driving forces, and there seems to be little regard for the kind of world future generations will inherit. Most drinking water comes from bottles, and it is becoming more difficult to get food that is free from toxins of one kind or another. In this promise, Jesus speaks of purity of heart, of hearts that are free from pollution, corruption, and deceit. There has never been a bullet fired, or a bomb planted that did not begin within the heart of some individual. The human heart can be a fountain of wonderful good, or a source of very destructive evil. 'Wash the evil from your heart, so that you may be saved.' (Jer 4:14) 'What comes out of a person is what can make him unclean, for evil designs come out of the heart: theft, murder, adultery, jealousy, greed, maliciousness, deceit, indecency, slander, pride, and folly. All these evil things come from within and make a person unclean.' (Mk 7:20-23) 'From the abundance of the heart the mouth speaks.' (Mt 12:34)

'My strength is as the strength of ten, because my heart is pure.'
What a wonderful blessing it is to have a heart that is pure, and
free from all the ugliness that can accumulate there. No wonder
Jesus points to the innocence of children as being the ideal for
people in his kingdom. Satan cannot have any part in the kingdom of God and, therefore, the heart must be exorcised of all deceit and impurities if it is to belong in that kingdom.

The pure of heart are single-minded, uncomplicated, and
truthful. They could never be devious, manipulative, cunning,
or deceitful. Their 'yes' is 'yes', and their 'no' is 'no'. They are
genuine, sincere, and authentic. They can be depended on, and
to have such a person as a friend is to have found a treasure.
They are simple people, in the very best meaning of that word.
They would find it difficult to survive in politics or public life,
but many of them do, despite the pressures to compromise and
make shady deals. Jesus said that such people will/can see God,
and that is not surprising. Because they are genuine themselves,
without hidden agendas, they tend to see the very best in others.
The day I feel good about me, I think you're OK too! On the
other hand, God help you when I'm not too happy with myself!
A man walks in from work, and draws a kick on the dog! The
poor dog did nothing wrong, but the man's anger has to get out
someway! The pure of heart are the ones who can live with
themselves and, because of that, they are able to live with others.

God is to be seen in all things good and beautiful, and the
pure of heart are attracted to such things. They make excellent
company, because there's no hidden agenda, and they're not
into taking offence, harbouring resentments, or bearing grudges.
They are uncomplicated in their sincerity and warmth, and are
predictable in their dependability and loyalty. Jesus tells us that
God blesses such people, and that blessing is so obvious. They
are blessed in themselves, and are a great source of blessing for
others. If they can see God, then they are able to overlook so
much of the pettiness, ugliness, and small-mindedness that be-
devil the lives of so many. Pope John XXIII set himself the guidelines of seeing everything, overlooking most, and correcting a
little. Such people have been touched by God, just as Jesus
touched the eyes of the blind, and restored their sight. They are
clear-sighted people, who are not looking at the world through

jaundiced glasses, but see things as they are. Some people see only what they want to see, and can be very short-sighted when it suits them. The pure of heart are authentic and, when I am authentic, I mediate life to those around me. The words of this promise say that the pure of heart will see God. I have chosen to reflect on them as people who already see God, through the purity and clarity of their vision.

# Forentiveness

*If you forgive anyone's sins, they are forgiven.*
*If you refuse to forgive them, they are not forgiven. (Jn 20:23)*

When I first came across this promise many years ago, I was given to understand that it had to do with Jesus instituting the Sacrament of Confession, or Reconciliation as we now call it. I now know this to be untrue. I understand this sentence to refer to any of us who read it. This, in effect, gives it a much more serious content, and has very real implications for all of us. I understand this to mean exactly what it says. If I am the one who is hurt, then I am the member of the body through whom the hurt came. Therefore, it is through me that the forgiveness must go, if that situation is to be rectified. That can be quite disturbing if I interpret it this way. It means that I can actually block God's forgiveness to another person. Let me explain further. If I hurt someone, it is not enough to tell God that I'm sorry. I don't think God wants me to tell him that I love him, praise him, thank him, or I'm sorry, unless the people in my life hear it first. 'Whatever you do to the least of these my brothers, I take as being done to me.' (Mt 25:40) The repercussions of this are frightening if I follow it to its logical conclusion. Does it mean that someone, long deceased, is still unfree, because forgiveness never came from me to that person? Obviously, I don't know, but I'm inclined to consider this as a possibility. This must surely raise the bar in the whole forgiveness stakes and, to understand Jesus correctly, one must give serious consideration to the whole area of forgiveness. For a generation like mine, which was reared on weekly confession, there was never a great deal of emphasis on a simple statement of Jesus, 'If you forgive those who sin against you, your heavenly Father will forgive you.' (Mt 6:14)

If what I'm suggesting is actually true, then the church must take greater responsibility for its teaching in the whole question of forgiveness. Even as he was dying on the cross, Jesus was praying for those who were killing him. (Lk 23:34) I don't think we can tip-toe around this one, no matter how uncomfortable it may make us. To err is human, to forgive is divine. I am not at all implying that it is easy to forgive. Some people have been very seriously abused, damaged, and traumatised. The effects of their suffering will last throughout their lives. There is no question that they will ever forget what happened to them. And here I must make a very important distinction. It is easy to confuse forgiveness with forgetting. There is no connection between them, and if I confuse these concepts, I'll have serious problems with forgiveness. I don't have any switches or erase buttons in my brain, and I cannot control the faculty of memory. Let us isolate the whole area of forgiveness for a moment, and leave forgetting to one side. I have to begin somewhere. I suggest that this should be in the area of praying for the person who offended me. This may raise the hackles. Easy does it! At first, the words may choke me, and I may hope that God is not listening. Maybe I should back off a little, and start further back. How about asking for the grace to be able to pray for the other person? This should be much easier. At least I would like to be able to forgive, even if I am convinced that I cannot. Hold on to that idea. Don't let go, even if it seems that you are making no progress whatever. By continuing to open my heart to the possibility of being able to forgive some day, I have every right to expect God to come to the rescue, to meet me more than half-way on this one. I am absolutely certain, if I hang in there, slowly but surely, I will find a greater willingness to forgive and, eventually, I will find myself praying for that person. 'To forgive is divine.' Once I continue the praying, I will discover a healing of the hurts. This, of course, will be gradual, but noticeable. Eventually, I will discover a desire within me to let go of the whole thing, and put it all behind me. Once again, I stress that this will take time. The hurt may have continued over a period of time, and I shouldn't expect the forgiveness and healing to be instantaneous. Remember we left the whole idea of forgetting to one side? Let's return to that now, for a few moments. I will never forget but, as the healing progresses, the memories will be less painful. The process of healing has begun and not only are you freeing someone else, you are also freeing yourself. If you have a resentment against another person, it's as if you were drinking poison and expecting the other person to die. I believe that one of the many reasons why

Jesus lays so much emphasis on forgiveness is that it can free
and liberate so many people. Unforgiveness is an unrelenting
bondage.

> *There is forgiveness of sins for all who turn to me.*
> *(Lk 24:47)*

This promise must be seen within the overall mission of Jesus. In
other words, it's not just a bright idea he plucked out of the air
one day, when he was feeling good about the world. This is from
the very core of his message. He came to call sinners. If they
were called, they must have been called somewhere – they were
called to come to him. If they were called to come to him, it must
have been for a purpose – they were called to seek forgiveness
for their sins. We've all heard of someone saying that things
were so desperate that 'I didn't know where to turn to'; in other
words, I could see no exit, or way out of this dilemma. Jesus actually calls himself The Way. (Jn 14:6) In this simple statement
he declares a clear and unconditional policy: anyone who comes
to him will receive forgiveness of their sins. There is no contradiction between the thought that Jesus came looking for sinners,
and sinners having to turn to him. He is certainly looking for
sinners, of course, but even when he finds them, he is powerless
to help until they turn to him and accept his offer.

What exactly is meant by 'forgiveness of sins'? Sin is a lie,
and it continues the disobedience and disbelief of the garden. It
is listening to a voice that is not God's, and coming under a different influence. When Adam and Eve fell for the lie in the garden they came under new management, as it were, and could no
longer 'walk with God in the cool of the evenings'. Sin continues
to alienate us from God, to take over the place of God in our
heart, and to sell us empty promises. Forgiveness of sin means
to unravel and expose all the lies, to rescue us from the bondage
of addiction, compulsion, or slavery, and to set our feet back on
the road of peace again. Forgiveness of sin is an extraordinary
act of love, because sin was something we had freely chosen,
and our choice was to turn away from God, in the pursuit of
some selfish interest. To turn back to God is to admit that we
were wrong. It is a turning back to the truth. When Adam and

Eve sinned, all they had to do was to tell God what they had done. Instead of doing that, Adam blamed Eve, and Eve blamed the devil, and God could do nothing for/with them. In a way, we have done much the same since then. There would never be a war if somebody somewhere was only willing to say, 'I'm sorry. I was wrong.' It seems very simple, and it really is very simple. If a couple knelt down before me to get married, and they hadn't a lot of sense, or a lot of money(!), I would go ahead with the wedding if I thought they had enough forgiveness in their hearts; because, if they have, their love will survive. 'How often should I forgive my brother?' Peter asked Jesus. 'Seven times seven?' 'Seventy times seven,' was Jesus' reply. (Mt 18:21-22) Anyone who turns to Jesus is brought straight back to the garden, and to the bosom of the Father's love. Jesus tells us that the Father is always on the lookout for sinners, and once they appear on the horizon, he runs to meet them, hug them, and welcome them home. (Lk 15:20) If Jesus was on this earth for three minutes, instead of thirty-three years, I think he could have given us the core message of the gospels in the story of the Prodigal Son. That, in effect, is the gospel encapsulated. 'Come back to me with all your heart. Don't let fear keep us apart. Long have I waited for your coming home to me, and living deep within my love.' Jesus assures us that, even if we've got pig's food all over our faces, there's a big welcome awaiting us once we turn to come home. Once again I point out that this forgiveness of sins is offered to all who turn to Jesus. Just before he died on the cross, we see a wonderful example of this in practice. On one of the crosses hung a man who may never have said a prayer in his life. His life had come to a bad end and, in his own opinion, deservedly so. Just before he died, he turned to Jesus and asked for help, and he was offered heaven right there. (Lk 23:42-43) This is quite a dramatic and convincing demonstration of the words of Jesus' promise.

> *If you forgive those who sin against you,*
> *your heavenly Father will forgive you. (Mt 6:14)*

If Jesus had died in any other way, e.g. falling out of the boat and drowning, the cross would still be a powerful sign of a meaningful religion. The cross represents the strong and central relationship between the vertical and the horizontal. The vertical represents God and me, while the horizontal represents me and others. The balance between the two is thus: what comes from God to me must go sideways to those around me, or it ceases to come from God. The more forgiveness I give to those around me, the more forgiveness flows from God to me. If I do not forgive, I am not forgiven. It's as simple as that. In the one simple prayer Jesus taught us, we ask God to forgive us our sins, as we forgive those who sin against us. (Lk 11:4) We are backing ourselves into a corner here, because we are clearly stating the conditions under which we ask for forgiveness. I think of this as more common sense than cleverness on God's part. It makes sense, and it stands to reason that there should be a direct link between how we treat others, and how we want God to treat us. For those of us brought up on confession, this simple truth may have lost its impact. If I forgive, I am forgiven – whether I go to confession or not. If I wrote out every sin I ever committed, illustrated it with diagrams(!), translated the lot into several languages, and then went to confession to the pope in any language, not one of my sins are forgiven if I have unforgiveness in my heart towards another human being. There is absolutely no way around this simple diktat, and I am left with no choice. I am happy about this because, knowing the human mind as I do, we tend to look for exit clauses, or escape hatches, when the net begins to close in on us. If I want forgiveness, I am left in no doubt what I should do to receive it.

When I stress how simple all of this is, I am not at all implying that it is ever easy. Far from it. We all have a strong desire to be proven right, to be vindicated, to appear as the victim rather than the perpetrator. Our pride is at stake here. There is a tendency to 'milk' the role of victim for as long as possible, because it gives us a certain control over another. With human resources alone, I can never become a forgiving person. This is very definitely the work of the Spirit within, and forgiveness is one of the special gifts of the Spirit. People who possess a forgiving spirit give real witness to the presence of God's Spirit within them. Indeed, I would suggest that it is one of the surest signs that I have God's Spirit because, of myself, I just don't have what it takes. Pride is very demanding, and always wants its own way. It always demands its pound of flesh. Even if, by human effort, I succeed in burying the hatchet, it is very likely that I mark the spot, ready to dig it up at very short notice.

I ask myself: 'Do I want to have my sins forgiven?' Obviously I do. Then I am faced with a decision. I have no other choice than to forgive others, and there's no way around that. I pray for the gift of forgiveness. I pray for those who have hurt me. This is being proactive, because this just doesn't happen of itself. Forgiveness of others is something to which I must bring my full attention and commitment. On human instincts alone, I could be wholeheartedly committed to getting even, to reaping revenge, to settling the score. When I decide to forgive, I must follow through on that with zeal and enthusiasm. Forgiveness is not just 'forgetting about it', letting bygones be bygones, letting sleeping dogs lie. It is something very positive, very definite, and very active. My forgiveness is not contingent on the other person seeking forgiveness through an apology. I do not have to make a song and dance out of my forgiveness. It may be good, and, indeed, necessary, to let the other person know that I have forgiven, but this is not always necessary. In fact, the other person may be blissfully unaware of having hurt me, in the first place. Once I am sure that, in my heart, I have actually forgiven the other, there is no need for any follow-through, unless that person comes to me. Usually life will provide me with opportunities to demonstrate through attitude and action that all is well, and that all is forgiven. In doing this, I have freed the other person and, in the process, I have freed myself.

*When you are praying, first forgive anyone you are holding a grudge against, so that your Father in heaven will forgive your sins too. (Mk 11:26)*

For whatever reason, with all the talks I heard, and all the books I've read on prayer, this particular approach never came through too clearly. It makes sense as I look at it, but I cannot remember it ever playing a large part in my own prayer. I see now that this was a serious oversight on my part. This promise is different from the previous one in several ways. The most obvious one, of course, is that forgiveness is presented as a prior condition for any authentic prayer. In a previous promise, I wrote about praying for the grace to forgive another. In that case, of course, forgiveness is not yet present, but is not far away, because of the subject of my prayer. To simplify things, I want to deal with this promise as Jesus telling us that we must rid our hearts of unforgiveness before we can pray with any kind of sincerity. The other side of that coin is, 'When you bring your gifts to the altar, and there you remember that someone has something against you, leave your gifts before the altar, go and be reconciled with that person, and then come and offer your gifts.' (Mt 5:23-24) This forgiveness works both ways when it comes to prayer. If prayer is a raising of my mind and heart to God, how can this be genuine if my heart if filled with resentment towards another, or if someone else is hurting because of my words or actions?

It is important to clarify what I mean by prayer. I am not thinking of saying prayers. I could teach a parrot to say a prayer, but I could never teach a parrot to pray. Prayer is not so much a question of me talking to God who doesn't hear, as God talking to me who won't listen. Real prayer can be very risky, because I may hear things I'd prefer not to hear. It is much safer to keep talking, so that God doesn't get a word in edgeways. Jesus came to comfort the afflicted, but he also came to afflict the comfortable! I would suggest that, when I put myself in a situation of prayer, the Spirit makes use of the opportunity to remind me of certain things that should be attended to first. Indeed, I would go so far as to say that this, in itself, is very much part of what prayer involves. Once I present myself before the Lord, I must be willing to listen to whatever he wishes to tell me; indeed, to give this a much higher priority than anything I might want to say to him. Thus, forgiveness is not an addendum to prayer, but is central to it. Prayer changes things. Prayer is a journey along the road to honesty, integrity, and truth. It is a cleansing process, something that purifies and frees the heart. The organ God gave me with which to pray is my heart, not my tongue. If my heart is not praying, then my tongue is wasting its time. When I come before God, I must be willing to open out the canvas of my life, right out to the very edges. No hiding, no denying, no excusing. Allowing God see what he sees. It has to be one of the most

important encounters possible for a human being. Adam, blamed
Eve, and Eve blamed the devil! The greatest lies I tell in life are
the ones I tell myself. It is only when I can become totally honest
with you and with others, that I can hope to become honest with
myself. To bring God into that formula faces us with a much
more serious situation. God knows me through and through. 'O
Lord, you know me; you have scrutinised me. You know when I
sit and when I rise; from far away you discern my thoughts. You
observe my activities and times of rest; you are familiar with all
my ways. Before a word is formed in my mouth, you know it entirely. O Lord, you are there if I ascend to the heavens; you are
there if I descend to the depths. If I ride on the wings of the
dawn, and settle on the far side of the sea, even there your hand
will guide me, and your right hand will hold me safely.' (Ps 139)
The more I reflect on this promise the more obvious and logical
its implications appear. I said at the beginning that I had never
been too aware of this particular condition for prayer, so I'm
grateful that I've had this opportunity to look at the whole thing
again, and add a very definite and clear guideline to my attitude
when I next come before the Lord.

### *I have come to call sinners,*
### *not those who think they are good enough. (Mk 2:17)*

Jesus came with a mission, and he never had any doubt what
that mission was. He came in obedience to the Father, to carry
out the Father's will in everything he did and said. It is obvious
then, that the Father sent him to seek us out, and to invite us to
come back to the garden. It is clear that he foresaw one of the
major problems, i.e. those who considered themselves good
enough would neither listen to, nor accept him. Religion is external, it's what we do; it's about rules and regulations, and it's
about control. Spirituality is internal, it's what God does in us,
and it's about surrender. Jesus found it almost impossible to
convert religious people, and it was they who eventually
brought about his death. They were highly indignant that he
should suggest that they had need for conversion. He had no
problem with the outcasts, the broken, and the public sinners.
They flocked to him, and listened to his every word. Obviously,

there is none of us good enough, so Jesus referred to those who *think* they are good enough. Spiritual pride is the most destructive form of pride. Ordinary pride, if there could be such a thing, is placing myself above and ahead of others. Spiritual pride can have me placing myself above God, and having him beholding to me for being so good. The Pharisee stood up in the Temple, and told God what a good person he was. (Lk 18:11-13) Instead of 'Praise the Lord', his prayer was 'Praise me, Lord'! What an abomination such an attitude must appear in the eyes of God. I remember, in the innocence of youth, how I thought of Lucifer or Adam and Eve daring to assume the place or privilege of God. Life has shown me that religious people can easily do the same, while not been so evident, in such a travesty of truth.

Humility is to know my place before God. He is the Creator, I am the creature, the work of his hands. Jesus is the Saviour, the Redeemer; I am the sinner, the one caught in bondage to sin and human weakness. We are all sinners, and Jesus came to call all of us. However, only those who know and believe they are sinners will answer his call. He compares himself to a shepherd who knows his sheep, and they know his voice. (Jn 10:3) While visiting in the Holy Land, I witnessed this in practice. At a particular watering hole a few shepherds with all their sheep had gathered. After a while, one of the shepherds called out some word, and proceeded to walk away. Immediately certain sheep began running out of the group, and they formed a single line behind him, as they headed off across the sand dunes.

To make this promise more practical, I must listen with my heart to assure myself that I actually do hear his call. I know I am a sinner, of course, but do I hear the voice of the Saviour? Jesus said that the Spirit would convict us of sin. (Jn 16:8) It is the Spirit of truth that reminds us of the need for conversion, and the call to come to Jesus as Saviour. 'The Spirit will tell you all about me' says Jesus. (Jn 14:17) When the Spirit is active within us, we will always hear the call to conversion. There are two parts in our salvation: Jesus calling us as sinners, and our response to that call. 'Many are called ... but few choose to answer the call.' (Mt 22:14) I must scour my heart to ensure beyond all doubt that there are no areas which my spiritual pride may have convinced me are in good shape, and need not be brought to

Jesus. Rather than bring areas of my life to Jesus, I would suggest it is much safer to invite Jesus into our hearts, and ask him
to rid the temple of anything there that is not of him. I allow him
full access to all that I am, and I leave all decisions regarding my
need for conversion to him. I have no reason to trust myself, and
I can be quite selective in what I myself might come up with.
Let's just take these simple words as Jesus intended them. He
came looking for people like us; people who are only too deeply
aware of our need for a Saviour; people who, of themselves,
would be nothing better than sheep without a shepherd, or a
flotilla of boats on a stormy sea, without sails, rudders, or life-
jackets.

# Faith

*Blessed are those who have not seen, and yet believe.*
*(Jn 20:29)*

An atheist would believe if I could show the evidence and present the facts in such a way that they could not be denied. There would be little value in faith that is based on irrefutable proofs. John and Mary get married, and there would be little faith required if somehow I could give them proof that this is going to work. As I am being wheeled down into an operation theatre, it is not possible to give me any certain guarantee that this is going to work, and there won't be any complications, no matter how simple the surgery may be. Throughout our lives we have to act more in hope than with certainties. Even to the simple case of buying a car: it could be a 'lemon', or it could be trouble-free for years. If I needed the proof first, I would never do anything. This applies particularly to my dealings with God. Death can still hold its fears for the best of us. We are venturing into the unknown, and sometimes we find ourselves clinging to hope by our finger nails. The merit of our faith and hope is in the trust that it calls for. Don't ask me to trust God until you have convinced me that God really cares for me, and has my welfare at heart. There are people to whom I can pour out my heart, because I trust them to treat that confidence with respect and reverence. There are people in whom I would never confide, because I have no reason to trust them. There are incidents in the gospel that absolutely amaze me. How could that little woman approach Jesus in the certain knowledge that if she touched but the hem of his garment she would be healed? (Mk 5:25-33) How was the centurion able to believe that if Jesus said but the word his servant would be healed? (Lk 7:2) I could continue with many such questions. The only opinion I can come up with was that these people saw something very special in Jesus, and they acted on what they saw. Their vision opened up infinite possibilities, and this was greatly helped by their own personal sense of powerlessness. 'I can't, but he can' seems to have been their heart-felt conclusion. The combination of their own helplessness and their conviction of his innate power for good were the two ingredients that brought about the miracle.

Faith is a journey. At Bethlehem, the shepherds were told the message by angels, which is fairly reliable authority, and yet they decided to 'go to Bethlehem to see these things for ourselves'. (Lk 2:15) The woman at the well brought out all her friends to meet Jesus. At the end of the story, they turned to the woman and said to her, 'Now we believe, but not because you told us, but because we have seen for ourselves.' (Jn 5:42) Both groups began with information, but without proof. They acted on the information, and ended up with the proof. That is what I mean when I say that the atheist would require the proof first. There is something beautiful about faith because, of necessity, it must involve love at some level. Faith is a response to love, and the more I am convinced of God's love, the more ready I am to trust him. St Thérèse of Lisieux was so convinced of God's love that she trusted him totally in all things. Towards the end of her life, when she was in the throes of darkness, and there was absolutely no proof or evidence that God even existed, her stubborn clinging to the belief that he still was watching over her brought her through, when she could easily have yielded to despair. This is called 'blind faith', and this is what Jesus has in mind in the words of this promise. Faith is not knowledge, like knowing that Jesus is God. Satan knows that. At best, this can be nothing better than mental assent. Real faith is in my feet, as I step out to do things that my head could never suggest. At the beginning, as he stepped over the side of the boat (Mt 14-29), Peter was acting on blind faith, and while he kept his eyes fixed on Jesus, he was able to walk on the water. Unfortunately, he turned his attention to the wind and the waves, and he lost his nerve and began to sink.

I learned to walk by walking, and to talk by talking. I learn to trust by trusting. Every time I step out in faith, my faith grows a little. The action comes first, and the proof will follow. In this is my growth. Faith implies action, and it grows through action. This promise of Jesus is a very simple invitation to take him at his word and, like Peter, to step over the side of the boat; but, unlike Peter to keep our eyes fixed on Jesus, so that my faith can grow through experiencing his fidelity to his promises, and the reliability of his word. 'Heaven and earth will pass away before my word shall pass away.' (Mt 5:18)

> *If you have faith as small as a mustard seed,*
> *you could say to this mountain 'Move', and it would move.*
> *(Mt 17:20)*

I remember the first time I saw a mustard seed. It was in the Garden of Gethsemane, of all places. The seeds were very black, and really tiny. There was no way I could pick up one with my fingers, so the only way I could hold them was to pick up some with a piece of cellotape, and paste them inside the cover of my Bible. I remember being profoundly impressed as I looked at the mustard trees that had been there since the time of Christ, and my mind couldn't possibly hope to comprehend how such a tree could possibility come from such a tiny seed. Jesus was such a superb teacher. He could / would point to something as he spoke of it, and be quite dramatic in his presentation. He used images that were familiar to them all. They would have known what a grain of mustard seed was like, and how tiny it was. The contrast here is very powerful. Jesus can hold a grain of mustard seed in his hand, and it is so tiny that his listeners take his word for it, because there's no way they could see. On the other hand, Jesus points to a mountain in full view of all, and he makes a direct connection that must have grabbed everybody's attention. There is no way they could imagine the mountain moving, no matter what force or power was exercised (long before the time of hydrogen or nuclear bombs). This was surely an attention-getter, and one way to focus attention fully on the whole question of faith.

There is great power in faith. That is the content of Jesus' message. Indeed, I would go so far as to say there's infinite power in faith. God works in and through faith, and therefore the possibilities are infinite. Just as the little woman drew healing from Jesus by touching the hem of his garment (Mk 5:25), so we can draw everything from God's heart through our trust and faith.

What is faith, and in whom is it placed? The second part of

the question is the most important part. My faith is in a God of infinite love, who created me, and who goes guarantor for me in everything that is needed to live a full life, and to share that life for eternity. My faith is in a God who is infinitely dependable, and completely reliable, and whose word is inviolable. 'God makes us holy by means of faith in Jesus Christ, and that is applied to all who believe, without distinction of persons. Because all sinned and all fall short of the glory of God; and all are graciously forgiven and made holy through the redemption effected in Jesus Christ. For God had given him to be the victim who, by his blood, obtains our forgiveness, and this is a matter of faith ... God makes us righteous and holy through faith in Jesus Christ.' (Rom 3:22-26) It can help if we look at things this way: look at what Jesus has already done. We are not being sold a pig in a poke here. Follow his journey all the way to Calvary, and to Easter. Then continue to reflect on the legacy he left, and on the presence, power, gifts, and activity of the Spirit. I can then ask myself if this person is worthy of my trust. Another translation of the above quote is, 'In this is our salvation, his blood and our faith.' Our salvation is based on what Jesus has done, and how I respond to that. My faith grows through the exercising of that faith, just as I learned to walk or talk. The more I act out of faith, the more I involve the Lord in everything I do and say, the stronger that faith becomes, until it becomes second nature to me. There comes a time when I would never venture into any situation without consulting him, and involving the power, presence, and action of his Spirit. The power of the Spirit is as vital to my spiritual life as breath is to my body. If I stop breathing I die. It's as simple as that.

The evolution of the grain of mustard seed is a very slow process, but it is one that continues day in, day out. 'A man scatters seed upon the soil. Whether he is asleep or awake, be it day or night, the seed sprouts and grows, he knows not how. The soil produces of itself; first the blade, then the ear, then the full grain in the ear.' (Mk 4:26-28) 'Imagine a person who has taken a mustard seed and planted it in his garden. The seed has grown, and becomes like a small tree, so that the birds of the air shelter in its branches.' (Lk 13:19) Growing in faith is not something I can personally control or effect. It is the action of God's Spirit

within. With the Spirit come the gifts, and it is the gifts that produce the fruit. Jesus came across a tree with green leaves on it,
but no fruit, and he cursed the tree, so that it withered. (Mt
21:19) Faith is both a gift and a virtue. The gift of faith is pure gift
from the Spirit, and when I exercise it, it produces fruit, which
results from my use of the gift. The choice is mine. I can choose
to exercise the gift and produce abundant fruit. I can develop the
gift, and it can grow within it, like yeast in the dough, until the
whole mix is effected by it. There is no limit to the effect of this
faith, and this is highlighted by Jesus who speaks of even up-
rooting a whole mountain, and casting it into the sea. This, of
course, is neither necessary nor desirable, but is a powerful way of
stressing the extraordinary power that is placed at out disposal.

### *Blessed are they who hear the word of God and keep it.*
### *(Lk 11:28)*

By the very fact of me writing this, and you, gentle reader, reading this, we both can claim to have heard the word of God in
many ways, and on many occasions. The Pharisees also heard
the word of God, and we can be sure that Satan listened to every
word that Jesus spoke. Jesus had many things to say about listening to his word. 'They who come from God listen to God's
words.' (Jn 8:47) 'This people will listen and listen, but not understand.' (Mt 13:14) 'Be careful then how you listen.' (Lk 8:18)
'Why do you not understand my message? It is because you cannot bear to listen.' (Jn 8:43) We are all familiar with people who,
after speaking to them for some time, turn to us and ask, 'Sorry,
what did you say?'! They hadn't heard a word we said. The
words quoted above were spoken about Mary, Jesus's mother.
Someone from the crowd spoke of how really blessed she was to
have borne and nurtured such as he. Jesus added to that comment with much higher acclaim. He spoke of his mother as
someone who heard the word of God, and held on to it. 'As for
Mary, she treasured all these words, and continually pondered
them in her heart.' (Lk 2:19) The word of God is like a seed that is
sown in our souls. One of Jesus' most powerful parables is the
one of the sower that went out to sow his seed. (Lk 8:5-8) The
man scattered the seed with prodigal generosity, without any

thought to whether it grew or not. His job was to sow, and it was up to the soil whether it grew or not. When Jesus sent his disciples to preach the good news of the kingdom (Lk 10:1-16), they were to *preach* the news, and leave it to the listeners whether they chose to accept it or not. If they refused to listen, the disciples were to shake the dust of that town from their feet, and move on elsewhere.

There are two very important verbs in this promise. The first is *hear*, and the second is *keep*. Obviously, I have to hear the word before I can keep it. Another important phrase is the word of God. The word of God is not a word, as in a dictionary. It is a message, as in 'Have you had any word from John yet?' I hear the message, and this implies that it received my attention, and entered both my head and my heart. To hear, in this case, has more to do with attitude of heart than with ability to hear. I could hear the words, but not the message. Words, of themselves, have very little meaning. It's the spirit in the words that makes all the difference. I meet people who ask me how I am, and I don't go into any great detail in my reply, because I'm not convinced that they really are anxious to know! On the other hand, I can meet someone who asks me how I am, and I reply at some length, because I sense a spirit of concern in their words. I could tell you some painful truths that it may not be easy for you to hear but, because the words are spoken in love, you listen to me and accept what I say. Alternatively, I could say the same things to you and hurt you deeply, because the words are coming across as an attack on you. Hearing the word of God is to absorb the Spirit that is in that word. It is a way of being touched by the Spirit. 'Say but the word, and my servant shall be healed.' (Mt 8:8) 'At your word I will let down the net.' (Lk 5:5) There is a power in the word of God, and to hear that word is to be empowered and healed. To keep that word is to treasure it, to ponder it, to cherish it, and to allow it take root within my heart. The word of God is like the seed sown by the man who went out to sow the seed. 'The seed is the word of God.' (Lk 8:11) To keep that word is the surest way of ensuring that the word grows within me. Jesus is the Word of God and, in Mary, that Word became flesh. (Jn 1:14) One can only wonder at the perfect state of Mary's heart, where the word of God was sure to find good soil, and where that word would surely produce abundant harvest. No wonder Jesus spoke these words about his mother, who did in such a perfect way what each of us is called to do.

> *I assure you, if you have faith, and don't doubt, you can do things like this (withered tree), and much more. (Mt 21:21)*

As I read these words, I find myself arguing a little point of detail, even if only to reassure myself. I can understand the need for faith, but I can also allow for the occasional doubts. I don't see any great contradictions, because I believe that doubts can often accompany faith. Let me explain. My focus is on Jesus, and on his promises, and I place everything in his hands. To experience the occasional niggling doubt does not mean that I have taken anything back from him. Once I become aware of the doubt I dispel it and, in doing so, my faith continues to grow. In practice, I can never claim to have faith that is completely devoid of doubts. When the doubts surface, I choose the path of faith, and there's no harm done. If the doubts take over, I am placing great obstacles in the way of the Lord working in, for, and through me. The doubts of which I have spoken at the beginning of this reflection are not those that replace or displace faith. My faith is always there, and it is strong enough to override all little anxieties and concerns about the outcome. If I speak of faith as a gift of the Spirit then, of course, there are no doubts, because faith is pure gift in this case. If, however, I speak of faith as a virtue, then it can be quite a long haul before my faith becomes strong enough to exclude all possibility of doubt. As a gift of the Spirit, faith is all-powerful and can do anything; while, as a virtue that I practise, and in which I grow, it will pass through many a stormy sea. Peter could step over the side on the boat in a spontaneous act of trust (Mt 14:29), and start walking on water. That was OK until Peter himself took over, through his awareness of the human danger involved. His own personal faith was insufficient to keep him afloat, and Jesus had to reach out to take his hand, and hold him up. I like to think that Jesus smiled at Peter this time, because Peter was so good that he just rushed into things, with all the goodwill in the world, without any great insight into where the power came from! He just wanted to get to Jesus; but, like many of poor Peter's good intentions, it came unstuck.

The context of this promise is when Jesus cursed the tree that had no fruit, and it withered. The apostles expressed amazement at this, and Jesus spoke this promise in reply. It's not a question that Jesus wanted them or anyone else to go around cursing and withering trees. He was just using the tree as an example, telling them that they could do much greater things than that. I remember when I heard this first that I was surprised at such a possibility. I wouldn't dare think of any of us doing greater things than Jesus did. I think I understand now what Jesus meant by this. He himself was engaged in a battle with the forces of evil. Satan was the prince of this world. (Jn 16:11) Satan offered Jesus all the kingdoms of this world if Jesus would adore him (Lk 4:6), because they were Satan's to give. However, when Jesus has completed his mission on earth, and the Spirit has come to complete his work, the grip of Satan will be released, and God's power will flow freely to his people. It is then that they will be able to do signs and miracles in his name, because he will have passed on all of his power and authority to them. From the very beginning, the Pentecost Church witnessed this new power at work and, indeed, these miracles would be the evidence of all those who believed in him. (Mk 16:17-18) He spoke to his apostles about receiving power from on high, and thus they would become his witnesses to the very ends of the earth. (Acts 1:8) They would receive the power, but they must also accept the responsibilities that go with such power. Going forth with this power, Jesus, through them, would become Lord in his kingdom and his victory over the evil one would be preached to the ends of the earth. One of the greatest witnesses, of course, would be his victory over death through his resurrection. Death entered the world through the work of Satan, as did sin and sickness, which were not part of God's creation. Their witness would be one of the triumph of good over evil, and the Spirit working through them would effect even greater signs and miracles than were witnessed in the ministry of Jesus.

# Resurrection

*I am the resurrection and the life.*
*(Jn 11:25)*

When God created, he looked at each item and said 'It is good.' (Gen 1:25) There were three 'baddies' that entered into that creation, through original sin, and they were sin, sickness, and death. Jesus tells a story about a farmer who sowed good wheat in his field. (Mt 13:25-30) After a while his servants came and asked 'Was that not good wheat you sowed? Where did the weeds come from?' 'An enemy has done this,' the farmer replied. (The word 'Satan' means enemy.) The good seed represents God's creation, which was good. The weeds are sin, sickness, and death, which were not part of God's creation. The servants asked if they should pull up the weeds, but the farmer said, 'No, leave them to me, lest in pulling up the weeds, you pull up the wheat as well.' Jesus came to remove the weeds of sin, sickness, and death. It is in reference to this that Jesus calls himself the resurrection and the life. He would personally remove the weed of death from our midst, and what had been a serious problem, would now be turned into a great blessing. When I say that Jesus removed the weed of death, I am not, of course, implying that he made it so that we don't now have to die. He changed the nature of death, not the reality. 'It is in dying that we are born to eternal life.' As things now stand, death is but the beginning of real life.

Let me put it this way. Death is like a pile of sand at the end of my life, which I can take and sprinkle, fist by fist, each day of my life, through the many little ways in which I have to die to myself in living my Christian vocation. In other words, death is something I do during my life and, when the end comes, it is my ascension. If I wait till the end of my life to die, it may be too late. When was the last time you died for someone? 'Greater love than this no one has, that a person should lay down a life for a friend.' (Jn 15:13) My life is made up of little dyings, as I die to my pride, possessions, comfort, opinions, interests, etc., for the sake of others. Everytime I put another before myself I die a little

229

to my own selfishness. This way of being is what dying *is* for the
Christian, and this dying is totally life-giving to myself and to
others. In other words, in the ordinary use of the word, death
has been rendered without a sting. 'Death has been swallowed
up by victory. Death, where is your victory? Death, where is
your sting?' (1 Cor 15:54-55) 'Dying, you destroyed our death,
rising, you restored our life.' Jesus died but once, but his 'yes' to
the Father (Calvary) can be repeated again and again. That 'yes'
is what we call Eucharist or Mass. The chalice represents the
death of Jesus. 'Father if it's possible, let this chalice pass from
me.' (Lk 22:42) Before offering the chalice at Mass, I place a drop
of water in the wine. In doing this, I am offering my little deaths
to the death of Jesus. That water comes from the water of my
baptism, which I bring back to the Lord drop by drop. In doing
this I am adding my 'yes' to Jesus to his 'yes' to the Father. In
this way I am sharing in the death and resurrection of Jesus. All
my little deaths would have no value in themselves; but, when
they are joined to the death of Jesus, they take on an eternal
value. Yes, indeed, Jesus is the resurrection and the life, and it is
a wonderful privilege to be able to share fully in his victory, and
in his triumph. He has turned things around completely, and
what was a great curse on humanity can now become one of its
greatest blessings. Because of Jesus, my death can be the greatest
moment of my life, when I am freed from the limitations of the
body, and I become everything that God created me to be.

> *The dead will hear my voice, and those who listen will live.*
> *(Jn 5:25)*

To be able to discover hope in death is a wonderful victory indeed, because, of its very nature, death is something that our
human nature can only see as an enemy. Our strongest human
instinct is self-preservation and, in general, nobody likes to die.
We often hear it said that as you live, so shall you die, and I have
witnessed this in the lives and deaths of many. I don't think of
God sending me anywhere when I die; rather will he eternalise
the direction I choose to travel in now. In other words, if I hear
his voice when I am alive, and heed that voice, it is to be expected
that I will hear his voice even after I die. 'The final enemy to be

defeated is death.' (1 Cor 15:26) If I may take a little liberty with
the gospels for a moment just to stress a particular point: Jesus
took two major risks in his life, and unless the Father proved
that he was present with Jesus at all times, Jesus might well have
lost the battle. The first risk was when he went down into the
waters of the Jordan in Baptism. In doing this, he was taking on
his shoulders all the sins, brokenness, and weaknesses of humanity. This would have been too much for him, and he would
never have come up out of that water, unless a miracle happened. And the miracle did, indeed, happen. The heavens were
opened (Lk 2:21), and the Spirit was seen to come upon him in
visible form, as the Father's voice boomed from the heavens,
'This is my beloved Son in whom I am well pleased.' Jesus came
up out of the Jordan with all human weaknesses on his shoulders, but with the power of God within him. He had survived
his first great risk. The second risk was when he bowed his head
in death. If there was no one there to catch him, he was gone forever. The fact is that the Father was there, and the life he had
surrendered so generously was restored to him, and he returned
to his apostles in the glory of a whole new life. It is important to
stress that Jesus was not restored to life, like Lazarus, who still
had to die. Jesus passed through death, into a life in which death
is non-existent. He thus survived that second great risk. At the
first victory, we are told that the heavens were opened. At this
second victory, 'the veil of the Temple was rent in two'. (Lk
23:45) Yet one more door was opened and, for the first time in
their history, the Jews came right into the Holy of Holies, which
had been totally out of reach to them before. This is pure symbolism, of course, in so far as the Holy of Holies was thrown
open to them but, even to this day, no Jew, except the High
Priest, would dare set foot in the Holy of Holies in the Temple.
The outcome of both events meant that the gates of heaven were
opened once again. 'Let us, then, with confidence, approach
God, the giver of grace; we will obtain mercy and, through his
favour, help in due time.' (Heb 4:16)

Jesus said that he was the Way, the Truth, and the Life. (Jn
14:6) He also said that he came that we should have life, and
have it in abundance. (Jn 10:10) In the promise on which we are
now reflecting, he tells us that, in life and in death, his voice will

continue to be spoken to us. In other words, even if you die, you
will continue to live. (Jn 11:25) Jesus can give abundant life, and
he can restore abundant life; life even greater than before. The
choice is ours. We can choose life, or we can choose death. If we
decide to follow Jesus, and to walk in his way, we have chosen
the path to life. He is our Moses, leading us through the Red Sea
of death into the Promised Land. 'Dying, you destroyed our
death; rising, you restored our life.' If I listen to his voice now, I
will hear his voice then. He is eternally faithful, and will never
abandon us, or leave us in the storm. He is faithful in life and in
death, and with him as a friend, we have nothing to fear. 'Who
will separate us from the love of Christ? Will it be trials, or anguish, persecution or hunger, lack of clothing, hunger or sword?
... No, in all of this we are more than conquerors, thanks to him
who has loved us. I am certain that neither death nor life, neither
angels or spiritual powers, were they from heaven or from the
deep below, nor any creature whatsoever will separate us from
the love of God, which we have in Jesus Christ, our Lord.' (Rom
8:35-39)

### On the third day I will be raised from the dead.
### (Mt 20:19)

The apostles were faced with some great enigmas. Jesus dis-
played a power that was awesome to behold. Not only did he
confront the most powerful religious leaders of his day, but he
also challenged, overcame, and routed Satan, with all his power
and cunning. And in the height of those glory days, he spoke of
dying. This must have been a real shock to the system for the
apostles. Indeed, it is reasonable to assume that they never really
believed that this would happen. Jesus had faced down his accusers on several occasions and, even when they did try to kill
him, by throwing him over a cliff, he walked freely away. (Lk
4:29) If they didn't really believe that he would be killed, it is
reasonable to assume that they didn't take the words of this
promise very seriously. Certainly, when the crunch came, they
failed miserably in every area. Peter tried to prevent him going
to Jerusalem, because of the danger. (Mk 8:33) Later, Peter drew
a sword to defend him, so that he would not be arrested. (Jn

18:10) When he was arrested, their world came tumbling down around them, and they ran in all directions. Obviously, the reality of Jesus' words had not got home to them at all. No matter what he said about rising from the dead, they just couldn't get their heads around the idea that he was actually going to die in the first place. When he died, they certainly didn't hang around, waiting on him to rise again on the third day. Two of them were on their way to Emmaus. (Lk 24:13-33) They were very downcast, because the glory days were over, and all their dreams for the future were shattered. Jesus, in the disguise of a traveller, caught up with them, and they explained the reason for their despondency. They even told him that they had heard a rumour that he had risen from the dead but, of course, they didn't believe this, and kept heading for home. Here we have two disciples who probably heard the words of this promise. The worst has happened, but there is no indication whatever that anything Jesus said about rising from the dead had got through to them at all.

Jesus came with a mission; which is something I have stressed again and again throughout these reflections. I don't have any great insights into the finer points of Jesus' life, but I can accept that his life was a constant revelation to himself. This would have been his reason for spending nights alone, in prayer, on the mountain-side. (Lk 6:12; 9:18; 11:1) What lay ahead may have been revealed to him over a period of time. I'm not sure when he became aware that he would have to pay the ultimate price for his obedience to the Father, and for confronting the evil one on his home ground. I like to think that the revelation about his death was followed very quickly by the assurance of his resurrection. Because of his complete trust in the Father, he could never have accepted that his mission would be a complete failure. He came to redeem us, and to lead us out of bondage, and I'm sure he trusted the Father's plan sufficiently to hold on to the belief that his mission would be carried through to completion. As he understood his mission, it was just unthinkable that death should have the final victory. 'If Jesus had not risen from the dead, then our faith is in vain, and we are still in sin,' St Paul tells us. (1 Cor 15:17) If Jesus were to die, then he would surely have to rise again, or his whole mission would have been in vain. I imagine that, once Jesus accepted the logic of his death, accepting the certainty of his resurrection would have been easier. The apostles would have been saved a great deal of heartbreak had they really listened to what Jesus told them. It is possible that they were so involved in their own prestige, and glorious future, that they just didn't hear anything they didn't want to hear. However, with God, all is well. It's ironic that the future mission of the apostles was to be witnesses to his resurrection to every corner of the globe. (Acts 1:8) It is possible that you and I could fall into the same trap, by failing to fully believe the full import of the resurrection of Jesus for each one of us. The apostles had an excuse but, two thousands years later, I don't accept that we have an excuse.

### *The Son will raise from the dead anyone he wants to.*
### *(Jn 5:21)*

One of the most human incidents in the gospels is the one where Jesus raised the widow of Naim's son from the dead. (Lk 11:17) For this woman, life had hit an all-time low. Her husband had died, and now her only son was dead. She must have felt very alone in the world, even though the story speaks of a large crowd of the townsfolk accompanying the funeral. Into this dark moment stepped Jesus, and everything was changed utterly. I could understand him raising Lazarus from the dead, because Lazarus and his sisters were close friends of Jesus. (Jn 11:1-43) In the case of the widow's son, no one had asked him to intervene, and it is possible that no one in the crowd may have recognised him, or even heard of him. In another scene, we have Jairus, an official of the Temple, coming to beg him to intervene for the sake of his daughter. One version has Jairus asking Jesus to come and heal her and, before he got there, word came that she had already died. (Mk 5:21-24, 35-43) Another version has Jairus asking Jesus to come with him because his daughter has already died. (Mt 9:18-19, 23-26) Anyhow, the outcome of both versions is that Jesus took the little girl by the hand and raised her to life again. Remember the words of the promise we are considering: 'The Son will raise from the dead anyone he wants to.'

Water represented both death and life for the Hebrews. The

absence of water could mean death, just as the presence of too much water could also mean death. For people living in a desert country, water was a very precious commodity, and an oasis was a source of life for man and beast. When Jesus walked on water, he showed that he had authority over death. (Mt 14:26) Peter was given the opportunity to discover that he too could walk on water, but he lost his nerve, and failed the test. 'Keep your eyes fixed on Jesus, the author and finisher of our faith.' (Heb 12:2) If Peter had kept his eyes fixed on Jesus, he would not have had any problem. However, he took his eyes off Jesus, and became concerned about the wind and the waves. It wasn't Jesus' fault that he nearly drowned! Jesus did save him, and could easily have made it easy for Peter to succeed, but Peter needed to learn a simple but basic lesson. If he concentrated on himself he was in trouble; if he kept his eyes on Jesus, anything was possible.

'Then a leper came forward. He greeted him respectfully, and said, "Lord, if you want to, you can make me clean." Jesus stretched out his hand, touched him, and said "I want to, be clean again",' (Mt 8:2-3) I could imagine Jesus being taken aback by the fact that the leper wasn't sure that he would want to heal him. In the promise on which we now reflect Jesus tells us that he can raise from the dead anyone he wants to. Do I believe that? I believe that if I do, then Jesus will raise me from the dead, and bestow on me eternal life. I think of Jesus as wanting to raise all those who trust him to do so. There is no doubt about his power to do this. The X factor is whether I believe that he will do it. Faith is a response to love, and the question is whether I believe that he loves me enough to intervene on my behalf. Faith is the ingredient that I contribute. Without faith, Jesus can do nothing for me. He didn't go around healing anybody; he went around with the power to heal, and the person along the roadside had to make a decision. 'Do you believe I can do this?' was the question he put to many of those who stopped him. (e.g. Mt 9:28) The only limits to what Jesus can do for, in, and through us are the ones we ourselves set. When he returned to Nazareth 'he couldn't work any miracles there because of their lack of faith.' (Mt 13:58) His hands were tied, as it were, because although he was more than willing to give, they were totally unwilling to receive. Jesus has arranged things in such a way that he places the onus on us to provide the conditions for his power to be effective. When he met the man at the pool (Jn 5:2), he asked him, 'Do you want to be healed?' He was leaving it to the man to decide whether he would be healed or not. Resurrection and eternal life is offered to all of us, and it is up to us to decide whether we want it or not.

# Those Who Love Me

*If anyone acknowledges me publicly here on earth, I will acknowledge that person before my Father in heaven. (Mt 10-32)*

Jesus misses nothing, and is fully alert to all that is happening in our lives. He knows when we acknowledge him publicly and, as in the case of Peter, he knows when we deny him. Christianity is about attracting, not about promoting.

*You write a new page of the gospel each day, through the things that you do, and the words that you say. People read what you write, whether faithful or true. What is the gospel according to you?*

My actual life, more than mere words, should bear witness to my beliefs. I myself can become the message, rather than anything I say. The messenger becomes the message. If I go into your house, and tell you I have chicken-pox, when I actually have measles, which do you think you'll catch? What else is our calling, as Christians, than to bear witness to Jesus and to his message? Each of us can give that witness in a different way, just as the ministries within the church are so varied, and so multi-faceted. 'There is diversity of gifts, but the Spirit is the same. There is diversity of ministries, but the Lord is the same. There is diversity of works, but the same God works in all. The Spirit reveals his presence in each one with a gift which is also a service. To one is given to speak with wisdom, through the Spirit. Another teaches according to the same Spirit. To another is given faith, through which the Spirit acts; to another, the gift of healing, and it is the same Spirit. Another works miracles, another is a prophet, another recognises what comes from the good or evil spirit; another speaks in tongues, and still another interprets what has been said in tongues. And all of this is the work of the one and only Spirit, who gives to each one as he so desires.' (1 Cor 12:7-11) It is not possible to be a Christian without having the Spirit in us, and having that Spirit work through us. Therefore, as Paul describes above, because of the presence of the Spirit, we are all called to different roles and ministries within the Body. Each one of us can reflect a different aspect of the personality of Jesus Christ. It is obvious that, if we do that, he will present us as the rewards of his salvation, before the throne of his Father in heaven. 'My Father is glorified when you become my disciples, that is, when you bear much fruit.' (Jn 15:8)

Obviously, we acknowledge Jesus publicly more through the lives that we live, than any words we may say. 'Who do you say that I am?' (Mt 16:15) is a central question in the gospels. I won't find the answer to that question in a book; it is to be found only in the human heart. If Jesus is Saviour, then he has complete control of yesterday, so I am not burdened down with guilt and self-condemnation. If he is Lord, then he is completely in control of my future, and I have no fear what the future holds if he holds the future. If he is God, then I can walk with confidence and trust today, because 'nothing is impossible for God'. (Lk 1:37) If I am riddled with guilt, paranoid about tomorrow, or frozen with fear today, then I cannot be giving much witness to Jesus in my life. I am not, of course, speaking of somebody with a nervous disorder, or some condition over which they have no control. Under normal circumstances, it's when the chips are down that I discover and give witness to the reality of Christ in my heart. 'Always have an explanation to give to those who ask you the reason for the hope that you have.' (1 Pet 3:15) Any worthwhile growth in my own Christian life has always been at times of conflict or struggle. Patience in suffering, forgiveness when hurt, support for a just cause – all these are ways of witnessing to Jesus in our lives. 'By this will all people know that you are my disciples, if you have love, one for another.' (Jn 13:35)

Before I can acknowledge Jesus publicly, it is important that he attain a proper level of acceptance within my heart, before being translated into action. I'm not saying these two dimensions can be separated, because they go hand in hand. What I mean is that it is only when the message becomes internalised that it will automatically begin to be evidenced externally. If I have 'Come and seen', I will automatically 'Go and tell'. I cannot give what I haven't got. What a privilege it is for us to know that Jesus acknowledges us before his Father in heaven. It would be good to remember that when we engage in self-condemnation, worry, or anxiety of every kind. 'Your heavenly Father knows your needs.' (Mt 6:8) How could we possibly be so truly blessed, and not give witness to that fact?

*Because they love me, my Father will love them,*
*and I will love them. (Jn 14:21)*

It is possible to be thousands of miles from someone, and feel
very close to that person. On the other hand, I could be sitting
beside someone and feel that we are thousands of miles apart.
Jesus came among us here on earth, but he always kept very
close to the Father. 'I and the Father are one.' (Jn 10:30) 'They
who see me see the Father; they who hear me hear the Father
who sent me.' (Jn 14:9) 'The Father is in me, and I am in the
Father.' (Jn 10:38) Jesus never lost sight of the Father; that is why,
during his darkest hour, we can glimpse his real anguish when
he felt that the Father had abandoned him. 'My God, my God,
why have you forsaken me?' (Mk 15:34) Jesus came to represent
the Father; therefore, he would take everything that happened
to him as happening to the Father as well. If we reject him, we
reject the Father also. In this promise we are told that if we love
him we open ourselves, not just to his love, but to the Father's
love also. It is interesting to see the parallels that Jesus makes between himself and the Father, and us and our neighbour. He
came to obey the Father, and he expects us to obey him. (Jn
15:12) 'Whoever receives anyone I send receives me, and whoever
receives me, receives the one who sent me.' (Jn 13:20) Of course
Jesus became human, but there is more to him than that. I can
listen to him, think of him, and obey him, and completely overlook the fact that coming in touch with him is to be in touch with
the Trinity. This is awesome when we reflect on it. The original
sin was that mere humans thought they could become as good
as God, or become as powerful as God. The story of redemption
is to make it possible for us to share in the fullness of God's life
and power. No wonder St Augustine exclaimed, 'Oh happy
fault, that merited so great a Redeemer.' Not only is God able to
repair a wrong, but he can restore the individual to a greater
level of strength than before. Even my sins can be turned into
good, because any compassion I have has come out of my brokenness. Jesus garners the nuggets of wisdom from the past, the
great lessons life has taught me, entrusts them to me, and blows
the chaff away.

Loving Jesus opens the treasuries of heaven. Through him

come all the blessings of heaven. Not only is he the Way to heaven (Jn 14:6), he is also the channel through which heaven comes down here. After his ascension, he shared this role very especially with the Spirit, who would complete his work on earth. If there is such a thing as a shortcut to heaven, then Jesus is that way. If I come to him, I come to the Trinity, and whatever I offer, or make available to him, is also accepted by the Trinity. Love is always active, always creative. If Jesus and the Father love us, it means that they continue to create us, to transform, to complete us. Creation is on-going, just like a time of gestation. We are in the womb of God, being formed in the image of Jesus Christ. When I was in my mother's womb, I was being formed in human fashion. That process of gestation is continuing, as I am brought one giant step beyond, to share in the very nature of God. Loving Jesus is something I show, rather than something I feel. 'If you love me you will obey me.' (Jn 15:10) In obeying Jesus, I am sharing in his mission which was essentially one of obedience, as an antidote to the original sin of disobedience. To obey him is to align myself as closely as is possible with him, and that, of course, is pure love. In human relationships we tend to shy away from the concept of obedience as being necessary for human love. In former times, a couple getting married pledged themselves 'to love, honour, and obey'. It's a while now since I heard such words at a wedding! Our love for Jesus, however, is a bond between sinner and Saviour, and salvation can only be perfected through obedience, which involves repenting of sin, which is one of disobedience.

*To those who are open to my teaching, more understanding will*
*be given, and they will have an abundance of knowledge.*
*(Mt 13:12)*

There is a particular gentleness in these words: not threatening, demanding, or commanding. To open my heart and mind to his teaching is to become open to all of his graces and blessings. Being open to his teaching is more than just listening to him, and agreeing with what he says. Of necessity, it must include a response that involves decision, action, and conformity. His teaching changes us, as we are brought from information to formation, to transformation. His Spirit enters our hearts through his teaching, and that is why we get more understanding, and an abundance of knowledge. His teaching is so much more than mere words. It forms our hearts, changes our attitudes, and nourishes our spirit. When we send children to school it is for so much more than merely collecting knowledge. The most important things they learn in school do not come from the text books. Filling the memory with facts will do nothing to form the person, or develop social virtues. The word 'education' comes from the Latin *educare*, which means to lead out, or to bring forth. It implies discovering the gifts that are within, and calling those gifts into life. For example, if a child doesn't have a gift for music, the parents will spend money in vain when they pay a music teacher. I have come across children who had a real mental block when it came to maths or languages, but could make or do anything with their hands. We are all familiar with the very learned 'professor' type, who couldn't change a wheel, or drive a nail.

Opening my heart, mind, and soul to his teaching involves a journey with him. As Jesus journeyed with the disciples on the road to Emmaus (Lk 24:13-35), he opened their hearts before he opened their eyes to recognise him. He explained to them what they had failed to understand, and he unveiled for them the real message of the scriptures. His teaching had such an effect on them that they experienced their hearts burning within them as they listened to him. (Lk 24:32) His teaching has an extraordinary power to heal a wounded heart, or to bring light into a soul in darkness. Walking with Jesus is like the pupil sitting at the feet of the guru. Martha was busy in the kitchen, while Mary sat at his feet and listened to his words. (Lk 10:39) When Martha objected, and complained to Jesus, asking him to tell her sister to help her, Jesus told her that 'there is only one thing necessary, and Mary has chosen the better part, and it will not be taken away from her.'(Lk 10:42) 'Not on bread alone do people live, but on every word that comes from the mouth of God.' (Mt 4:4) There is a hunger in the human heart to which St Augustine referred when he said, 'You have made us for yourself, O Lord, and our hearts can never be at rest until they rest in you.'

There is a wonderful richness in this promise. We are promised more understanding, and an abundance of knowledge.

At one stage or another in our lives, we have waited for someone to fulfill a promise which was to our advantage. It is not possible to consider a promise as generous as the one Jesus makes.
A special dimension of this promise, of course, is that we know
he will be faithful to it. All of the riches are ours if we open our
hearts to his teaching. 'Speak, Lord, your servant is listening.' (1
Sam 3:9) This is the very heart of prayer, which is so much more
than just saying prayers, which can sometimes imply, 'Listen,
Lord, your servant is speaking.' Every promise of Jesus is important, of course, but this one is particularly important, easy to understand, and is loaded with wonderful and extraordinary
blessings.

### *In just a little while the world will not see me again, but you will. (Jn 14:19)*

On the morning of the ascension, as the apostles stood looking
up into heaven, an angel appeared to them and asked them
'Why are you standing looking up into heaven?' (Acts 1:11)
Jesus told us where we can see him now. We don't have to look
up to heaven, because we can find him in those around us. In
*Cry the Beloved Country*, Alan Paton writes, 'Do not look for me
just in the sanctuaries, or in the precise words of theologians, or
in the calm of the countryside. Look for me in the place where
people are struggling for their very survival as human beings.'
'Whatever you do to the least of these my brothers and sisters,
that you do onto me.' (Mt 25:40) Jesus tells his disciples that they
will see him. They will see him because they will be people of
love and, where love is, God is, because 'God is love'. (1 Jn 4:8)
My vocation as a Christian is to be Christ to others, and to see
Christ in others. Notice the order in which this is presented. If I
could see Christ in others, there would be little thanks to me for
loving him. However, when I begin by *being* Christ to others, I
am acting out of love, and not because of anything I see. 'Happy
are they who have not seen, and yet believe.' (Jn 20:29) In fact,
many of those to whom I may have to minister may not be
Christ-like in any way and, on a human level, it would be impossible to see Christ in them. The world would never see Christ
in the poor, the marginalised, the disabled. In many cases it is

obvious that the world sees nothing good whatever in such
people. In some of the more cruel incidents in history, such
people have been annihilated, as in Germany during the last war.
People of conscience, in many countries today, are keeping constant pressure on governments to ensure that such people receive their basic human rights. It is sad that we should speak of
giving people their rights, because they already have those
rights, even if they cannot exercise them.

There are many ways in which I can see Jesus, apart from seeing him in others. I can see him at work in my life, I can see him
very clearly among the saints of my day, those canonised and
those who need never be canonised. I can sit in his presence,
close my eyes, and use my creative imagination, seeing him in so
many different ways. As I sit before him, I can imagine how he
looks, what happens when he comes to sit beside me, or walk
with me along a beach. I can spend as long as I wish in such a
prayer, and see him and, of course, hear him. The best way, of
course, to see him is in those around me. 'She's really very nice
when you get to know her' is a phrase with which we're all
familiar. I get to know another through listening, and spending
time with that person. My time is one of the greatest gifts I can
give another. Those who are depressed, bereaved, lonely, or ill
are very much in need of my time. It's sad when I become so preoccupied with the urgent that I haven't time for the important.
Any worthwhile ministry to another must surely include time
and attention. Quite often all the other wants is a listening ear.
Jesus asked his disciples to love others as he loved them. (Jn
15:12) They had seen how he treated the lepers, the tax collec-
tors, the prostitutes, and the crippled. 'I have given you an example, so that as I have done, so should you do.' (Jn 13:14-15) He
came 'to do and to teach'. (Acts 1:1) He did the action himself,
and then he asked them to do the same. He made it very clear
that his preference was for the least of the brothers and sisters.
He never curried favour with the powerful, or those in authority.
Through his actions and his teaching his disciples would surely
have known how they were to behave towards others. They obviously did, because, even among those who had no idea who
the early Christians were, or what they were about, there was an
awareness that 'these Christians love one another'. Jesus had

actually said, 'By this will all people know that you are my disciples, if you have love one for another.'(Jn 13:35)

It is an extraordinary privilege for us to be able to see Jesus
every single day of our lives. This is a very real expression of
prayer and spirituality. Whatever I do for others, Jesus takes as
done for him. On our journey home to eternal life, it is wonderful to be aware that Jesus is travelling with us. It is the best possible preparation for that eternal life, when those to whom we
now minister will join us in unending happiness. It is very much
the work of the Spirit to reveal Jesus to us. 'The Spirit will tell
you all about me.' (Jn 16:13) It is the Spirit that focuses our vision,
and enables us see things that the world could never see, because the world just doesn't want to see. There are none so blind
as those who don't want to see.

# Love

*God blesses those who are hungry for justice,*
*for they will receive it in full. (Mt 5:6)*

Justice is more important that charity. Charity inspires me to give you something that is mine; justice involves giving you something that is yours by right. Justice is becoming more and more important in today's world; or rather, it is being highlighted much more. With the explosion on the communications highway, we are more aware of injustices around the world, and more and more people with social awareness are beginning to take up the cudgel for the deprived, and to become a voice for the voiceless. Within the church there is an organisation called 'Peace and Justice', very appropriately called, because peace without justice is not peace at all. We could shoot or starve all the troublemakers and, perhaps, put an end to riots and disturbances, but peace is so much more than the absence of war. Thank God, there are people who are really hungry for justice; this could equally be called a thirst for justice. They are driven by a sense of outrage, by the glaring inequalities, and by the apparent indifference of those who could do something about it. In recent times, all globalisation conferences between the world's super powers have attracted ferocious protest, and violent opposition. It is obvious that the will is not there, to any great degree, among the powers that be to do anything about the situation. Politics is the art of compromise, and big money interests hold the reins of power. If a business is labour intensive, they move to the far east, where the pay packet is so much smaller. If it is financially intensive, they move to the west, where the capital is available. They are in business to raise money, obviously, and there's very little sentiment or concern for individuals when big money is at stake.

The second part of this promise is very consoling indeed. On a human level, it is so easy to become discouraged, because the struggle seems like a David and Goliath all over again. However, as in that first encounter (1 Sam 41:54), God's power is greater than all human power, and he can do for us all those things that we never could do for ourselves. If the Spirit touches our hearts, and instills in us a genuine concern for the welfare of others, and a real hunger for fair-play and justice, then I will have access to a power that no earthly power can ever defeat. There are so many levels of injustice that we all come up against the issue, even in our own backyard. While half the world is dying of hunger, the other half is on a diet, in an attempt to get down the weight. The scandal is that there is more than sufficient food, but it is not evenly and properly divided. On the other hand, there can be great injustice within a family, where a mother is stretched to her limit to feed her children, while her husband is sitting on a high stool in the local pub, solving the problems of the world. In recent times, we have had revelations about migrant workers housed in disgraceful conditions, and receiving only a percentage of that to which they were entitled. There is very little sympathy for such selfish exploiters out there, which shows that most people are in favour of fairness and justice.

Most of the public efforts for justice in today's world are certainly not the monopoly of the Christian churches, although they are quite involved. It matters not where the help comes from, if it alleviates suffering, and corrects injustice. 'John said to him, "Master, we saw a man who drove out demons by calling upon your name, and we tried to stop him, because he was not following us." Jesus answered, "Do not forbid him, for no one who works a miracle in my name can soon after speak evil of me. For whoever is not against us is for us".' (Mk 9:38-41) The Spirit can work in and through all of us, and a sure sign that the human heart is right is when a person is seen to be committed to justice, and fair play for all.

> *God blesses those who are merciful,*
> *for they will be shown mercy. (Mt 5:7)*

The cross is an ideal symbol of a meaningful religion, even if it wasn't ever connected with the death of Jesus. The balance between the vertical and the horizontal bars is very significant. What comes down to us from God must go sideways to others. This promise reminds us that if mercy goes from us to others, that it will most certainly come to us. My dictionary defines mercy as 'Compassion shown by one to another who is in his power, and has no claim to kindness.' In other words, mercy is a gift that is given, which cannot be earned or merited. It comes from a heart that contains compassion, which is a very special way of loving. Compassion is a form of pity that inspires one to share or help. We speak of God as being a God of compassion, and we read that 'Jesus had compassion for the multitudes for they were like sheep without a shepherd.' (Mt 9:36) 'The blind men cried out to Jesus "Take pity on us, sir." Jesus had pity on them, and touched their eyes.' (Mt 20:31-34) The word compassion is mentioned frequently in the letters of Paul and James, for example. 'Have kindness and compassion for one another.' (Phil 2:1) 'You must clothe yourselves with compassion.' (Col 3:12) 'The wisdom that comes from above is pure and peace-loving. Persons with this wisdom show understanding, and listen to advice; they are full of compassion and good works.' (Jas 3:17)

Jesus tells a story in the gospel to highlight this very important point. It is worth quoting it in full, because it contains the very promise under reflection. 'A king decided to settle the accounts of his servants. Among the first was one who owed him ten thousands pieces of gold. As the man had nothing to repay him, the king commanded that he be sold as a slave with his wife, children, and all his goods as payment. The official threw himself at the feet of the king, and said "If you give me time, I will pay back everything to you." The king took pity on him, and not only set him free, but even cancelled his debt. This official then left the king's presence and met one of his companions who owed him a hundred pieces of money. He grabbed him by the neck, and almost strangled him, shouting "Pay me what you owe!" His companion threw himself at his feet and asked him "If you give me time, I will pay everything." The other did not agree, but sent him to prison until he had paid all his debt. The others saw what happened. They were indignant, and so they went and reported everything to their lord. Then the lord summoned his official and said, "Wicked servant, I forgave you all that you owed when you begged me to do so. Should you not have had pity on your companion as I had pity on you?" The lord was now angry, so he handed his servant over to the court until he had paid all his debt.' (Mt 18:23-34) This story presents a teaching of Jesus in a very clear and unambiguous way. There is no escape. If I don't show mercy to others, I cannot expect mercy from God. On the other hand, I can assure myself of mercy through the mercy that I show to others. This is only right and proper, and I don't think anybody could argue with it. Jesus entrusts us with many decisions effecting our own welfare. If we forgive, we are forgiven. 'As you would that people should treat you, you should treat them in like manner.' (Mt 7:12) The choice is ours, and a lot of our happiness is within our grasp, if we follow the advice and teachings of Jesus. God blesses those who are merciful, and I'm fairly sure that his blessing extends beyond the boundaries of mercy. Having a merciful or compassionate heart is a wonderful condition to be open to great and wonderful outpourings of God's love and blessings on us.

> **God blesses those who are gentle and lowly,**
> **for the whole earth will belong to them. (Mt 5:5)**

This is one of the most beautiful teachings of Jesus. He returns to it again and again, and on a few occasions he placed a child in the midst of the crowd to point out the power that resides in the heart of an innocent child. As I live my Christian vocation, there is no room for muscular Christianity, or for being a member of 'the white-knuckle club'. There is a power in gentleness and humility that the world cannot deal with. It was a source of amusement, as well as edification, when Mother (Blessed) Teresa arrived in Oslo to receive her Nobel Peace Prize. There were two limousines sent to meet her at the airport, one for her, and one for her luggage! The authorities were at a complete loss about how to treat her. She had no interest whatever in guards of honour and in sumptuous banquets. She had accepted the prize, and she came to collect the money to bring it back to her starving people. It was obvious that the authorities were in awe in her presence, because she exuded a power they had never before experienced. Mahatma Ghandi and Martin Luther King refused to strike back, so they were shot, because there was a power in their gentleness that the world could not deal with, or overcome. The bully is essentially a coward, and is completely unable to deal with gentleness and humility. I have known teachers and youth leaders who had extraordinary control over those in their charge, simply because they refused to scream, to threaten, and to bully. Many of those in their care were loud, aggressive, and disruptive because, since their earliest years, they were subjected to shouting, correction, and verbal and physical abuse. When their teachers or leaders refused to go down that road, the youth were free from all aggression, and became totally biddable and co-operative. Violence begets violence. We see that only too clearly in Iraq at the moment. The US and British went in there, and pounded every city and town until they had subdued the country. They then began a programme to rebuild the country. For the sake of world peace and order, I hope they succeed, but its not possible to build peace out of the muzzle of a gun. Peace cannot be imposed, because all that does is to allow a head of steam to build up, and to explode into violence at a later date.

There must be extraordinary potential for real power within the human heart. That power comes from humility, which is truth, and the many ways in which humility can be expressed. The facts are always friendly, and I never have to change my tune, to manipulate, or to coerce. Sometimes, with the worldly logic of politics, might seems to presume a right. The essence of this promise is that right can produce a might, a strength of character, and an inner power that the world cannot overcome. 'Lowly', in the context of this promise, is but another word for humility, which is an acceptance of reality, something that enables one to live in reality. I have known a few recovering alcoholics who went back to drink because reality was too painful for them. Rather than face up to things as they are, they choose the deadly anesthetic of alcohol to numb their feelings and thinking. At the heart of all recovery programmes is a straightforward admission that I am beaten, and I surrender. 'We admitted that we were powerless over alcohol, and that our lives had become unmanageable' (First of Twelve Steps). The victory is in the acceptance of the powerlessness, because it is only 'the truth that will set us free'. (Jn 8:32) Normally admitting defeat could be seen as failure, but never when that is the truth about how things are. To be gentle and lowly is not to make exaggerated claims to greatness, something that sets one up for a fall. This promise of Jesus tells us that the earth will be ours. That is quite a triumph, without a drop of blood being shed, or a voice being raised. Yes, indeed, there is real power in meekness and humility, and there is no way that, of myself, I could earn this, claim this, or demand it.

### God blesses those who mourn, for they will be comforted.
### (Mt 5:4)

Grief is the price we pay for love. If you never want to cry at a funeral, then don't ever love anyone. That would be an awful price to pay, and it would be far more preferable to carry around the box of tissues. To feel sorrow or regret over the loss of another is an expression of love. Human life is becoming cheaper by the day, and our morning papers report a murder or two on the front page alone. Murder is not a new phenomenon, of course, as the story of Cain and Abel show right at the beginning of creation. (Gen 4:8) Because this is one of Jesus' promises, we can safely take it that he is referring to those who genuinely grieve the loss of another. In former times in Ireland, there were groups of people called 'keeners' (Irish for 'weepers') who made a living out of being available to weep and mourn in the homes of those who died. When Jesus arrived at the house of Jairus, 'and saw the flute players and the excited crowd, he said "Go away! The girl is not dead. She is only sleeping!" And they laughed at him.' (Mt 9:23-24) It is interesting that, when he had cleared all the mourners out of the house he selected a chosen few to surround her bed, before he raised her from the dead. He chose her parents, and two of his own close friends, and this group would have represented those who were genuine in experiencing the pain of loss when the girl died. That same quality would make them excellent support company as he reached out to restore life to the girl.

Under normal circumstances, it's quite normal to mourn the dead. Bereavement is like an amputation; you lose a leg, but you will walk again if you are patient and give the wound time to heal. Time is the greatest healer, and often the only one when a loved one passes away. I don't wish to confine our reflection to mourning for a friend or relative who has died. There are people

who really do care about others, and can hurt deeply, and become really effected by a tragedy that may have happened at the
other end of the world. Some time ago, two young girls went
missing in a village in England. Anxiety for their welfare, and
shock at the discovery of their bodies, shocked the nation. There
was something about their innocence, and the evil that befell
them, that touched the hearts of everyone, and there was
mourning on a national scale. In recent years we have had genocide, ethnic cleansing, and serial killing as never before witnessed. The greatest loss here would be if we became immune to
such shocking events, and they failed to evoke the sense of outrage that they merit. From time to time a television programme
presents us with the details and graphic realities of one such
atrocity, and it is never easy viewing. I think, when possible, it is
no harm to confront us with such events, and evoke a personal
response from within us for the fate of people who shared this
planet with us, but who lived at such a distance that they may
not have caused us any great concern. I believe that love has no
boundaries, and the person with a loving heart will feel for the
pain of any other human being, no matter where they have lived
on our planet. I'm sure we all know those who can get genuinely
upset at the tragic loss of a human life, no matter where the
place, or what the circumstances. These are people who have a
real affinity with their fellow humans, and they feel the pain
when others suffer. I like to think that this is a reflection of the
kind of heart Jesus possessed. He wept at the tomb of Lazarus
(Jn 11:34), and when he overlooked Jerusalem. (Lk 20:41) I'm
sure he wept on many another occasion, because of the great
love in his heart. He could feel strongly for those who suffered,
and on many occasions we are told how he took pity on people.
To have the heart and the Spirit of Jesus within is a sure guarantee that I will definitely join others in their grief, and share their
sense of loss.

# Peace

*I am leaving you with a gift, peace of mind and heart.*
*(Jn 14:27)*

Peace is what we experience when our relationships are the way they ought to be. There are very few problems that are not relationship ones; not getting on too well with God, myself, or others. Peace of mind and heart is, indeed, a beautiful gift, and only Jesus can give it. We sometimes hear it said about persons, 'He's awfully scattered'; 'She's all over the place'; 'He badly needs to get himself together'. The opposite to this is togetherness, wholeness, or what is sometimes called holiness. Peace of mind and heart is certainly a gift, and it is something really worth praying for. Our prayer should be greatly strengthened by this promise. Jesus offers it, and it's up to us whether we want to accept it. To have peace of mind and heart is to be a source of great blessing to those around. This is more evident when we witness the opposite in operation. A man returns from work, and draws a kick on the dog. The dog did nothing wrong, but there is so much anger inside that it comes out in all the wrong ways, and anybody is liable to come within the line of fire.

When Jesus made this promise, it was as if he was declaring his last will and testament, before he died. He left us with many things, and with many promises. He was going to send the Spirit to complete his work among us. He was going to prepare a place for us, and when the time was right he would return to bring us, so that where he was, we also would be. Many of the promises had to do with the future. The promise under reflection now, however, is in the present, and is something that holds good right now as I write. It is a mistake to 'box' the gospels into a time-frame of two thousand years ago. This promise is spoken to me today. The gospel is now, and I am every person in the gospel. It is today that I am offered peace of mind and heart. This promise has profound implications, and it merits our sincere and close attention. I believe we all need peace of mind and heart. Jesus offers us this gift. He doesn't give it to us, because it's up to us to decide that we want it. He offers us peace, but we're free to die from ulcers if we choose! I stress the word 'peace' here. The gift is there for all who want it. It cannot be earned, nor do I have to be good enough. It is the gift itself that will change me to become more worthy after I receive it. There is the fallacy that I have to work on myself, get my act together, and be good enough, and then Jesus will give me peace of mind and heart. In fact, it is the very opposite approach that is needed. I come to Jesus exactly as I am, completely devoid of any rights to claim anything. If I do have a right it is because I haven't a hope on my own, and this approach always attracts his mercy and compassion. I ask for the gift, and I receive it. It is then that I begin to exercise the gift, and great changes can begin to happen in my life.

It is good to be definite and positive in my openness to this gift. Even as I write, or you read these lines, your heart can open to the reception of this gift. The only 'yes' in my whole life the Lord is interested in is my 'yes' of now. This is not a promise that I need spend much time reflecting on. Rather it is a promise that I should act on. It is an extraordinary promise indeed, but anyone who knows anything about the heart of Jesus would not be in the slightest bit amazed at such wonderful generosity, and genuine and practical love.

> *God blesses those who work for peace,*
> *for they will be called children of God. (Mt 5:9)*

Notice that Jesus doesn't say 'Happy are they who have peace', but 'Happy are they who are peacemakers'. Peacemakers, of course, need peace within their own hearts before they can be effective in bringing peace to others. A peacemaker is someone who is reasonably reconciled with himself/herself, and by reason of that reconciliation is capable of being an instrument of reconciliation in the lives of others. There are times that we have more war-mongers than peacemakers, but part of the peacemaker's work is quiet diplomacy in the background, and does not get the publicity of the war-monger. Thank God for some wonderful peacemakers in today's world, and we have always had people like that. We speak of winning the war, and then find it more difficult to win the peace. To win the peace is to win over the minds and hearts of people, and unite them in a common endeavour for good. In some of the more recent conflicts, where sides were involved in genocide, and ethnic cleansing, it is almost impossible to bring such irreconcilable forces together. To some extent, this is happening even now, but we must accept that opening of this promise, where we are told that God blesses those who work for peace. Without God's blessing, their task would be impossible. Working for peace is working on changing minds and hearts, and only God can do that, through the work of his Spirit. From the beginning of creation, the Spirit continues to hover over creation, bringing order out of chaos. The Spirit of truth convicts and convinces us of our sins. There would never be a war if someone, somewhere, was willing to say, 'Sorry. I was wrong.'

While armies travel across the world to oust dictators, or to subdue terrorists, our national army have had a very unique role for many years now. Our contribution is to provide soldiers for a peacekeeping role in several countries. Several of them have died in the process, but they were victims of violence, and not casualties of war. Some of our politicians have been peace-brokers in some of the areas of conflict, and they certainly have the support and the admiration of our nation. Despite our own turbulent past, at heart, most people are very much in favour of peace. The title 'children of God' is indeed one of extreme privilege, and is a wonderful reward for taking a stand on the side of peace. God is love, and children of God are those who promote love in any way they can. Promoting love through reconciliation is a unique and practical expression of love. It is tangible love, and it benefits so many at the same time.

Working for peace, of course, is something that any of us can become involved in. I can start in my own home, because it is said that the most difficult place to practise the gospel is in my own kitchen. Every single one of us encounters situations where reconciliation is needed. We don't go around like a fire-brigade, of course, stopping all fires. Our intervention might well be sharply rejected as interference. What I'm talking about here is something that starts with myself, and works out from there. If I myself have peace of mind and heart, then I am very likely to be invited to assist in bringing reconciliation to the lives of others. This is not just being an arbitrator, as in a trade dispute. It can involve the simplest of situations, and the nearest of friends and acquaintances. The only real qualification, of course, is to be a source of peace myself. What I have within my heart is what I bring to each and every situation. If I have turmoil in my heart, then I will bring turmoil to the situation, where I ought to bring reconciliation. In working for peace, the one person who is sure to benefit most from all of my efforts is myself.

> *The peace I give isn't the peace the world gives.*
> *(Jn 14:27)*

Peace is not the absence of war, but the presence of something tangible and real. It is freedom from disorder of any kind, and implies a friendliness that allows for peaceful co-existence with others. Peace is a very important gift of God. Right from the beginning of the entry of Jesus into our human journey, there was an offer of 'peace on earth to those of goodwill'. (Lk 2:14) One phrase of Jesus' appears puzzling at first glance. 'Do not think that I have come to bring peace on earth. I have not come to bring peace, but a sword.' (Mt 10:34) He goes on to explain that his coming will cause conflict, in that people will be faced with a decision. We are either with him, or against him. If Jesus joined a gathering of people anywhere in the world today, in no time at all they would be divided down the middle, because they would be forced to decide for him, or against him. During his life on earth, there were those who hung on his every word, and there were those who listened to what he said, so as to use it as evidence against him. Politics in the art of compromise. Jesus wasn't into the business of compromise in any way. He was very clear and definite where he stood on any particular issue, and he had no hesitation in calling to order those who chose to vacillate, or compromise in any way. On the other hand, to those who listened and took him seriously, he could change his statement about the sword rather than peace, and bestow his peace on them, and tell them that his peace was now theirs.

The peace Jesus gives is something positive, and is a source of powerful blessings in the lives of those who receive it. He used the word 'peace' on many occasions, especially after his resurrection. His first words, when he appeared among them, were 'Peace be with you.' (Jn 20:21) His peace was a sharing in the riches of his own soul. No earthly power, like the UN or NATO can bring peace to the world. All they can hope to do is stop a war, which will break out somewhere else in a very short time. That is not the peace of which Jesus speaks. He specifically mentions that, lest we be in any doubt. In fact he calls it '*my* peace', and that must be very special indeed.

Because this peace is the peace of Jesus himself, it must have a great power in it. It was the peace within him that enabled him raise his hand over the stormy sea, and say 'Peace, be still' (Lk 8:24), and the whole sea became calm immediately. He was exercising his own peace as a power over disturbance and turmoil. Sometimes we read of a siege at a house, where somebody is holed up in the house, threatening to kill someone within if attacked. It is then that negotiators are called in, to talk with the person, to attempt to bring calm to the situation, to cool things down. Apart from professional expertise, it is obvious that such people should themselves be people of peace. Peace can be transmitted through words, and attitudes. One couldn't imagine anything but words of peace and reconciliation coming from a person whose heart is filled with peace. The presence of this peace is evidence of the presence of the Spirit. Peace is one of the fruits of the Spirit. The promise of Jesus still holds good today, except that his peace is transmitted through his Spirit, who is here to complete his work among us. To open my heart to this gift, to yearn and long for it, to ask for it, is a prayer that is sure to be answered. 'If each before his own door swept, the whole village would be clean.' 'Let there be peace on earth, and let it begin with me.' If I really want peace on earth, then I must begin with my own heart. If I have the peace of Christ there, then that will go out from me through my words and actions, and will touch the hearts of those I meet. I cannot have the peace of Christ without giving it away to those around me.

# Index

## KINGDOM OF GOD

Seek first the kingdom of God, and everything else will be added to you. (Mt 6:33)                                                                124

Blessed are the poor in spirit, for theirs is the kingdom of heaven. (Mt 5:3)                                                                          126

Unless you are born again, you cannot enter the kingdom of God. (Jn 2:3)                                                                              128

I assure you that, when I sit on my throne in the kingdom, you have followed me will also sit on thrones. (Mt 19:28)                         130

The good news about the kingdom will be preached throughout the world, so that all nations will hear it, and then, finally, the end will come. (Mt 24:14)                                                              132

Blessed are those who suffer for the cause of justice, for theirs is the kingdom of heaven. (Mt 5:10)                                         133

## TREATMENT OF OTHERS

If you give even a cup of cold water to one of the least of my followers, you will surely be rewarded. (Mt 10:42)                             136

Do not judge others, and you will not be judged. (Mt 7:1)          137

Whatever measure you use in giving, will be used to measure what is given back to you. (Lk 6:38)                                              139

I, the Son of Man, will come in the glory of my Father, with his angels, and will judge all people according to their deeds. (Mt 16:27)     141

If you give, you will receive. (Lk 6:38)                            143

Stop criticising others, and you will not be criticised. (Lk 6:37)    145

I assure you, whatever you do to the least of my brothers and sisters, I will take as done for me. (Mt 25:40)                                146

## SHEEP

I am the good shepherd. The good shepherd lays down his life for his sheep. (Jn 10:11)                                                        149

I am the gate for the sheep. (Jn 10:7)                             150

Those who come in through me will be saved. (Jn 10:9)             152

I will give them eternal life, and they will never perish. (Jn 10:28)    153

No one will snatch them from me, for the Father has given them to me. (Jn 28:29)                                                              155

I have other sheep too. I must bring them also, and they will listen to my voice, and there will be one flock, and one shepherd. (Jn 10:16)   156

I came that you should have life, and have it in abundance. (Jn 10:10)                                                                        159

Those who obey my commandments are those who love me.
(Jn 14:21)                                                                 198

### CHILDREN

Anyone who becomes as humble as this child, is the greatest in the
kingdom of heaven. (Mt 18:4)                                    201

Anyone who welcomes a little child like this, on my behalf, is welcoming me. (Mt 18:5)                                                  202

Let the little children come to me, for the kingdom of heaven belongs to
such as these. (Mt 19:14)                                       204

Those who exalt themselves will be humbled, and those who humble
themselves will be exalted. (Mt 23:12)                     206

God blesses those whose hearts are pure, for they will see God.
(Mt 5:8)                                                               208

### FORGIVENESS

If you forgive anyone's sins, they are forgiven. If you refuse to forgive
them, they are not forgiven. (Jn 20:23)                     211

There is forgiveness of sins for all who turn to me. (Lk 24:47)     213

If you forgive those who sin against you, your heavenly Father will forgive you. (Mt 6:14)                                                214

When you are praying, first forgive anyone you are holding a grudge
against, so that your Father in heaven will forgive your sins too. (Mk
11:26)                                                                 216

I have come to call sinners, not those who think they are good enough.
(Mk 2:17)                                                             218

### FAITH

Blessed are those who have not seen, and yet believe. (Jn 20:29)    221

If you have faith as small as a mustard seed, you could say to this
mountain 'Move', and it would move. (Mt 17:20)        223

Blessed are they who hear the word of God and keep it. (Lk 11:28)    225

I assure you, if you have faith, and don't doubt, you can do things like
this (withered tree), and much more. (Mt 21:21)        227

### RESURRECTION

I am the resurrection and the life. (Jn 11:25)                229

The dead will hear my voice, and those who listen will live.
(Jn 5:25)                                                             230

On the third day I will be raised from the dead. (Mt 20:19)    232

The Son will raise from the dead anyone he wants to. (Jn 5:21)    234